W9-ACK-095

DATE DUE

			PRINTED IN U.S.A.

Entrepreneurship, Geography, and American Economic Growth

Knowledge has become the primary fuel for economic growth in the twenty-first century. Through the mechanism of knowledge spillovers, the full potential of knowledge as the fuel for economic growth expands with the increasing interaction of people. The authors present a knowledge spillover theory of entrepreneurship to explain geographic variations in local rates of economic growth. Central to entrepreneurship is the process of discovering an opportunity to create value through innovation. Entrepreneurs are rewarded for transforming knowledge into new products and bringing them to market.

The 1990s showed that growth in the American economy is dependent on knowledge spillovers among primarily college-educated workers who start new businesses to profit from ideas they develop into competitive new products and services. Using comprehensive annual business data from the U.S. Bureau of the Census, the authors find that the regions with the highest rates of new-firm formation are the fastest-growing economic areas.

The "industrial policies" of the 1980s did not prove effective at increasing growth or competitiveness, because they were based on traditional models of economic growth, which assume stable populations of business firms. Policies to support higher rates of regional growth should focus on seeding entrepreneurship. Such policies promote occupational choice, enable the commercialization of new technology, and enhance the spillovers of knowledge.

Zoltan J. Acs is University Professor in the School of Public Policy, George Mason University, and a Research Scholar at the Max-Planck Institute for Economics, Jena, Germany. Previously he was a Research Fellow at the U.S. Bureau of the Census and Chief Economist at the U.S. Small Business Administration. Professor Acs has published more than 75 scholarly articles in leading academic journals, including *The American Economic Review* and *The Review of Economics and Statistics.* His primary research interests are entrepreneurship, technological change, and economic development. He is the founder and editor of *Small Business Economics,* the leading international journal in entrepreneurship, and the recipient of the 2001 Small Business and Entrepreneurship Research Award given by the Swedish Foundation for Small Business. His most recent publications are *Innovation and the Growth of Cities* (2002), *Entrepreneurship, Small & Medium-Sized Enterprises and the Macroeconomy* (1999), and *Small Firms and Entrepreneurship: An East–West Perspective* (1993).

Catherine Armington has provided expertise on socioeconomic data development and econometric modeling for major government and international agencies, including the U.S. Small Business Administration (SBA), U.S. Bureau of the Census, U.S. Department of Labor, Wharton Econometric Forecasting Associates, and the OECD. She began construction of business microdata for measurement of turnover and growth in U.S. businesses as a Senior Research Analyst at the Brookings Institution in 1980 and analyzed these early data in "Small Businesses: How Many Jobs?" (1982) with M. Odle. At the Bureau of Labor Statistics she developed techniques for linking establishment data from the Unemployment Insurance system to construct a longitudinal establishment and enterprise database. For the Office of Advocacy of the SBA she defined the Longitudinal Establishment and Enterprise Microdata for use at the Census Bureau's Center for Economic Studies. As ASA/NSF/Census Research Fellows the authors investigated patterns of employment growth in manufacturing and services and then turned to analysis of new firm formations.

Entrepreneurship, Geography, and American Economic Growth

ZOLTAN J. ACS

George Mason University

CATHERINE ARMINGTON

Lawrence W. Tyree Library
Santa Fe College
3000 NW 83rd Street
Gainesville, Florida 32606

CAMBRIDGE
UNIVERSITY PRESS

CAMBRIDGE UNIVERSITY PRESS
Cambridge, New York, Melbourne, Madrid, Cape Town, Singapore, São Paulo

Cambridge University Press
40 West 20th Street, New York, NY 10011-4211, USA

www.cambridge.org
Information on this title: www.cambridge.org/9780521843225

© Zoltan J. Acs and Catherine Armington 2006

This publication is in copyright. Subject to statutory exception
and to the provisions of relevant collective licensing agreements,
no reproduction of any part may take place without
the written permission of Cambridge University Press.

First published 2006

Printed in the United States of America

A catalog record for this publication is available from the British Library.

Library of Congress Cataloging in Publication Data
Ács, Zoltán J.
Entrepreneurship, geography, and American economic growth / Zoltan J. Acs,
Catherine Armington.
p. cm.
Includes bibliographical references.
ISBN 0-521-84322-7 (hardcover)
1. Entrepreneurship – United States.   2. New business enterprises – United States.
3. Industrial location – United States.   4. United States – Economic conditions.
I. Armington, Catherine   II. Title.
HB615.A32   2006
338′.040973–dc22   2005025468

ISBN-13   978-0-521-84322-5 hardback
ISBN-10   0-521-84322-7 hardback

Cambridge University Press has no responsibility for
the persistence or accuracy of URLs for external or
third-party Internet Web sites referred to in this publication
and does not guarantee that any content on such
Web sites is, or will remain, accurate or appropriate.

Contents

Contents

Tables and Figures

Tables

Figures

Preface

This project originated several years ago while the authors were ASA/ NSF/CENSUS Research Fellows at the Center for Economic Studies (CES) at the U.S. Bureau of the Census, Washington DC, under grant SBR 980894. The authors were fortunate to have limited access, through CES, to comprehensive U.S. microdata, including all recent firm formations, which they grouped into labor market areas. Over the years, several papers were written using this LEEM (BITS) database at CES.

This research was initiated and supported by the Kauffman Center for Entrepreneurial Leadership at the Ewing Marion Kauffman Foundation, as the first step of a larger project to analyze the causes of regional differences in new firm formation rates in the United States. The research was carried out at CES under the title "U.S. Geographical Diversity in Business Entry Rates." Subsequent research was funded by the National Science Foundation under grant SES-0080316 and was carried out at CES under the titles "Evaluation of New Service Firm Entries in the Standard Statistical Establishment List" (SSEL) and "The Geographic Concentration of New Firm Formations and Human Capital: Evidence from the Cities," working paper CES 03–05 (2003). The U.S. Small Business Administration funded the final phase of the project under grant SBAHQ03M534 under the title "Using Census BITS to Explore: Entrepreneurship, Geography and Economic Growth" (2005). Finally, the generous financial support of the Doris and Robert E. McCurdy Distinguished Professorship at the University of Baltimore is acknowledged.

For valuable comments, the authors would like to thank Andre van Stel, Philip Cooke, David J. Storey, David B. Audretsch, Attila Varga, Paul

Reynolds, Olav Sorenson, Sharon Alvarez, Larry Plummer, Peter Nijcamp, Curtis J. Simon, Roger Stough, Ariel Pakes, Josh Lerner, Dale Myers, Michael Camp, Denny Dennis, Scott Shane, Per Davidson, Bo Carlsson, Pontus Braunerhjelm, Brian Headd, Carl Schramm, Roy Turick, Ronnie Phillips, John Haltiwanger, Sam Youl Lee, Richard Nelson, Anders Lundstrum, Lois Stevenson, and seminar participants at the University of Maryland at College Park; The University of Pecs; The Tinburgen Institute, Amsterdam; The Ohio State University; the School of Advanced Studies, Pisa, Italy; Cambridge University; the 2002 Babson Entrepreneurship Research Conference; the Uddevalla Symposium 2003 in Uddevalla, Sweden; and the 2003 American Economic Association meetings. The paper that Chapter Five is based on won the 2002 Babson Kauffman Entrepreneurship Research Conference's National Federation of Independent Business Award for Excellence in Research. We would also like to thank the *Journal of Urban Economics* for permission to include much of our article in Chapter Four and *Center for Urban and Regional Analysis* for permission to use our articles in Chapters Three and Five. We would also like to thank Ning Li and Alex Acs for valuable assistance in preparing the manuscript and Scott Parris of Cambridge University Press for making this process as easy as possible. Finally we would like to thank Ed Malecki and the Center for Regional Analysis at The Ohio State University for preparing the map on the jacket and the Federal Reserve Bank of Kansas City for permission to reproduce the figure on the cover as well as in Chapter Three.

All the data shown have been released for public disclosure, in compliance with the confidentiality procedures of the Census Bureau. Research results and conclusions expressed are those of the authors and do not necessarily indicate concurrence by the Bureau of the Census or the Center for Economic Studies. All errors and omissions are our responsibility.

CHAPTER ONE

Introduction

Modern economic development is to an important extent determined and driven by the emergence of the knowledge economy (Jorgenson, 2001). Advances in technical and organizational knowledge have been identified as key drivers of economic growth. Access to knowledge is generally recognized as a key condition for innovation, improved standards of living, and international competitiveness (Jones, 2002). This seems to imply that there is something new about growth being based on knowledge, as if knowledge is more important today than in the past. While this may be true, it may very well be misleading. It has long been the consensus among economists who have studied the problem that long-term growth is always based on the growth of technical and organizational capabilities (Chandler, 2000).

However, according to Peter Howitt (1996), what is new about knowledge from the economist's point of view is that we are now beginning to incorporate it into our framework of analysis. Even more importantly, we are dealing with knowledge not as an extraneous outside influence but as one of the main factors whose evolution we seek to explain as the outcome of economic forces. Although many of the ideas of the new growth theory go back to writers such as Joseph Schumpeter, it is only with the work of Paul Romer (1986) and Robert Lucas (1988) that economists were able to incorporate these ideas into simple dynamic, stochastic, general equilibrium models.

One of the advantages of the new growth theory is that it supports more relevant discussion of regional issues. While the Kaldorian approach to growth (Kaldor, 1961) also pointed to a need for regional economic policies, the new growth theories suggest that such policies would need to

1

be more supply oriented, focusing on innovation, infrastructure, and ecological sustainability, rather than on the traditional simplistic tools of local demand stimuli through subsidies and lower interest rates. The new growth theory also has important implications for entrepreneurship research. By shifting the focus from the demand side of the economy to the supply side of the economy, and from tangible to intangible inputs, growth theory is now much better aligned with Schumpeterian insights on innovation. The emphasis on knowledge and technological change gives us an operational way in which to think about the sources of opportunity and how the opportunity set may be expanded and exploited. While these new growth theories give us better insights into the role of knowledge in economic growth, they only hint at how knowledge leads to innovation. This book addresses these gaps in our understanding of the processes underlying growth.

We build on two previous empirical studies. *Innovation and Small Firms* (Acs and Audretsch, 1990) examined the question "Why should entrepreneurship emerge as a driving force of the U.S. economy precisely when both technical change and globalization seem to play an unprecedented role in the national welfare?" However, this first book did not answer the question "Why is innovation important to national welfare?" *Innovation and the Growth of Cities* (Acs, 2002) demonstrated that innovation is the driving force of the growth of cities and regions. Innovation is not an autonomous miracle; it emerges out of knowledge creation and adoption. However, this second book did not answer the question "Why is entrepreneurship important for regional growth?"

The current work bridges the gap between these related but disparate works. We suggest that variations in entrepreneurial activity, and agglomeration effects, could potentially be the source of different efficiencies in knowledge spillovers and ultimately in economic growth. In other words, we try to answer the question *"What is the role of entrepreneurial activity and agglomeration effects in economic growth?"* As early as 1976, *The Economist* magazine wrote about the coming entrepreneurial revolution, and in 1985, then-President Ronald Reagan announced that "we are living in the age of the entrepreneur." David Hart at the Kennedy School of Government at Harvard University, discussing the dot-com bubble in the late 1990s, wrote, "The Entrepreneurship fad rested on a foundation of fact. New companies made a significant contribution to economic growth in the past decade, both directly and by stimulating their more established competitors" (Hart, 2003, 3). And, Edward Lazear at Stanford University wrote, "The entrepreneur is the single most important player in a modern economy" (Lazear, 2002, 1).

Schumpeter After Romerian Insights

In *The Theory of Economic Development* (1911 [1934]), Schumpeter unveiled his concept of the entrepreneur against the backdrop of economic development. He looked upon economic development not as a mere adjunct to the central body of orthodox economic theory, but as the basis for reinterpreting a vital process that had been crowded out of neoclassical economic analysis by the static general equilibrium theory. He draws attention to the role of the entrepreneur, who is a key figure and plays a central role in his analysis of capitalist evolution.

Schumpeter uses a blend of economics, sociology, and history to arrive at his unique interpretation of "the circular flow of economic life." He shared the view with Marx that economic processes are organic and that change comes from within the economic system. It is the entrepreneurs' social function that is central to his theory. Schumpeter made the entrepreneur into a mechanism of economic change. The system is driven by innovation, and the innovator makes things happen; for Schumpeter, this is the role of the entrepreneur (2005).

Schumpeter makes a distinction between the innovative function of the entrepreneur and the financial function of the capitalist. For Frank Knight (1921), a member of the Chicago School, the entrepreneurial and capitalist functions are inextricably intertwined. Entrepreneurs must finance themselves, must bear the risk of failure, and by definition are recipient income claimants. Thus, for Knight, the superior foresight of the entrepreneur and his willingness to bear financial risk must go hand in hand. However, Schumpeter wrote, "If we choose to call the manager or owner of a business an 'entrepreneur' then he would be an entrepreneur of the kind described by Walras, without special function and without income of a special kind" (1911 [1934], 45–46).

The entrepreneur, as a member of a social class, is what gives rise to continued self-generated growth. According to Robert Heilbroner (1984, 690), it is the "essentially unadventurous bourgeois class that must provide the leadership role, it does so by absorbing within its ranks the free spirits of innovating entrepreneurs who provide the vital energy that propels the system. In Schumpeter's theory the entrepreneur is the person who innovates. In this system, the underlying 'pre-analytic' cognitive vision is thus one of a routinized social hierarchy creatively disrupted by the gifted few."

Three decades after the original publication of *The Theory of Economic Development* in 1911, it was the large corporation and the rise of socialism that drew attention to Schumpeter's gloomy prospects for economic progress. As Schumpeter himself wrote in 1942 in *Capitalism, Socialism, and Democracy,* the ideologically plausible capitalism contains no purely economic reason why capitalism would not have another successful run. The socialist future of Schumpeter's drama, therefore, rested wholly on extraordinary factors. When large corporations take over the entrepreneurial function, they not only make the entrepreneur obsolete but also undermine the sociological and ideological functions of capitalist society. As Schumpeter ([1942] 1950, 134) himself wrote in the classic passage:

> Since capitalist enterprise, by its very achievements, tends to automatize progress, we conclude that it tends to make itself superfluous – to break to pieces under the pressure of its own success. The perfectly bureaucratized giant industrial unit not only ousts the small or medium-sized firms and "expropriates" the bourgeoisie as a class, which in the process stands to lose not only its income but also what is infinitely more important, its function. The true pacemakers of socialism were not the intellectuals or agitators who preached it but the Vanderbilts, Carnegies and Rockefellers.

As the large firm replaces the small- and medium-sized enterprise, economic concentration starts to have a negative feedback effect on entrepreneurial values, innovation, and technological change. Technology, the means by which new markets are created, and source of that "perennial gale of creative destruction" that fills the sails of the capitalist armada, may die out, leading to a stationary state.[1] This view of the future

---

[1] This inherent tension between innovation in hierarchical bureaucratic organizations and entrepreneurial activity has been more recently echoed by Oliver Williamson (1975, 205–206), who suggested a division of labor between large and small firm innovation: "I am inclined to regard the early stage innovative disabilities of large size as serious

of capitalist society held by Schumpeter ([1942] 1950) was not universally accepted. John Keynes (1963) was much more optimistic about the economic prospects of our grandchildren.

Nevertheless, in long-run economic progress, prosperity gives way to stagnation when the rate of basic innovation remains at a low level. This of course did not happen, at least not in the capitalist world. Why was Schumpeter wrong about the future of capitalist society? We believe he made this mistaken forecast in part because he was writing at a point in time when the world was indeed on a socialist trajectory after the Russian Revolution, with communism spreading throughout Eastern Europe and China. He did not err by missing the essential feature of the class struggle – the principal driving force of history – the struggle between "elites and masses, privileged and underprivileged, ruler and ruled." He erred by underestimating the deep-rooted nature of the entrepreneurial spirit buried within American civilization. While for Marx the principal struggle is between privileged and underprivileged, for Schumpeter, as in the transition from feudalism to capitalism, the quintessential struggle is between "elites and elites: merchants and aristocrats, entrepreneurs and bureaucrats, venture capitalists and Wall Street" (Acs, 1984, 172).

Perhaps Schumpeter did not see – partly because of his European background – that the entrepreneurial spirit would emerge from America's past and rise to challenge, engage, and extinguish the embers of bureaucratic hegemony, bringing to an end the era of monopoly capitalism. Bruce Kirchhoff (1994), building on Schumpeterian dynamics, demonstrated that entry of new business is a necessary condition for economic development if long-run market concentration and declining innovation rates are to be avoided. The reemergence of entrepreneurship in the United States during the 1980s, and the positive channeling of it, must be seen as triumphs of the capitalist system. Of course, other countries also experienced a revival of capitalism during this time period, most notably

---

and propose the following hypothesis: An efficient procedure by which to introduce new products is for the initial development and market testing to be performed by independent inventors and small firms (perhaps new entrants) in an industry, the successful developments then to be acquired, possibly through licensing or merger, for subsequent marketing by a large multidivisional enterprise.... Put differently, a division of effort between the new product innovation processes on the one hand, and the management of proven resources on the other may well be efficient."

in the UK under Margaret Thatcher. For a discussion of the different institutional frameworks, see Michael Porter (2000) on Japan, Woltgang Streech and Kozo Yamamura (2002) on Germany, Honah D. Levy (1999) on France, and Charlie Karlsson and Zoltan J. Acs (2002) on Sweden.

Where does all this leave Schumpeter, the early Schumpeter, that is? The answer is provided by R. Nelson (1992, 90) who wrote:

> In his *Theory of Economic Development*, Schumpeter is curiously uninterested in where the basic ideas for innovations, be they technological or organizational, come from. Schumpeter does not view the entrepreneur as having anything to do with their generation: "It is not part of his function to "find" or "create" new possibilities. They are always present, abundantly accumulated by all sorts of people. Often they are generally known and being discussed by scientific or literary writers. In other cases there is nothing to discuss about them, because they are quite obvious" (Schumpeter, 1911 [1934], pp. 88).

While Schumpeter did not worry about where opportunities come from, a generation of economists spent the better part of a half century trying to figure out the relationship between technology, economic growth, and public policy (Nelson, Peck and Kalachek, 1967). After the Romer revolution, however, we now realize that the opportunity set is expanded and that economic growth is explained, to a large extent, by investments in knowledge and human capital (Jones, 2002). A second generation of new growth theorists recognized that Schumpeter's entrepreneurship was missing from these models, and they incorporated entry through "R&D races" into the model (Aghion and Howitt, 1992).

While this was a step forward, the essence of agency was missing from these models. There is a "missing link" between new growth theory and entrepreneurship theory. In Schumpeter we have no explanation of where opportunity comes from, or how it is expanded, and in Romer the Schumpeterian entrepreneur is missing. These models assume that knowledge and economic knowledge are the same and that knowledge spillovers are ubiquitous. Acs, David Audretsch, Pontus Braunerhjelm, and Bo Carlsson (2004) identify entrepreneurship as the "missing link" in converting knowledge into economically relevant knowledge. Thus, the development of new growth theory reinforces the seminal contributions made by Schumpeter a century ago on the importance of entrepreneurship and innovation for economic development.

The Definition of the Entrepreneur

In colloquial English, entrepreneurship has at least two meanings. First, entrepreneurship refers to owning and managing a business on one's own account and risk. Within this concept of entrepreneurship, a dynamic perspective focuses on the creation of new businesses, while a static perspective relates to the number of business owners. Second, entrepreneurship refers to entrepreneurial behavior in the sense of seizing an economic opportunity. At the crossroads of behavioral entrepreneurship and the dynamic perspective of occupational entrepreneurship has risen a new discipline (Sternberg and Wennekers, 2005).

The entrepreneur, according to Mark Casson (2003, 225), "is someone who specializes in taking judgmental decisions about the coordination of scarce resources." The term *someone* emphasizes that the entrepreneur is an individual. The term *judgmental* implies that the decision cannot be simply a routine application of a standard rule. The idea that the perception of opportunities is subjective, but opportunities are objective, has a long history in the theory of entrepreneurship. It is most clearly expressed in Frederick Hayek (1937). Knight (1921) expressed the same idea in somewhat different language when he introduced the distinction between risk, which is objective, and uncertainty, which is subjective, and identified uncertainty bearing as the economic function of the entrepreneur (Casson, 2005; Alvarez and Barney, 2005). As G. L. S. Schackle wrote, "The entrepreneur is a maker of history, but his guide in making it is his judgment of possibilities and not a calculation of certainties" (in Hebert and Link, 1982, viii).

We view entrepreneurship as what happens at the intersection of history and new technology (Acs and Audretsch, 2003, Chapter 1). History is the codified record of what has happened in the past, and new technology changes the future. This leads to two useful concepts. First is the stock of technical knowledge, what one might think of as codified language and knowledge. The second is the technology opportunity set, which consists of all the opportunities that have not been exploited. Investment in new knowledge increases the technology opportunity set and sharpens our ability to gaze into the future. This leads to a simple definition of entrepreneurial activity that involves the discovery, evaluation, and exploitation of opportunities within the framework of an individual-opportunity nexus.

According to Scott Shane (2003), this definition involves some assumptions. They are

- the existence of market and technological opportunities;
- differences between people to recognize opportunities;
- the decision to exploit under conditions of uncertainty;
- some form of innovation;
- the creation of a means-end vehicle to exploit the opportunity.

The nature of the vehicle to exploit opportunities depends on the mix of the exploitation and discovery matrix. The four types of ventures discussed in the literature are independent start-ups; spin-offs; acquisitions; corporate ventures.

When one looks at these four vehicles to exploit new opportunities, it becomes clear that the first three have empirical counterparts in the real world. Many large corporations engage in both the spin-off of existing operations and the acquisition of independent start-ups. However, corporate venturing does not have an easily identifiable empirical counterpart in the business world. By far the most popular vehicle for exploiting newly discovered opportunities is the independent start-up.

While independent start-ups are difficult to conceptualize in the empirical world, two types of empirical data exist for studying it. The first is self-employment data, a legal definition as much as an economic one, however. The self-employed work on their own account and do not work for wages. Self-employment data have been used to investigate many aspects of entrepreneurship, including occupational choice questions, financial constraints, and the characteristics of entrepreneurs (Parker, 2004). The second operational measure is the founding of a new business with employees, which may or may not be incorporated. New firm formation implies that the new venture is independent of any existing business currently in operation. It is not a subsidiary or branch establishment of any existing business. This measure has been used to study industry evolution, including new firm formation, firm survival, firm growth, and firm exit (Audretsch, 1995b).

Therefore, the operational definition of entrepreneurial activity used in this book is the *new firm formation:* the process whereby an individual or group of individuals, acting independently of any association with an existing organization, creates a new organization (Sharmes and Chrisman, 1999). Thus, our definition operates outside the context of a previously established organization and is consistent with the early Schumpeter (1911 [1934]).[2]

Geography: The Unit of Analysis

To investigate the relationship among entrepreneurship, geography, and economic growth, we need to analyze differences across local economic areas that are big enough to comprise the local labor and consumer markets. Cities and their broader integrated economic areas provide much more suitable units than do states or nations (Lucas, 1988). The local economic areas centered on primary cities tend to function as open economies, with a tremendous internal mobility of capital, labor, and ideas. These city-based economic areas are much more homogeneous units than those defined by the political boundaries of states. Cross-national analysis is complicated by the barring of factor mobility across national boundaries; national policies that encourage industrial diversification, reducing the gains from internal factor mobility; and distortions from the aggregation of diverse socioeconomic regions within countries. City-based regions allow us to look at fairly integrated units of economic growth without these concerns (Glaeser, Scheinkman, and Shleifer, 1995).

Within the United States, there are many levels of geographic units that have some economic data associated with them. Most politically defined units, including states, counties, cities, and towns, have boundaries that rarely represent the borders of functional economic areas. Furthermore, most of the data collected for these politically defined units are based on where people live, rather than where they work or shop. Data based on the location of business establishments (where people work) are needed for measuring the effect of location-specific economic growth, productivity, employment, and other economic factors. These data are also collected for various political units – particularly for states and counties.

The city proper has the advantage of being a smaller geographic unit, within which there is reasonably integrated economic and social activity, which might be important for spillovers operating in dense areas. However, city boundaries are often quite arbitrary relative to the local

---

[2] This work does not include self-employment in its empirical analysis. We define self employment as working for profit alone and not for wages.

patterns of economic activity, and their relatively small size means that neighboring political units may substantially influence them. In addition, while cities and towns usually collect some economic data, these data are rarely comparable across areas because they tend to vary with the details of local regulations and tax laws.

State- and county-level business data collected by the federal government are generally comparable across all the states, but most states are composed of multiple, diverse economic areas. Therefore, analyses of economic data based on states as geographic units usually suffer from aggregation problems due to the diversity of economies with a state. On the other hand, many integrated local economic areas cross both state and county boundaries, and both people and businesses flow freely back and forth across these boundaries, so that the economic behavior of agents within a given state or county may be significantly affected by unmeasured influences from adjacent areas in other states or counties.

Metropolitan Statistical Areas (MSAs) are multicounty units that are defined to include all of the densely populated areas surrounding the larger cities. These geographic units do a better job of ensuring that people both live and work within their boundaries. However, until 2000, they were based primarily on residential population densities, with only secondary consideration for where people worked. In addition, MSAs are periodically redefined to keep pace with changing urban population patterns, and they exclude large areas of the country whose local economies are not centered on large cities.

The geographic unit of analysis chosen for this study, Labor Market Areas (LMAs), substantially avoids all of the problems associated with the aforementioned units. These LMAs are aggregations of the 3,141 U.S. counties into 394 geographical regions based on the predominant commuting patterns (journey-to-work). Each LMA contains at least one central city, along with the surrounding counties that constitute both its labor supply and its local consumer and business market.[3] Many of the 394 LMAs cut across state boundaries, to better

---

[3] These LMAs are defined according to the specification of C. M. Tolbert and M. Sizer (1996) for the Department of Agriculture, using the Journey-to-Work data from the 1990 U.S. Census of Population. They are named according to the largest place within them in 1990. Some LMAs incorporate more than one MSA, whereas others separate some of the larger MSAs into more than one LMA, depending on the commuter patterns. A few smaller independent (usually rural) Commuting Zones have been appended to

represent local economic areas. The LMA unit of observation has the advantage of including both the employment location and the residence location of the population and labor force within the same area. A wide variety of data collected at the county or Zip-code level can be aggregated to construct LMA-level data. Finally, the 394 LMAs together cover the whole country, so that their data can be aggregated to U.S. totals, and all areas are represented.[4]

American Economic Growth

The time span of this book is the last decade of the twentieth century – the decade sandwiched between the fall of the Berlin Wall in 1989 – the collapse of communism – and the end of the longest period of peacetime economic expansion in U.S. history (Stiglitz, 2002). This entrepreneurial decade was the epicenter of no fewer than three simultaneous revolutions, namely, an information technology revolution (Jorgenson, 2001), the information and communication technologies (ICT) revolution, and a global institutional revolution (Stiglitz, 1997). The impact of these three revolutions on the U.S. economy was evident when William Jefferson Clinton was reelected president of the United States in 1996. The economic anxiety of four years earlier was no longer to be found (Garten, 1992).[5] After a quarter century of painful ups and downs, the U.S. economy appeared to be doing extraordinarily well. According to Lawrence H. Summers, then deputy treasury secretary, "The economy seems better balanced than at any time in my professional lifetime" (*Washington Post*, December 2, 1996). It seemed clear that the U.S. economy had restructured, moving from an industrial economy to

adjacent LMAs so that each LMA had a minimum of 100,000 population in 1990. Alaska and Hawaii each are treated as a single integrated LMA. See Paul Reynolds, 1994 for further discussion of LMAs.

[4] We code the location of each establishment according to its initially specified state and county in the LEEM, because our primary interest is in the location of new firm formations. The few businesses that report operating statewide (county = 999), or are missing their county code, have been placed into the largest LMA in each state.

[5] During the early days of the decade, economic thinking was summed up by Jeffrey E. Garten (1992, 221), then under secretary of commerce in the first Clinton administration: "Relative to Japan and Germany, our economic prospects are poor and our political influence is waning. Their economic underpinnings – trends in investment, productivity, market share in high technology, education and training – are stronger. Their banks and industry are in better shape; their social problems are far less severe than ours."

an information economy, and had made a transition to the twenty-first century.

The Data

In order to test hypotheses about how and why regions differ in their firm formation rates and growth of employment, one needs a database, representing all industry sectors, that distinguishes business establishments from firms, identifies start-ups of new firms, and specifies the location and changing employment of each establishment through time. The research underlying this book depends crucially on use of the Longitudinal Establishment and Enterprise Microdata (LEEM) database that the Bureau of the Census has constructed for the Office of Advocacy of the U.S. Small Business Administration (SBA) for study of entry, survival, and growth in different types of businesses. This LEEM file facilitates the tracking of employment, payroll, and firm affiliation and (employment) size for the more than 14 million establishments that existed at some time during 1989 through 2001.

This LEEM database (which the Small Business Administration refers to as the Business Information Tracking Series, or BITS) is a unique product of the complex register that Census maintains, with information on all businesses in the United States. This Standard Statistical Establishment List, or SSEL, is updated continuously with data from many other sources, but its underlying coverage is based on new business names and addresses from the Master Business File of the Internal Revenue Service. Therefore, *every business* in the United States that files any tax return is covered by the SSEL, and IRS data from quarterly payroll tax filings (including employment only for the March 12 payroll period) are used to provide comprehensive annual updates on all U.S. employers.

Census's annual County Business Patterns (CBP) publication provides aggregate data on all active (with positive annual payroll) private sector establishments, except those in agricultural production, railroads, private households, and large pension, health, and welfare funds. These tables are constructed by tabulating microdata that are selected from the SSEL and extensively edited both at the establishment level (relative to the previous year's data) and at various aggregate levels. The edited microdata supporting the CBP provide the starting point for Census's Company Statistics Division to produce their annual Statistics of U.S. Business files for each year since 1988. For this, firm-level data are constructed by aggregating data for all establishments belonging to each enterprise (industry-wide and country-wide), and the firm-level data are attached to the records of each firm's component establishments. These firm-level data are tabulated and processed for disclosure for the SUSB (public) database of the Census Bureau.

A Longitudinal Pointer File is then constructed to link each year's establishment record to the prior year's record for the same establishment, allowing for possible changes in identification numbers or ownership of continuing establishments. The LEEM files are constructed by merging annual SUSB files using the Longitudinal Pointer Files to create a single longitudinal record for tracking employment and ownership of each establishment that appears in any of the annual files, beginning with 1989 data.

The LEEM provides far more accurate and comprehensive longitudinal data on U.S. private sector businesses than any other source of business data in America. In comparison with the longitudinal business data available for most other countries, the LEEM data offer broader coverage of both national and local economies, with more complete linkages between business firms and their owned establishments, and with more comprehensive tracking of establishments across ownership and legal changes. See Appendix A for a more detailed explanation of the construction of the LEEM, and the specification of "firm formations" in the LEEM that was used for the empirical analysis in this book.

Business Age Versus Business Size

What is the relative contribution of entrepreneurial activity to economic growth?[6] In the traditional growth model, the entry of new large plants played a predominant role, through their economies of scale, while new small firms were assumed to be less efficient and expected to decline

---

[6] While the primary contributions of new firms are probably in the area of facilitating innovation and increasing productivity (see Schumpeter's "creative destruction" discussions, 1942), this study is limited to analyzing their impact on local employment, as a proxy for local growth.

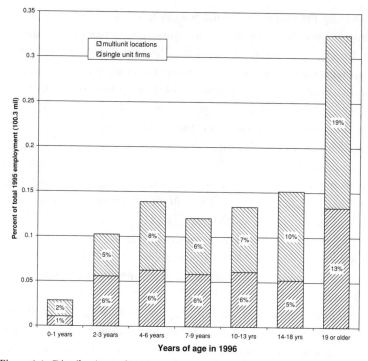

Figure 1.1. Distributions of 1995 employment by age and type of establishment.

and exit over time. In the new growth theory, the focus has shifted from economies of scale to externalities, where new firm formation plays a predominant role (Sutton, 1997).

In order to gain some insight into the relative contributions of new organizations (age less than two years) to economic growth, we have separated all establishments into age groups, based on the number of years since they reported their first payroll costs. We have further distinguished these establishments according to whether they constitute single-unit firms or are components belonging to multiunit firms (whose secondary establishments are commonly called plants, subsidiaries, or branches). We then tabulated and plotted the 1995 distributions of total U.S. private nonfarm employment and net employment change from 1995–1996, classified by the age of establishments, for those in single-unit firms and in multiunit firms. This year was typical of the decade.

The employment distribution in Figure 1.1 shows that new establishments that are less than two years old account for only 3% of total employment, and those that are new firms (single-unit establishments) account for just 1% of employment, or a third of the total. However, in the subsequent two years, the balance between new firms and new multiunit locations changes, so that establishments under four years old of each type account for 7% of total employment. Obviously, both de novo firms and new secondary-location establishments contribute new employment opportunities. However, this shift in employment shares during the first four years suggests that new firms either have higher growth rates or higher survival rates than the new secondary locations, in spite of the expected managerial and financial support that secondary locations get from their owning firms.[7]

Establishments that are at least 10 years old account for 60 percent of total employment – most people are employed in older establishments. Contrary to a popular image of insecure jobs in obsolete production facilities, the typical older establishment offers jobs with good prospects for continued employment. Note also that the majority (36% vs. 24%) of employment in these older establishments is in those belonging to multiunit firms. Because many successful single-unit firms either expand by starting up secondary locations or are acquired by other firms, this dominance by multiunit firms is to be expected for older businesses.

Figure 1.2 shows 1995–1996 net job growth distributed by the age and type of establishments. The class of establishments that were less than two years old accounts for all of the positive net job growth. All other age classes of establishments lost employment on average, whether they were single-unit firms or multiunit locations. Among the older age classes, the share of losses by firm type was roughly proportional to their share of employment, with the exception of the oldest group. Establishments over 18 years old that belong to multiunit firms incurred a disproportionately large share of losses. This is consistent with the trend during the last two decades of the twentieth century of a shift toward both smaller plants and fewer large firms. According to John Haltiwanger and C. J. Krizan (1999, 94), summarizing their discussion of the distribution of growth across firm types, "for employment growth, it looks as if the more important factor is age and not size. Put differently, most small establishments are

---

[7] A long tradition of studies of the determinants of new manufacturing plant entry (secondary location) has focused on tax rates, transportation costs, and scale economies at the plant level (Bartik, 1989). In this study, we will not examine the impact of new multiunit establishments since we are focusing on the entrepreneurial behavior of individuals who create new firms with employees.

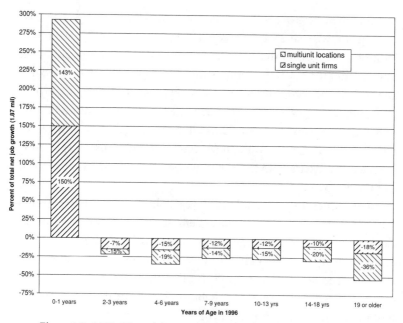

Figure 1.2. 1995–96 net job growth by age and type of establishment.

new. Thus, the role of small business in job creation may simply reflect the role of births and in turn young establishments."[8]

Figure 1.3 plots the firm formation rates of the LMAs against their employment growth rates between 1991 and 1996. Note that the variation in the firm formation rate is rather small, while the variation in employment growth rates is much larger. The regression line estimated through these has an R squared of 0.58 for the 394 Labor Market Areas suggesting that differences in formation rates account for 58% of the differences in growth rates.[9] Moreover, it is clear that the relationship is a good reflection of the overall pattern, not a consequence of a few outliers.

---

[8] During the past 25 years, there has been a significant research agenda examining the relationship between job creation and firm size. This literature suggests that size is an important variable and that there is an inverse relationship between firm size and job creation (Kirchhoff and Greene, 1998). However, several studies have concluded that the earlier claims of job creation by small firms were overstated and that there was in fact no relationship between job creation and firm size, after controlling for age and industry (Davis, Haltiwanger, and Schuh, 1996). While these findings also are not without their critics (Carree and Klomp, 1996, among others), it is clear that firms of all size do create some jobs.

[9] These results are similar to the 0.37 R-squared found at the country level for the Global Entrepreneurship Monitor (2002) for 38 countries.

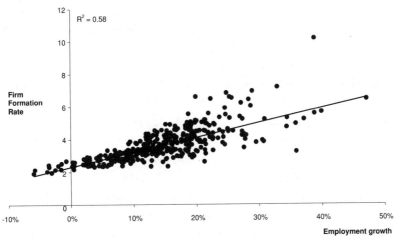

Figure 1.3. Firm formation rate and employment growth in Labor Market Areas.

What Are the Research Questions?

Three distinct questions form the basis of the empirical analysis of this book. They are as follows: from growth theory (1) the role of knowledge in economic growth; from the new economic geography (2) the role of agglomeration of knowledge; and from entrepreneurship theory (3) the role of cultures, competition, and occupational choice (Glaeser, 2000).

Two of these questions have been examined extensively in the literature. First, a significant number of papers confirm the connection between the initial level of human capital in an area and later growth in that area. In two important essays, Curtis Simon and Clark Nardinelli (1996, 2002) estimate the connection between human capital and city growth over a much longer time period in the United States and Great Britain. S. Glendon (1998) confirms their evidence and shows that the primary effect of human capital is not due only to the fact that high human capital cities tend to have high human capital industries. The presence of human capital may increase new idea production and the growth rate of the city-specific productivity level. James Rauch (1993) further documents the importance of human capital spillovers by showing that nominal wages and housing prices rise together in cities with the average level of human capital.

As long as the knowledge necessary for technological change is codified (i.e., it can be studied in written forms either in professional journals and books or in patent documentations), then access to it is essentially not constrained by spatial distance; among other means, libraries or the Internet can facilitate the flow of that knowledge to the interested user no matter where the user is located.

However, in case knowledge is not codified, because it is not yet completely developed, or it is so practical that it can only be transmitted while knowledge is actually being applied, the flow of knowledge can only be facilitated by personal interactions. For the transmission of such tacit knowledge, spatial proximity of knowledge owners and potential users appears to be critical (Polanyi, 1967). The new economic geography literature provides a general equilibrium framework where spatial economic structure is endogenously determined simultaneously with equilibrium in goods and factor markets (Fujita, Krugman, and Venables 1999; Krugman 1991a). The need for the integration of the two schools is clear; if one takes into account that agglomeration facilitates knowledge spillovers (according to the new economic geography) and knowledge spillovers determine per capita GDP growth (according to the new growth theory), then it is not an unrealistic assumption that spatial economic structure affects macroeconomic growth.

Finally, the role of entrepreneurship in city and regional growth has not yet been extensively examined. While anecdotal evidence abounds about the importance of entrepreneurial activity, systematic evidence is lacking. While competition has an unequivocal positive impact on growth, how to measure it has remained an issue. While the mechanism by which knowledge spillovers are realized remains illusive, we suggest in this book that entrepreneurship provides one avenue by which knowledge spillovers impact an economy, producing a knowledge spillover theory of entrepreneurship.

Organization of the Book

The efficiency of transforming knowledge into economic applications is a crucial factor in explaining macroeconmic growth. New growth theory treats this factor as *exogenous*. The theory offers no insight into what role, if any, entrepreneurship and agglomeration play in the spillover of tacit knowledge. The answer to this question can be pursued through the lens of the "new economic geography" and the newest wave of entrepreneurship research. We pursue a better understanding of both the relationship between geography and technological change and that between entrepreneurship and technological change because these lines of research may prove fruitful in better explaining variations in economic growth. Thus, this book remains a solid economic study for an economic audience, while offering a conceptual bridge to related non-economics-based social science fields.

The key assumptions of the new growth theory are developed and evaluated in Chapter Two. New growth theory emphasizes the crucial role of knowledge spillovers in macroeconomic growth, but leaves out the regional dimension, although substantial evidence has been provided in the recent empirical economics literature that a significant share of knowledge spillovers is localized. The new economic geography extends this framework by pointing to both the interplay between spillovers and agglomeration and the resulting cumulative regional growth, but it leaves out the macroeconomic dimension. The theory of entrepreneurship focuses on the role of an individual-opportunity nexus in explaining knowledge spillovers. We provide an interpretive model of this interplay.

Chapter Three examines the regional variation in entrepreneurial activity. While much attention was focused on new firm formation in the 1980s, rising levels of unemployment motivated that literature. In this chapter, we examine recent developments in the new growth theory and the new economic geography to increase our understanding of the spatial perspectives of economic growth, and offer a knowledge spillover theory of entrepreneurship. We regress entrepreneurial activity on unemployment, entrepreneurial culture, industry specialization, population and income growth, business density, and human capital for all 394 Labor Market Areas, distinguishing six industry sectors.

We refine our investigation of the impact of differences in local human capital resources and agglomeration on local differences in new firm formation rates in Chapter Four, focusing on the rapidly growing service sector. Previous studies have found that higher educational attainment levels lead to higher rates of growth. We suggest that the primary mechanism promoting higher rates of growth from education is through knowledge spillovers. This chapter empirically investigates how the new firm formation rates are influenced by human capital differences, while controlling

for other regional characteristics. We find that the greater sectoral specialization of existing businesses within a sector contributes to greater
entrepreneurship, but that this relationship of business specialization
outside of the sector has no positive effect on entrepreneurship. We also
find that higher levels of human capital, as well as the lack of it, lead to
more entrepreneurship, suggesting that both skilled and unskilled labor
is necessary for entrepreneurial growth.

Chapter Five asks a different question. Instead of inquiring "How
do a region's characteristics influence entrepreneurial activity?" we are
now interested in "How does entrepreneurial activity influence economic
growth?" as conditioned by spatial structure. We regress economic growth
on entrepreneurial activity, agglomeration effects, and human capital
and find that entrepreneurial activity is significantly positively related to
growth, suggesting that entrepreneurial activity may be the mechanism by
which spillovers are transmitted. Moreover, we find that agglomeration
effects beyond higher firm formation are negatively related to economic
growth. Finally, we find that higher levels of human capital lead to higher
rates of growth beyond their impact on entrepreneurship. Chapter Six
offers a summary of our research findings and insights for theory.

Chapter Seven examines the potential role of entrepreneurship policy
in economic development. If societies perform better only if they are
entrepreneurial, then entrepreneurship policy may play an important
role in economic development. For this purpose we define entrepreneurship broadly: *the process by which agents transform knowledge into wealth
through new firm formation and growth, and then reconstitute wealth into
opportunity for all through philanthropy.* Our definition of entrepreneurship leads us to develop an overarching framework for examining
entrepreneurship policy at the level of the agent, the firm, the economy,
and society at large.

CHAPTER TWO

Entrepreneurship, Geography, and Growth

Introduction

For the past two decades, scientists, policymakers, and the general public have been fascinated by the new product innovations by entrepreneurs in "Silicon Valley" (Acs, 2002). Their introduction of improvements in computers, software, semiconductors, biotechnology, and a host of other innovations have come to dominate industry after industry throughout the world. This uneven distribution of innovative activity across space has led to a host of questions about the causes and consequences of disparate economic growth (Bresnahan, Gambardella, and Saxenian, 2001).

If we are to understand why some regions grow and others stagnate, there are three fundamental questions that need to be answered (Acs and Varga, 2002). First, why and when does economic activity become concentrated in a few regions, leaving others relatively underdeveloped? Second, what role does technological change play in regional economic growth? Third, how does technological advance occur, and what are the key processes and institutions involved? In order to answer these three questions, we draw on three separate and distinct literatures that have a long and distinguished history, and all three have been recently reexamined. They are the new economic geography (Krugman, 1991a), the new growth theory (Romer, 1990), and the new entrepreneurship (Acs and Audretsch, 2003).

While each of these three literatures sheds some light on the relevant questions, none completely explains the larger questions about divergent regional growth. The new economic geography answers the question of why economic activity concentrates in certain regions but not

21

others, but leaves out entrepreneurship and economic growth. The new growth theory explains the causes of economic growth, but leaves out regional consideration and ignores the key processes and institutions involved in entrepreneurship. Finally, the new focus in entrepreneurship research suggests that the question of how opportunities are discovered, evaluated, and exploited remains a central issue in both economic-based and psychological-based research on entrepreneurship (Shane and Venkataraman, 2000). However, this research does not address the question of where opportunities come from or what role spatial structure plays.

This chapter develops the key assumptions of the new growth theory to help us better understand the economic relationship between growth, geography, and entrepreneurship. Our premise is that entrepreneurial activity translates new knowledge into innovation that sustains the growth of cities through thick labor markets and localized knowledge spillovers. The second section discusses why economies grow. The third section examines neoclassical growth theory, and the new growth theory is discussed in section four. The fifth section examines the relationship between the new economic geography and economic growth. Section six examines the importance of entrepreneurship and new growth theory. Section seven presents a simple entrepreneurship-based model of endogenous growth.

Why Do Economies Grow?

Contemporary theories of economic growth can be traced all the way back to mechanisms suggested by the classical economists, such as Adam Smith, David Ricardo and Thomas Malthus. But the more coherent building blocks of modern growth theory originated in the advances made in the beginning of the twentieth century. Important cornerstones were provided by F. Ramsey (1928), who explicitly introduced an intertemporal optimization economic structure, which was then further elaborated by Irving Fischer (1930). A more formal growth model in the Keynesian tradition was presented by Roy Harrod (1939) and Evsey Domar (1946). Exogenous savings and investment rates were paired with low substitutability of factors of production and a fixed supply of labor. Still, it was not until the neoclassical economists entered the scene that research on growth gained momentum.

Neoclassical Explanations of Growth

A major leap forward in understanding growth stems from the work by Robert Solow (1956) and Trevor Swan (1956). They proposed a general equilibrium solution to growth, based on an aggregate production function exhibiting traditional properties (constant returns to scale, substitutability among production factors, etc.). In steady state, capital would grow at a rate determined by the increase in the labor force and consumers' rate of time preferences. Consumers are willing to postpone consumption – that is, to save – for one period, provided that the return on those savings is at least as large as the increases in prices during the same period. Thus, given the increase in labor supply, savings are channeled into investments such that marginal productivity of capital complies with those conditions. As a consequence, growth would cease when the marginal productivity of net investments reached a certain level, that is, steady state was attained. The model was closed, and a well-defined and decentralized equilibrium was attained.[1]

The problem was that this did not conform to the observed patterns of growth within the last centuries. Growth-accounting exercises revealed that something else was also taking place. As shown by Solow (1957), after accounting for the contributions provided by additional labor and capital, there remained a sizeable part of growth to be explained. Solow attributed that unexplained effect to technical progress and knowledge-enhancing processes in general, and the effect became known as Solow's "technical residual." However, the mechanisms that resulted in technical progress and knowledge accumulation were still unspecified.

Hence, despite the progress made in modeling and understanding the growth process, the model suffered from the fact that the main part of growth was determined in an exogenous manner not captured by the model. The most promising attempts in the neoclassical tradition to account for that shortcoming were the models of Kenneth Arrow (1962) and Eytan Sheshinski (1967), suggesting that learning-by-doing was an important by-product of production that diffused into the economy, but their models were not fully integrated into a growth context.

In the aftermath of the contributions provided by Solow, Arrow, and others, research on growth nearly vanished from the academic agenda,

---

[1] See Barro and Sala-i-Martin (1995) or Gylfasson (1999) for a survey of the literature.

mainly because of the ambiguous empirical support that existing models attained.[2] There was a general awareness that the missing element was knowledge, an insight that was far from new. Scholars as far back as Alfred Marshall (1890) had noted that knowledge is the most prominent engine of growth, a view also emphasized by Hayek (1945?), Knight (1921, 1944), and L. McKenzie (1959). Still, the technical complexities in incorporating knowledge into growth models discouraged research in this field for a considerable time.

Central to the neoclassical theory of economic growth as formulated in Solow (1957) is the production function. Assuming that capital does not depreciate, labor force does not grow, and technology does not change over time, the production function has the form of

$$Y = F(K, L) \tag{2.1}$$

where Y represents aggregate production, K the capital stock, and L the labor force. $F(.)$ is the constant returns to scale production function. It is assumed that the capital stock grows without bounds. However, the growth rate of per capita income is bounded. Growth rate of per capita income is

$$g = s F_K(K, L) \tag{2.2}$$

where g is the growth rate of per capita income, s is the savings rate, and F_K is the marginal product of capital. Equation (2.2) states that per capita income grows as long as the marginal product of capital exceeds zero and savings is positive. However, assuming constant growth in the capital stock, per capita income growth approaches zero. Relaxing the assumptions of stable labor force and no depreciation of capital does not essentially change the main point of the model. The condition for a sustained per capita income growth in the long run is that the marginal product of capital, while decreasing as a result of continuous capital accumulation, should not fall below a positive lower bound.

Development in technology is an essential force to offset the negative effect of capital accumulation on per capita income in the neoclassical

---

[2] See also Kaldor (1961) and Denison (1967). See Rostow (1990) for a survey of the contributors to neoclassical growth theory.

model of economic growth. Introducing technological progress in the production function, it takes the form

$$Y = F(A, K, L) \tag{2.3}$$

where A stands for the state of technology. Assuming that A increases, it will increase the marginal product of capital, which will lead to a higher per capita income. As a result, in steady state the rate of technical development equals the rate of capital accumulation.

The essential role of technological progress in economic growth has been emphasized here. However, technological development itself remains unexplained in the neoclassical theory of economic growth. As a public good, it is considered to be exogenously determined, although (as data show in Solow 1957) the major portion of economic growth can be attributed to technological change, whereas capital accumulation (the main concern in the neoclassical model) explains only a fraction of it.

Primary attempts in the literature to endogenize technological progress include those of Arrow (1962), who introduced "learning by doing" in technological development; Lucas (1988), who modeled human capital as the determinant factor in technical change; and Romer (1986), who explicitly included research in the production function. In Arrow's formulation

$$Y_i = A(K)F(K_i, L_i) \tag{2.4}$$

the state of technology depends on the aggregate capital stock in the economy. Subscript i denotes individual firms. According to Lucas's model of endogenous technological change, it was spillovers from human capital accumulation, rather than accumulation of physical capital, that increased the technological level in the economy:

$$Y_i = A(H)F(K_i, L_i) \tag{2.5}$$

where H stands for the general level of human capital in the economy. In Romer (1986), it is assumed that spillovers from private research efforts account for increases in the public stock of knowledge. It could be written as

$$Y_i = A(R)F(R_i, K_i, L_i) \tag{2.6}$$

where R_i stands for the results of private research and development (R&D) efforts by firm i and R denotes the aggregate stock of research results in the economy.

The major conceptual problem with the formulation of endogenous growth in equations (2.4) to (2.6) is that in those models, the entire stock of technological knowledge is considered to be public good. However, as evidence suggests, new technological knowledge can become partially excludable (at least for a finite amount of time) by means of patenting. Not until the formulation of monopolistic competition by Avinash Dixit and Joseph Stiglitz (1977), applied in the dynamic context by Judd (1985), could we model economic growth within an imperfectly competitive market structure.

New Growth Theory

Romer (1990) combined the approach by Judd with learning-by-doing in innovation to create the first model of endogenously determined technical change with imperfectly competing firms.[3] At the core of the new growth theory is the concept of technological knowledge as a nonrival, partially excludable good, as opposed to the neoclassical view of knowledge as an entirely public good. Knowledge is a nonrival good because it can be used by one agent without limiting its use by others. This distinguishes technology from, say, a piece of capital equipment, which can only be used in one place at a time. Technology in many cases is partially excludable because it is possible to prevent its use by others to a certain extent. The excludability reflects both technological and legal consideration. Knowledge can be made partially excludable by the patent system and commercial secrecy. However, as Arrow (1962, 615) suggests:

> With suitable legal measures, information may become an appropriable commodity. Then the monopoly power can indeed be exerted. However, no amount of legal protection can make a thoroughly appropriable commodity of something so intangible as information. The very use of the information in any productive way is bound to reveal it, at least in part.

[3] This is not a complete survey of endogenous growth theory. For such surveys see, for example, Grossman and Helpman (1991); Helpman (1992); Romer (1994); Barro and Sala-i-Martin (1996); Nijkamp and Poot (1998); Aghion and Howitt (1998).

This partial nonexcludability of knowledge suggests that industrial R&D may generate technological spillovers. According to Gene Grossman and Elhanan Helpman (1991, 16):

> By technological spillovers we mean that (1) firms can acquire information created by others without paying for that information in a market transaction, and (2) the creators or current owners of the information have no effective recourse, under prevailing laws, if other firms utilize information so acquired.

There are many ways in which spillovers take place; for example, the mobility of highly skilled personnel between firms represents one such mechanism. Silicon Valley has a regional network-based industrial system that promotes learning and mutual adjustment among specialist producers of complex technologies. The region's dense social networks and open labor markets encourage entrepreneurship and experimentation, resulting in knowledge spillovers (Saxenian, 1994). Innovative activity may flourish best in environments free of bureaucratic constraints. A number of small-firm ventures have benefited from the exodus of researchers who fled from large firms, thwarted by managerial restraints, as in the case of Shockley Semiconductor Labs. These small firms exploit the knowledge and experience accrued from the R&D laboratories of their previous employers.[4]

New knowledge enters production in two ways – privately and publicly. First, newly developed technological knowledge may be used in production by the firm that invested in its development. Second, new knowledge may increase the total stock of publicly available knowledge by spilling over to other researchers, either informally or through scientific papers or patent documentation (Romer, 1990). As such, it increasingly contributes to further innovation and productivity in the research sector.

The most original contribution of Romer (1990) is the separation of economically useful scientific-technological knowledge into two parts. The total set of knowledge consists of the subsets of nonrival, partially excludable knowledge elements that can practically be considered as public goods, and the rival, excludable elements of knowledge. Codified knowledge published in books and scientific papers or in patent

---

[4] This section draws heavily on Acs and Varga (2002).

documentation belongs to the first group. This knowledge is nonrival since eventually it can be used by several actors at the same time and many times historically. On the other hand, it is only partially excludable, since only the right of applying a technology for the production of a particular good can be guaranteed by patenting, while the same technology can spill over to further potential economic applications as others learn from the patent documentation. Rival, excludable knowledge elements are primarily the personalized (tacit) knowledge of individuals and groups, including particular experiences and insights developed and owned by researchers and business people.

Equation (2.7) summarizes how the two types of knowledge interact in the production of economically useful new technological knowledge.

$$\mathring{A} = \delta \, H_A^\lambda \, A^\varphi, \tag{2.7}$$

where H_A stands for the number of researchers working on technical knowledge production and A is the total stock of technological knowledge available at a certain point in time, whereas $\mathring{A}$ is the change in technological knowledge resulting from private efforts to invest in research and development, and δ, λ and φ are parameters. Equation (2.7) plays a central role in the explanation of economic growth, since on the steady state growth path the rate of per capita GDP growth equals the rate of technological change ($\mathring{A}/A$).

The particular functional form of knowledge production in (2.7) is explained by the assumption that the efficiency of knowledge production is enhanced by the historically developed stock of scientific-technological knowledge. Even the same number of researchers becomes more productive if A increases over time.

In the words of Grossman and Helpman (1991, 18):

> [T]he technological spillovers that result from commercial research may add to a pool of public knowledge, thereby lowering the cost to later generations of achieving a technological break-through of some given magnitude. Such cost reductions can offset any tendency for the private returns to invention to fall as a result of increases in the number of competing technologies.

A is assumed to be perfectly accessible by everyone working in the research sector. However, as follows from the modification of Charles Jones

(1995a), spillovers from the stock of codified knowledge might not be perfect. Hence, the value of the aggregate codified knowledge spillovers parameter φ should be between 0 and 1.

However, this theory does not go far enough. Not only codified but also noncodified, tacit knowledge can spill over. The value of λ in (2.7) reflects the extent to which tacit knowledge spills over within the research sector and the economy at large. The process by which knowledge spills over from the firm producing it for use by another firm is exogenous in the model proposed by Romer (1990). That model focused on the influence of knowledge spillovers on technological change without specifying *why* and *how* new knowledge spills over. Yet the critical issue in modeling knowledge-based growth rests on this spillover of knowledge. New growth theory offers no insight into what role, if any, entrepreneurial activity and agglomeration effects play in the spillover of tacit knowledge. While the new growth theory is a step forward in our understanding of the growth process, the essence of the Schumpeterian entrepreneur is missed. As pointed out by Schumpeter (1947, 149), "the inventor produces ideas, the entrepreneur 'gets things done.' ... [A]n idea or scientific principle is not, by itself, of any importance for economic practice." Indeed, the Schumpeterian entrepreneur, by and large, remains absent in those models.

Consequently, despite the gains in terms of transparency and technical ease obtained by imposing strong assumptions in the endogenous growth models, these advantages have to be measured in relation to the drawbacks of deviations from real-world behavior. In our view, the result has been that the endogenous model fails to incorporate one of the most crucial elements in the growth process: transmission of knowledge through entrepreneurship, entry and exit, and the spatial dimension of growth. The presence of these activities is especially important at the early stages of new technology.

Assumptions

The knowledge-based growth model has three cornerstones: spatially constrained externalities, increasing returns in the production of goods, and decreasing returns in the production of knowledge. These drive the results of the model. They rely on assumptions related to (1) knowledge,

(2) technology, (3) firm characteristics, and (4) spatial dimension. We will now examine these assumptions in order to motivate the extensions of the model we consider necessary in order to better understand growth in a knowledge economy.

1. The distinguishing feature of new growth theory is the modeling of knowledge as the result of profit-motivated investments in knowledge creation by private economic agents. According to this formulation, knowledge is a nonrival, partially excludable good. Such formulation of knowledge as a key factor in the production function results in a departure from the constant returns to scale, perfectly competitive world of the neoclassical growth theory.

2. The production of knowledge is characterized by diminishing returns to scale: Doubling the inputs to research will not double the amount of knowledge produced. Hence, the result is an upper bound of knowledge that can be used in the production of goods. On the other hand, the production of goods is characterized by increasing returns to scale associated with increasing marginal productivity of knowledge, holding all other inputs constant. Still, even though growth rates may increase monotonically over time, the increase in the rate of growth is constrained by the decreasing returns to scale in knowledge production. The production function is:

$$F(k_i, x, K)$$
$$F_1 \geq 0, F_{12} \leq 0, F_2 \geq 0, F_{22} \leq 0, F_3 \geq 0, F_{32} \geq 0 \tag{2.8}$$

where k is knowledge production by firm i, and K is the sum of all new knowledge produced in period t, and x represents all other factors of production. This production function has the following properties: First, it is concave and homogeneous of degree 1 as a function of k_i and x, holding K constant, but convex in all arguments.[5] Second, it is assumed to exhibit globally increasing marginal productivity of knowledge from a social point of view. The implication is that production is convex in k_i for a social planner who is assumed to have the ability to set k_i at the optimum level. Or, to put

---

[5] Any concave function can be kept homogeneous by adding an additional factor to *x* that exempts production revenue. That, as Romer (1986) notes, could be entrepreneurial reward.

it differently, the aggregate production function for the whole economy is characterized by increasing returns to k_i; it is a strengthening of the increasing return assumption on knowledge (K). Assuming utility maximizing agents, these assumptions on production technology ensure that this dynamic model – in contrast to other models where consumption would grow toward infinity – results in a tractable, stable, and competitive equilibrium with increasing returns to scale.

3. The scale and number of firms are indeterminate.[6] However, firms are also assumed to be price takers, which implicitly means that there are many firms operating in competitive markets and earning zero profits. Even though the numbers of firms, entry rates, and the scale of operation cannot be determined in the model, the following assumptions are typically imposed: The number of firms is given (i.e., equals the number of individuals), no entry occurs (labor being constant), and all firms operate at the same level.[7] In principle, these models typically assume what amounts to a "representative" firm, which is supposed to capture microeconomic behavior.

4. The total stock of knowledge (K) is evenly distributed across space. However, this assumption is not supported in the literature on geographic knowledge spillovers. New technological knowledge (the most valuable type of knowledge) usually contains a strong element of tacitness that makes accessibility bounded by geographic proximity and by the nature and extent of the interaction among agents in agglomerated areas.

The basic shortcoming of the endogenous growth model is its failure to recognize that only some of the aggregate stock of knowledge (K) – normally from R&D – is economically useful, and that even economically relevant knowledge (K^c) is not necessarily exploited (or exploited successfully) if the transmission links are missing. We also note that some part of the general stock of knowledge is not in the public domain and

---

[6] In principle, from the social planners' view, the number of firms could range from a large number of atomistic firms to one single firm. Subsequent models have elaborated on somewhat more sophisticated market and firm structures, even though symmetry conditions remain (Fujita and Thisse, 2002).

[7] These simplifications mean that subscripts/indexes can be avoided and the inclusion of a representative, symmetric firm allows technical generalizations.

may not spill over easily from one carrier (agent) to another. Most knowledge, regardless of whether it is in the public or private domain, requires a certain absorptive capacity on the part of the recipients in order for successful transmission to occur.

Geography, and New Growth Theory

The fundamental geography question addressed by urban economics is why cities exist. The urban advantage in eliminating transport costs for goods captures the classic manufacturing cities example and is formalized by Paul Krugman (1991a, 1991b). Cities also facilitate the flow of ideas between individuals and firms. In dense urban environments, proximity enables workers to acquire human capital by imitating a rich array of role models and learning by viewing. If there is a greater variety of new ideas in cities, then these ideas may show up in new firms and improved production processes.

So long as the knowledge necessary for technological change is codified in written forms such as professional journals, web sites, patent documentation, and books, access to it is not essentially constrained by spatial distance; among other means, libraries or the Internet can facilitate the flow of that knowledge to the interested user, no matter where the user is located. However, where knowledge is not codified because it is private, or not yet completely developed, or is so practical that it can only be transmitted while being applied, the flow of it can only be facilitated by personal interactions. For the transmission of such tacit knowledge, spatial proximity of knowledge owners and entrepreneurs appears to be critical (Polanyi, 1967).

An important theoretical development is the recognition that geography provides a relevant unit of observation within which knowledge spillovers occur. The theory of localization suggests that geographic proximity is needed to transmit knowledge – especially tacit knowledge.

Adam Jaffe (1989) was the first to identify the extent to which university research spills over into the generation of commercial activity. His statistical results provided evidence that corporate patent activity responds positively to commercial spillovers from university research. Building on Jaffe's work, Maryann Feldman (1994) expanded the knowledge production function to innovative activity and incorporated aspects of the regional knowledge infrastructure. She found that innovative activity is conditioned by the knowledge infrastructure and responds favorably to spillovers from university research at the state level, strengthening Jaffe's findings.

Attila Varga (1998) built further on this solid foundation. His main concern was whether university-generated economic growth observed in certain regions and industries can be achieved by other regions. He extends the Jaffe-Feldman approach by focusing on a more precise measure of local geographic spillovers. Varga approaches the issue of knowledge spillovers from an explicit spatial econometric perspective and, for the first time, implements the classic knowledge production function for 125 Metropolitan Statistical Areas, yielding more precise insights into the range of spatial externalities between innovation and research and development.

The Jaffe-Feldman-Varga research into R&D spillovers takes us a long way toward understanding the role of R&D spillovers in knowledge-based economic development. A host of recent empirical studies have confirmed that knowledge spillovers are geographically bounded (Keller, 2002; Anselin, Varga, and Acs, 1997; Audretsch and Feldman, 1996; Jaffe, Trajtenberg, and Henderson, 1993; Acs, Audretsch, and Feldman, 1992 and 1994).

Knowledge spillovers from other (industrial or academic) research facilities can be channeled via different means, such as a web of social connections, the local labor market of scientists and engineers, or different types of consultancy relationships between universities and private firms. Agglomeration of research, industry, and business services is a significant factor in technological change, as it facilitates knowledge spillovers through entrepreneurship. How do such agglomerations emerge in space?

The new economic geography literature provides a general equilibrium framework where spatial economic structure is endogenously determined simultaneously with equilibrium in goods and factor markets (Fujita, Krugman, and Venables, 1999; Krugman,1991a). This is a real breakthrough in economics, given that before the appearance of the new economic geography, no school of economics since Johann Heinrich von Thünen's *Der Isolierte Staat* in the early nineteenth century had been able to build an economic model where the development of spatial structure is treated endogenously within a general equilibrium framework (Samuelson, 1983).

The most recent models in the new economic geography incorporate the effects of knowledge spillovers on the formation of spatial economic structure, in addition to providing the first attempts to explicitly integrate the two "new" schools of economics: the new growth theory and the new economic geography (Baldwin et al., 2003; Fujita and Thisse, 2002). The need for the integration of these two schools is clear if one takes into account that if agglomeration facilitates knowledge spillovers (according to the new economic geography) and knowledge spillovers determine per capita GDP growth (according to the new growth theory), then it is not unrealistic to assume that spatial economic structure affects macroeconomic growth.[8] This point has been emphasized by Krugman (1998, 172):

> It would not be surprising if it turns out that the market-size effects emphasized by the current generation of new geography models are a less important source of agglomeration, at least at the level of urban areas, than other kinds of external economies. It is, for example, a well-documented empirical regularity that both plants and firms in large cities tend to be smaller than those in small cities; this suggests that big cities may be sustained by increasing returns that are due to thick labor markets, or to localized knowledge spillovers, rather than those that emerge from the interaction of transport costs and scale economies at the plant level.

Thus, a closer connection between the endogenous growth models and entrepreneurship models seems necessary. In particular, as noted by Patricia Thornton and Katherine Flynn (2003, p. 401), knowledge is developed in certain regions where individual agents that choose to act upon acquiring new knowledge will most likely become entrepreneurs:

> [E]ntrepreneurship is increasingly the domain of organizations and regions, not individuals. These organizations and regions are environments rich in technological opportunity and resources and they have been increasing in numbers and in varieties – be they technology licensing offices, bands of angels, venture capital firms, corporate

---

[8] Unfortunately, empirical investigations in the area of agglomeration and macroeconomic growth are still relatively uncommon in the literature. The very few exceptions include Ciccone and Hall (1996), Ciccone (2002), and Varga and Schalk (2004).

venturing programs, or incubator firms and regions. These environments explicitly influence individuals by teaching them how to discover and exploit technological opportunities. These environments also specifically influence new ventures, providing resources to increase their rate of founding and survival. However, how these environments spawn new entrepreneurs and create new businesses remains relatively understudied.

Thus, the region and environment in which agents operate are crucial for the outcome. The fact that knowledge-producing inputs are not evenly distributed across space implies that regions (and countries) may not grow at the same rate, not only because they have different levels of investment in knowledge but also because they exploit knowledge at different rates. Even if the stock of knowledge were freely available, including the tacit and nontacit parts, the ability to transform that knowledge into economic knowledge, or commercialized products, would not be. Hayek (1945) pointed out that the partitioning of knowledge or information about the economy is the central feature of a market economy.

The key is that this knowledge is diffused in the economy and is not a given or a free good at everyone's disposal. Thus, only a few may know about a particular scarcity, or a new invention, or a particular resource lying fallow or not being put to best use. This knowledge is idiosyncratic because it is acquired through each individual's own circumstances, including occupation, on-the-job routines, social relationships, and daily life. It is this particular knowledge, obtained in a particular knowledge base, that leads to profit-making insight. The dispersion of information among different economic agents who do not have access to the same observations, interpretations, or experiences has implications for economic growth. Since this is not recognized in the endogenous growth model, we will suggest a different set of assumptions and outline an alternative structure of the model.

A principal assumption in the theory of endogenous growth is that for creating new sets of technological knowledge, the total stock of knowledge – A in equation (2.7) – and the addition to the stock of knowledge are freely accessible for anyone engaged in research. However, this assumption is not verified in the growing literature on geographic knowledge spillovers. New technological knowledge (the most valuable type of knowledge in innovation) is usually in such a tacit form that its accessibility is bounded by geographic proximity and/or by the nature and extent of the interactions among actors of an innovation system (Edquist, 1997).

Similar to the case of relaxing the neoclassical assumption of equal availability of technological opportunities in all countries of the world (Romer, 1994), a relaxation of the assumption that new knowledge (H_A) in equation (2.7) is evenly distributed across space within countries also seems to be necessary. The nonexcludable part of the total stock of knowledge should be classified into two portions: a perfectly accessible part consisting of already established knowledge elements (obtainable via scientific publications, patent applications, etc.) and a second, tacit element, accessible by interactions among actors in the innovation system.

While the first part is available without restrictions, accessibility of the second one is bounded by the nature of interactions among agents in a system of innovation. Research has found that the value of φ, the rate of knowledge spillovers from the stock of codified knowledge, is less than 1, with a value of around 0.8 for most developed economies. Here, technology commercialization could play an important role in increasing the rate at which existing knowledge is commercialized. Research indicates that the value of λ is much smaller in both the United States and in Europe. How to increase the value of λ is an important policy question; it appears to be influenced by both spatial considerations and entrepreneurship.

Entrepreneurial Activity and New Growth Theory

In new growth theory, the Schumpeterian perspective on exploiting knowledge spillovers accruing from aggregate knowledge investment is not adequately explained. In essence, these models assume that knowledge – defined as codified R&D – automatically transforms into commercial activities, or what Arrow (1962) classifies as economic knowledge. However, the imposition of this assumption lacks intuitive as well as empirical backing. It is one thing for technological opportunities to exist, but an entirely different matter for them to be discovered, exploited, and commercialized.[9]

---

[9] Acs and Varga (2002) suggest that if one is to understand endogenous economic growth, one needs to answer the questions of how technological advance occurs, and what are the key processes and institutions involved.

This gap in our prior understanding can be filled by the notion of entrepreneurial opportunity. An entrepreneurial opportunity consists of a set of ideas, beliefs, and actions that enables the creation of future goods and services in the absence of current markets for them. Entrepreneurship "seeks to understand how opportunities to bring into existence 'future' goods and services are created, discovered and exploited, by whom and with what consequences" (Shane and Venkataraman, 2000, 218). However, any discussion of opportunity requires an understanding of where these opportunities come from.

Existence of Opportunity

The traditional story told is that in most societies, markets are imperfect, thus providing opportunities for enterprising individuals to enhance wealth by exploiting imperfections. This is most clearly articulated in the work of Israel Kirzner (1997) where most markets are in disequilibrium. A second premise suggests that even if markets are in equilibrium, human ambition, combined with the lure of profits and the advancement of knowledge, will shift the equilibrium eventually. This premise is most often identified with Schumpeter's (1942) theory of creative destruction. Both Schumpeter's and Kirzner's theories are based on the underlying assumption that change is a fact of life. And the result of this natural process is both a continuous supply of lucrative opportunities to enhance personal wealth and a continuous supply of enterprising individuals seeking such opportunities. However, as we argued in the previous chapter, the entrepreneur has little to do with the *generation* of these opportunities.

So where do opportunities come from? There are four sources of opportunities. The first is disequilibrium within existing markets, due either to information asymmetries among market participants or to the limitations of technology to satisfy certain known but unfulfilled market needs. While we do not deny that disequilibrium exists, we argue that the exploitation of these opportunities will not lead to sustained technological change. The second is the emergence of significant changes in social, political, demographic, and economic forces that can be exploited for economic gain and are largely outside the control of individual agents. However, these cannot explain continuous growth. The third source of opportunity is the accumulated stock of knowledge (A) that exists in every society. However, the opportunities to exploit existing knowledge will diminish over time. New knowledge (H_A) in equation (2.7) is the fourth source. Many opportunities that have a systematic impact on future economic growth come from the R&D expenditures in the economy (Schmookler, 1966). Technological change is an important source of entrepreneurial opportunity because it makes it possible for people to allocate resources in different and potentially more productive ways (Casson, 1995). Without continued investment in research and development, the opportunity set exploited by entrepreneurs would dry up.

Entrepreneurial Discovery

If the opportunity set is in part created by the production of new knowledge, how are specific opportunities discovered and exploited? Here, the field of psychology helps fill the void in our understanding. The field of entrepreneurship has moved away from the "traits and characteristics" type of studies that sought to answer the question "Who is the Entrepreneur?" This line of research showed that the variance between entrepreneurs is as high as the variance between entrepreneurs and nonentrepreneurs (Gartner, 1989). The new cognition research focuses not on traits and characteristics (which are fixed and deterministic) but on the mental processes that entrepreneurs engage in to discover, evaluate, and exploit opportunities, which are not fixed and may be taught.

Audretsch (1995b) argued that human agency is necessary for the discovery of entrepreneurial opportunities. Individuals, whether they are working in an existing organization or are retired or unemployed at the time of their discovery, are the agents that discover opportunities. The organizations that employ people are inanimate and cannot engage in the discovery of opportunity. One important way in which people discover technological opportunity is through knowledge spillovers from others. Entrepreneurial discovery is in fact a process of knowledge spillover where knowledge is a nonrival good. Once entrepreneurs discover new opportunities that are only partially excludable, they have the chance to exploit them. While formal R&D creates opportunities in large firms and universities, it is frequently different individuals in different entities that carry out the exploitation of these opportunities.

New knowledge by itself may only be a necessary condition for the exercise of successful enterprise in a growth model. The ability to make the connection between new knowledge and commercial opportunity requires a set of skills, aptitudes, and circumstances that is neither uniformly nor widely distributed in the population. Thus, two people with the same new knowledge may put it to very different uses. It is one thing to have an insight, but an entirely different matter to profit from it. The incentive, capability, and specific behaviors needed to profit from useful knowledge or insight all vary among individuals, and these differences matter for explaining the exercise of enterprise.

There is an uncertainty in entrepreneurial activity that cannot be insured against or diversified away (Knight, 1921). Individuals vary in their perception of such downside risk, and in their aptitudes and capabilities to deal with and manage them. The significant issue is that individuals vary in how they process and interpret statistical generalities, and these variations may have significant but systematic impact both on the decision to become an entrepreneur and on the success of the endeavor.

The uncertainty inherent in new economic knowledge, combined with asymmetries between the agent possessing that knowledge and the incumbent organization making decisions about its expected value, potentially leads to a gap between the agent and the organization in their valuations of the knowledge. This initial condition of not just uncertainty but also greater degree of uncertainty vis-à-vis incumbent enterprises in the industry is captured in the theory of firm selection and industry evolution proposed by Boyan Jovanovic (1982).

Opportunity Exploitation

The decision to exploit an opportunity is influenced by nonpsychological factors like education, career experience, age, social position, and opportunity cost, as well as by psychological factors like motivation, core evaluation, and cognition. Once the decision to exploit is made, the entrepreneur must decide on the mode of opportunity exploitation. The discovery exploitation matrix gives us four ways in which to exploit an opportunity, depending on the individual's desire to exploit the opportunity him- or herself or on behalf of someone else. The four options are new firm formation, corporate venturing, acquisition, and finally a spin-off (Shane, 2003). The individual needs to make a decision to use a market, an existing firm, or a new venture.

Audretsch (1995b, 39) provides an insight into "[w]hy... economic agents start new firms instead of working through existing institutions." New firms allow the agent to best appropriate the expected value of new economic knowledge. Asymmetries in new economic knowledge, combined with the high costs of transacting that knowledge, lead to divergences in beliefs about potential innovations. If the expected value of new economic knowledge diverges greatly enough across economic agents, and in particular between the decision-making hierarchies of incumbent organizations, agents will have a greater incentive to form new firms.

If an agent has an idea for something different than is currently being practiced by the incumbent enterprise in terms of a new product or process idea, which we will term here as an innovation, it will be presented to the incumbent enterprise. Assuming perfect information, both the firm and the agent will agree on the expected value of the innovation. However, to the degree that any economies of scale or scope exist, the expected value of implementing the innovation within the incumbent enterprise will exceed that of taking the innovation outside of the incumbent firm to start a new enterprise. Thus, the incumbent firm and the inventor of the idea would be expected to reach a bargain, splitting the value-added to the firm contributed by the innovation (Audretsch, 1995b).

But, of course, as Knight (1921) and others emphasized, new economic knowledge is anything but certain. Not only is new economic knowledge inherently risky, but also substantial asymmetries exist between agents and firms. The expected value of a new idea, or innovation, is likely to be estimated quite differently by the inventor of the idea and by the decision makers of the firm confronted with proposed innovations. In fact, it is because of the uncertainties of information that Knight (1921, 268) argues that the primary task of the firm is to process imperfect information in order to reach a decision.

A Simple Theoretical Model

In order to remedy the limitations of the endogenous growth model and to specify the nature of the transmission mechanism that generates a diffusion of knowledge, we propose changing the assumptions on the spatial distribution of knowledge (knowledge spillovers) and the role of new firms (entrepreneurship). We retain the assumptions on technology and knowledge.

Assumptions

1. New firms are assumed to be the (primary) mechanism to transmit knowledge (K). K is transformed into economically relevant knowledge (K^c) via spillovers, which are exploited in new ventures regardless of whether the knowledge is new or existing, and whether it is scientific or some other kind of knowledge. Existing firms may learn and thereby add to their firm-specific knowledge, but we think of the results of such learning as taking the form of new ventures. This means that if there are no start-ups (whether as genuinely new firms or as new entities within existing firms), there is no spillover and hence no growth.

2. Each new firm represents an innovation. An innovation is any new combination of new or existing knowledge, as suggested by Schumpeter (1911 [1934]).[10] An important implication of this assumption is that firms are heterogeneous, not only in the size dimension but also in terms of all characteristics, such as absorptive capacity, strategy, technology, and product range, and all aspects of performance (profitability, productivity, etc.). However, new entrants, being less experienced than incumbents and frequently taking bigger risks, often make mistakes and fail. As a result, a high entry rate is necessary to sustain long-term growth.

3. There are no interregional spillovers, only local. Access to the stock of knowledge is assumed to be equal to all local entities, but the success in converting general knowledge into economically useful firm-specific knowledge depends on the absorptive capacity of each firm and hence firm characteristics. Both public and private knowledge is subject to spillover. Thus, in order to tap into the knowledge base in Silicon Valley, you have to be located in Silicon Valley.

---

[10] See also Knight (1921), Hannan and Freeman (1989), Acs and Audretsch (1990), Winter (1984), and Williamson (1985).

4. The conditions for knowledge transmission and hence new firm formation vary across regions. Policy and previous history (path dependence) determine the entrepreneurial climate in the form of infrastructure, regulation, attitudes, networks, technology transfer mechanisms, and so on.

5. Entrepreneurial ability is distributed unevenly (and exogenously) across individuals. They deploy their endowments of entrepreneurial capabilities to evaluate the knowledge accessible to them in reaching a decision how best to appropriate the returns from that knowledge; that is, they make profit maximizing intertemporal choices of whether to remain employees or become entrepreneurs (Knight, 1921.)

A Simple Theoretical Framework

The combined result of these assumptions, when added to the endogenous growth model, can be characterized as a filter (here defined in terms of entrepreneurship) that determines the rate at which the stock of knowledge (K) is converted into economically useful firm-specific knowledge (K^c):

$$0 \leq K^c / K \leq 1 \qquad (2.9)$$

Two conditions thus are decisive for an increasing stock of knowledge (through R&D and education) to materialize in higher economic growth; first, knowledge has to be economically useful and, second, *an economy must be endowed with factors of production that can select, evaluate, and transform knowledge into commercial use, that is, entrepreneurs.* If these conditions are not fulfilled, an increase in the knowledge stock may have no impact on growth. Similarly, regions with smaller knowledge stocks may experience higher growth than regions more abundantly endowed with knowledge due to superior links to the market.

The basic structure of the model implies that we have two types of firms. First, we have incumbent firms (I), which have a history and have accumulated knowledge over their lifetime,

$$k_{i,j,t}^I = f\left(\int_{t=0}^{\infty} k_{i,j,t}^I, K\right), \quad \sum_{i,j}^{n} k^I = K^I \qquad (2.10)$$

At each given point in time, firm-specific knowledge of the incumbent firms i in industry j depends on their previous investment in knowledge and on the size of K at time t. The already accumulated firm-specific knowledge within the incumbent firms has two implications for their ability to exploit new knowledge spillovers from K: First, the size of accumulated firm-specific knowledge determines their capacity to draw on spillovers (their absorptive capacity), and second, the degree of firm specificity constrains the absorption of knowledge spillovers. Hence, the incumbent firms' ability to exploit spillovers is determined by path dependence and the specificity of the accumulated knowledge.

The second type of firm is start-ups, that is, newly formed firms. These differ from incumbents, since their knowledge is not governed by path dependence and history to the same extent. Rather, it builds on an entrepreneur's ability to exploit an opportunity arising from aggregate spillovers,

$$k_{i,t}^S = f(K), \quad \sum_i^n k^S = K^S \tag{2.11}$$

Start-ups entering the market thus produce genuinely new products or use new processes. Note that K^S in period 1 becomes encapsulated in K^I in the subsequent periods. At the aggregate level (region/country), we would argue that the relationship between K^S in the previous period and K^I in the current period reflects the presence of entrepreneurship in an economy.

Both types of firms thus contribute to the exploitation of knowledge spillovers, albeit in different ways. Thereby they will narrow the gap between total spillovers (K) and the share of those knowledge spillovers that are commercialized. Yet, a complete mapping between K^c and K – implying perfect information in an unbound state space – is unrealistic. Rather, we postulate that

$$K^c = K^{cI} + K^{cS},$$

where

$$K^{cI} = \theta K, \quad K^{cS} = \lambda K; 0 \le (\lambda + \theta) \le 0.$$

hence,

$$K \ge K^c = K^{cI} + K^{cS}$$

and

$$K^c = (\theta + \lambda)K,$$

assuming for the moment that spillovers are independent of the spatial dimension. We can think of θ as the absorptive capacity of incumbent firms and λ as a proxy for entrepreneurship within an economy. In accordance with assumptions 1 and 2, the production function described in equation (2.8) then has to be modified to account also for entrepreneurship,

$$F(k_i, x, \lambda K) \qquad (2.12)$$

Thus, if entrepreneurship is nonexistent in an economy, knowledge spillovers will not provide the same solution as in the endogenous growth model with automatic and all-encompassing spillovers. In fact, it will then reduce to the neoclassical growth model. In addition, it is obvious that it is not only the size of K and the absorptive capacity of incumbent firms that matter but also the presence of entrepreneurs.

Conclusion

This chapter developed the key assumptions of the new growth theory to help us better understand the economic relationship among growth, geography, and entrepreneurship. If entrepreneurship is nonexistent in an economy, knowledge spillovers will not provide the same outcome for economic growth. The next three chapters examine the determinants of entrepreneurship in a regional context and the role that entrepreneurship plays in economic growth.

CHAPTER THREE

Regional Variation in Entrepreneurial Activity

Introduction

The regional dimension of entrepreneurship and new firm formation is clearly a subject of high interest, both in the United State and abroad (Lee, Florida, and Acs, 2004; Keeble and Walker, 1994; Mason, 1994; Audretsch and Fritsch, 1994; Reynolds, Miller, and Maki, 1994; Guesnier, 1994; Reynolds, 1994). In a recent study, M. Dunford and colleagues (2002) show that the single most cited issue of *Regional Studies* was the 1984 special issue on small firms and regional economic development. In the editorial of that issue (Storey, 1984), the focus was on seeking to justify the relevance of the topic. The need for justification was on three grounds, all of which in hindsight seem almost quaint, since they are now taken to be almost axiomatic. The first was that small firms were important as a source of economic dynamism and particularly job creation. Second was that while the 1980s saw the term "enterprise culture" used for the first time in the United Kingdom, the downside of "enterprise" was also highlighted. In particular, the low quality of many small-firm jobs was lamented. Thirdly, and perhaps most importantly, the articles themselves emphasized that the distribution of enterprise was spatially uneven, and that policies to promote enterprise could be spatially regressive, in the sense that the prosperous areas would benefit more than the less prosperous. The key contribution of that 1984 special issue was to highlight these differences, suggesting by implication that they mattered, in the sense that they reflected or caused economic prosperity.

Ten years later there was a clear acceptance of the regional variation in new firm formation rates. Why this was the case was less clear, and

45

it became the topic for the 1994 special issue of *Regional Studies*. As befitted the widening of interest in this topic, the contributions covered a much wider range of countries, including the United States, the United Kingdom, and Ireland – which had contributed to the 1984 issue – plus Sweden, France, Germany, and Italy. The focus was on seeking to explain regional variations in new firm formation rates, using broadly the same methodology for all countries.

The findings were striking (Reynolds, Storey, and Westhead, 1994). First, in all seven countries, the new firm formation rates were broadly similar. Second, the ratios of the rates in the highest and lowest regions within each country were also broadly similar. In other words, in all countries, the most entrepreneurial regions had formation rates that were between two and four times that of the least entrepreneurial regions. The third key finding was that the factors that "explained" this variation were also broadly similar. Urban regions with high rates of in-migration and a high proportion of employment in small firms had higher new firm formation rates. Disconcertingly, however, for those seeking to enhance the rates of new firm formation, the key influences were not clearly amenable to policymakers. Indeed, the instruments that were available, such as government assistance programs, local expenditure patterns, or even political parties, seemed to exert little or no explanatory power.

Several recent developments warrant a fresh examination of this subject. First, there have been important theoretical and empirical advances in our understanding of entrepreneurship. In many instances, entrepreneurship scholars drawing upon literatures in other disciplines have derived these advances. For example, recent theoretical developments in the new economic geography have increased our understanding of spatial perspectives. Jaffe (1989), Acs, Audretsch, and Feldman (1992 and 1994), Audretsch and Feldman (1996), L. Anselin, Varga, and Acs (1997, 2000), and W. Keller (2002) have all found evidence that knowledge spillovers are local. Second, new and more sophisticated databases have been developed that can better identify firm formation rates (Acs and Armington, 2005; Robb, 1999; Acs and Armington, 1998; Armington, 1997). Third, the recent evolution of the U.S. and other developed economies has been accompanied by regional shifts in economic activity away from traditional industrial regions to new regional agglomerations of high technology, creating an explosion in entrepreneurial activity and new firm formation (Acs, Carlsson, and Karlsson, 1999). Therefore, Acs and Storey recently reexamined the issue in a 2004 special issue of *Regional Studies*.

While much of the literature on new firm formation in the 1980s was motivated by high levels of unemployment in traditional industrial regions, much of the focus on new firm formation in the 1990s was motivated by new technology-based firms that were thought to be driving the economy. During the 1990s, the unemployment rate was at an all-time low in the United States, and there was little interest in the role of new firm formation as an explanation for reducing unemployment. The research focus shifted to the role of knowledge on rates of new firm formation, and the impact of these formation rate differences on economic growth.

A second important change has been the advances in both the quality of the data and the sophistication of the statistical analysis. An examination of the 1984 special issue shows that the focus was on collecting and presenting data on the topic; only simple tabulations of firm and owner characteristics were provided. In the 1994 special issue, a comparison was made between regions, but the most sophisticated analytical technique used was ordinary least squares (OLS), primarily because the data examined were a cross section. A decade later, however, the analysis is more sophisticated because of the availability of time series as well as cross-section data.

Finally, while the data quality and analysis have clearly improved over the three decades, drawing upon other academic disciplines has also contributed major analytical advances. Nowhere is this better illustrated than where entrepreneurship scholars have incorporated their concepts into economic production functions.

The purpose of this chapter is to reexamine the issue of regional variation in new firm formation rates in the United States. The next section of this chapter examines issues of measurement of new firm formation rates and discusses new sources of data. Then we discuss the theoretical background of the role of knowledge in new firm formation rates and present a knowledge spillover theory of entrepreneurship. This is followed by a discussion of the explanatory variables and the results of the estimation of the model, as well as several variations on it. A summary of the findings concludes this chapter.

Measurement of Firm Formation Rates and Industry Sectors

In this book, we study gross new firm formation rates, not the net change in numbers of firms or establishments in an area.[1] What we are investigating is not the equilibrium result of new firm formation and closure or acquisition of old firms, but the factors accounting for differences in rates of new firm formation. These capture local differences in entrepreneurship, restructuring, innovation, industrial evolution, and development. The factors contributing to explanations of local differences in firm deaths and in plant entry and exit, all of which affect the net numbers of establishments, are far beyond the scope of this study, and generally not strongly related to local human capital.[2]

We define six industry sectors for the analysis in this chapter and in Chapter Five, to better control for aggregation effects in regions with different distributions of industries. This considerably expands the industrial detail beyond that of previous studies, most of which were limited to manufacturing. Industry sectors are based on the most recently reported 4-digit SIC code[3] for the original establishment in each firm. For most firms (single location firms), this is the only establishment. For most of the few new multiunit firms, the industry classification of the primary location is the same as that of their secondary locations. The most recently reported SIC code was preferred to the first reported SIC because the precision and accuracy of these codes tend to increase over time, as Census often lists new establishments before detailed industry codes are available for them.[4]

---

[1] Most of the early analyses of "firm formation" were actually based on net changes in numbers of business establishments, because those were the only data widely available with regional and industry detail for the United States. Establishment counts include not only the primary location of all firms but also all secondary locations, such as chain stores, branch plants, warehouses, and multiple service locations owned or controlled by a multiunit firm.

[2] A long tradition of studies of the determinants of new plant entry has focused on tax rates, transportation costs, and scale economies at the plant level (Bartick, 1989; Kieschnick, 1981; Harrison and Kanter, 1978). Little work has been done yet on regional variation in exit, or closure, rates.

[3] The LEEM data are available through 2001 with SIC coding of industry, although Census had already begun the process of transitioning to the new North American Industry Classification System (NAICS) codes for classification of industry, or primary activity of each business location.

[4] There is a small number (10,000 to 16,000) of new firms each year for which no industry code is ever available. Most of these are small and short-lived. These have been added to the local market category, which is the largest of our sectors.

Industry sectors used in Chapters Three and Five, with share of total employment in 1991

Sector	Employment Share in 1991	Standard Industrial Classification
Local market	36%	1500–1799 and 6000–8999 except bus. services below (incl. construction, consumer and financial services)
Retail trade	21%	5200–5999
Manufacturing	20%	2000–3999
Distributive	13%	4000–5199 (transportation, communication, public utilities, and wholesale trade)
Business services	8%	7300–7399 and 8700–8799 (incl. engineering, accounting, research, and management services)
Extractive	1%	0700–1499 (agricultural services and mining)

These sectors identify industries that might differ in their sensitivity to regional supply and market conditions. For example, local services and construction businesses tend to be more sensitive to the level of local demand, while manufacturing may be more sensitive to the local supply of semi- and unskilled labor. Distributive businesses are concentrated in transportation hub regions, while extractive industries are dependent on the local supply and quality of natural resources.

The relative size of these sectors varies greatly. The local market sector is the largest, with 36% of total private sector employment, while extractive industries accounted for just over 1%, as shown in the table. While business services accounted for only 8% of employment in 1991, their gross increase in employment due to new firm formations between 1991 and 1996 was 44%, dominating the growth rates. Most of the other sectors gained around 25% in employment during that period, but manufacturing gained at only half that rate.

Firm formations include both new single unit firms (establishments, or locations) with fewer than 500 employees and the primary locations of new multiunit firms with fewer than 500 employees, firmwide. Those new firms that had 500 or more employees in their first year of activity appear to be primarily offshoots of existing companies. Further details on how new firm formations are identified on the LEEM, and why these rules were chosen, are provided in Appendix A.[5] The numbers of new firm formations are tabulated for each of the 394 LMAs for all industries together and for each of the six sectors defined here, based on new firms making their first appearance with employees in 1995 and 1996, and labeled as 1995 + 1996 firm formations. The two years of formation were aggregated to avoid having data disclosure problems in small LMAs in small industry groups. The new firm formations in each LMA in each year[6] were also tabulated, and used to calculate annual rates for all industries together.

Comparisons across regions among their absolute numbers of new firm formations would be more misleading than revealing because the economic regions vary considerably in size. Two approaches are used here for calculating comparable formation rates for regions. The first method standardizes the number of new firm formations relative to the number of establishments already in existence. This can be termed the ecological approach because it considers the amount of start-up activity relative to the size of the existing population of businesses (Hannan and Freeman, 1989). The second method, which can be characterized as the labor market approach, is to standardize the number of new firms relative to the total size of the local labor force. This labor force approach has a particular theoretical appeal in that it is based on the theory of entrepreneurial choice proposed by D. Evans and Jovanovic (1989). This latter approach implicitly assumes that the entrepreneur starting a new business is in the same labor market within which that new establishment operates. Regions do vary considerably in their average number of employees (or labor force) per establishment,[7] and so compared to the labor market approach, the ecological approach would result in relatively higher formation rates in regions where the average size of establishments is relatively high and lower rates in regions lacking many large establishments.

---

[5] See also Acs and Armington (2005) and Armington (2004) for further discussion of the use of LEEM (also known as BITS) data for this type of research.

[6] In fact, formation rates were calculated for each annual period from 1990 through 1998, but these were found to be quite consistent in their rank ordering across LMAs, and so averages of formations during two-year or three-year periods were used for most of the analyses in this book.

[7] In particular, manufacturing establishments generally are larger than others, and so areas with larger shares of manufacturing have relatively fewer establishments for their labor force size.

These two approaches are compared in Table 3.1, which shows annual firm formation rates for all U.S. states, based on both the labor market approach and the ecological approach (averaging 1995 and 1996 formations and dividing by the appropriate 1994 base). The U.S. firm formation rate for the United States as a whole is 3.85 firms per 1,000 labor force. This is somewhat higher than the earlier 3.20 firm formation rate reported by Reynolds for 1986 to 1988 (1994, 433). The parallel ecological formation rate is 13.0 firms per 100 establishments. Note that in this table, the states are ordered by their firm formation rates per 1,000 labor force. When the corresponding rates per 100 establishments are examined, the more extreme differences stand out. Thus, we see some very low formation rates per establishment among certain states with high formation rates per labor force – in Wyoming especially, and in Delaware, New York, and the District of Columbia. Conversely, Illinois and Minnesota stand out as having high firm formation rates per establishment, but low per labor force.

There are several observations about the variations across states in Table 3.1 that should be noted. Clearly, the areas with the highest firm formation rates are all in the West or South. Colorado, Florida, and Montana have the highest formation rates per labor force, and Nevada and Utah are highest when standardized by numbers of establishments. The lowest formation rates are all found in the Northeast and the Midwest. It is surprising that many states in the West that are sparsely populated, such as Montana, Wyoming, Nevada, and Idaho, have higher firm formation rates than most with denser populations. However, the states themselves are not very useful as a unit of economic analysis since substantial local differences are lost in their aggregation to political boundaries. There is much more variation among LMAs than among states. Figure 3.1 shows firm formation rates in LMAs for the whole United States. The general regional patterns remain, but the results are much more nuanced, with some low-performing areas in the West and a few very high performing ones evident in the East.

Table 3.2 shows the firm formation rates per 1,000 labor force, along with the actual numbers of formations and base number of establishments in the LMAs with the highest and the lowest firm formation rates.[8] The formation rates in LMAs range from a high of 10.18 firms

[8] The complete list of LMAs ranked by their firm formation rates is reported in Appendix B.

Table 3.1. *1995 + 1996 firm formation rates by state for all industries (ordered by formation rates per 1,000 labor force)*

	Avg Annual Firm Formations per 1994			Avg Annual Firm Formations per 1994	
	1,000 LF	100 Establ.		1,000 LF	100 Establ.
United States	3.85	13.0			
			South Carolina	3.94	13.3
Colorado	5.50	14.9	Missouri	3.90	12.6
Florida	5.48	15.1	California	3.84	12.8
Montana	5.45	14.1	Alabama	3.82	12.9
Wyoming	5.36	11.8	Kansas	3.80	12.8
Nevada	5.05	18.7	Louisiana	3.70	11.4
Idaho	5.01	15.4	Tennessee	3.66	12.9
Oregon	4.86	13.8	Rhode Island	3.63	11.5
Washington	4.75	14.2	Mississippi	3.61	12.0
Utah	4.68	16.9	North Dakota	3.56	9.8
Arizona	4.65	15.4	Virginia	3.53	12.7
New Mexico	4.44	13.9	West Virginia	3.51	11.2
Georgia	4.39	14.6	Hawaii	3.46	10.2
Maine	4.36	12.9	Nebraska	3.36	11.0
Vermont	4.36	12.6	Kentucky	3.36	12.1
New Hampshire	4.31	14.9	Massachusetts	3.34	12.6
Alaska	4.24	12.5	Minnesota	3.33	14.3
Arkansas	4.14	12.8	Michigan	3.32	12.3
Oklahoma	4.13	12.5	Illinois	3.31	13.0
South Dakota	4.12	12.7	Maryland	3.26	12.7
New Jersey	4.12	13.3	Connecticut	3.21	10.5
Delaware	4.08	11.5	Indiana	3.18	12.1
New York	3.98	11.9	Iowa	3.07	11.2
North Carolina	3.98	13.7	Wisconsin	2.99	11.2
Texas	3.98	13.5	Ohio	2.95	11.7
Dist. of Columbia	3.95	8.5	Pennsylvania	2.91	10.8

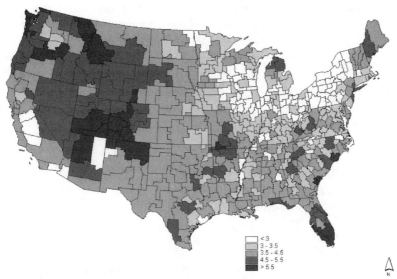

MAP PREPARED BY THE CENTER FOR REGIONAL ANALYSIS, OSU, APRIL 2003

Figure 3.1. Average annual firm formation rates in Labor Market Areas (1995 + 1996 formations per 1,000 labor force in 1994).

per 1,000 labor force, down to 2.06. These firm formation rates appear to be independent of regional size. For example, St. George UT, which is one-thirtieth the size of Miami FL, has an identical firm formation rate. The South and the West have the strongest new firm start-up rates, while the Northeast and the Midwest, which were formerly characterized by large-scale manufacturing, generally continue to lag behind the rest of the country. Dayton OH, for instance, was formerly dominated by the large-scale manufacturing of National Cash Register and has not yet restructured toward services.[9]

Finally, although not shown here, we found very little variation in annual firm formation rates over the time period studied. For example, the firm formation rate for Miami between 1991 and 1993 was 6.79 and between 1994 and 1996 it was 6.49. These figures are remarkably consistent, given that 1991 was a recession year. For Dayton OH, the parallel numbers were 2.34 and 2.54. The correlations between

[9] It is a well-documented regularity that both plants and firms in large cities tend to be smaller than those in small cities (Hoover and Vernon, 1959). This would suggest that smaller industrial cities might have the most difficulty restructuring.

Table 3.2. *1994 establishments and 1995 + 1996 firm formations and formation rates for LMAs (for labor market areas with high and low formation rates per 1,000 labor force)*

LMA	Biggest Place	1994 Establ.	Avg Annual Formations	Formations/ 1,000 LF
	United States	5,770,090	504,939	3.85
Highest 20 LMAs by formation rate				
287	Laramie, WY	5,898	887	10.18
72	Fort Myers, FL	14,543	1,782	7.20
352	Grand Junction, CO	4,319	613	6.95
71	West Palm Beach, FL	32,743	4,161	6.84
392	Bend, OR	4,608	625	6.61
393	Bellingham, WA	6,509	735	6.60
359	St. George, UT	3,187	536	6.54
70	Miami, FL	90,179	11,644	6.49
345	Missoula, MT	6,520	817	6.47
354	Flagstaff, AZ	6,037	835	6.44
69	Sarasota, FL	15,683	1,746	6.23
344	Bozeman, MT	5,696	682	6.03
353	Farmington, NM	3,157	417	5.92
88	Savannah, GA	8,734	986	5.67
15	Wilmington, NC	6,805	866	5.59
387	Longview, WA	5,025	514	5.57
298	Monett, MO	2,442	373	5.55
348	Santa Fe, NM	6,801	824	5.51
376	Reno, NV	11,736	1,356	5.38
78	Ocala, FL	6,079	661	5.34
Lowest 20 LMAs by formation rate				
134	Lima, OH	5,312	333	2.54
182	Olean, NY	4,677	282	2.54
213	Mankato, MN	5,430	353	2.53
139	Kokomo, IN	3,585	235	2.52
125	Dayton, OH	24,505	1,613	2.52
237	Galesburg, IL	2,861	180	2.51
165	Erie, PA	13,602	790	2.51
192	Harrisburg, PA	20,484	1,323	2.50
208	Springfield, MA	13,904	819	2.49
224	Sheboygan, WI	3,717	258	2.49
140	Muncie, IN	7,760	527	2.48

Table 3.2 *(continued)*

LMA	Biggest Place	1994 Establ.	Avg Annual Formations	Formations/ 1,000 LF
133	Findlay, OH	4,938	313	2.47
177	Syracuse, NY	22,325	1,317	2.46
126	Richmond, IN	2,127	130	2.31
178	Oneonta, NY	3,281	176	2.31
187	Sunbury, PA	3,509	206	2.28
183	Watertown, NY	4,342	246	2.28
219	Marshalltown, IA	2,360	129	2.18
179	Binghamton, NY	5,557	309	2.11
181	Elmira, NY	6,501	346	2.06

consecutive years of LMA formation rates varied from .90 to .94 during the nineties.

Knowledge as a Source of Entrepreneurial Opportunity

The starting point for most theories of entrepreneurship (innovation) is the knowledge production function (Griliches, 1979). The knowledge production function assumes that the firm is exogenous to the model and that the firm endogenously converts knowledge inputs into knowledge outputs (Jaffe, 1989). We assume a knowledge production function:

$$Q = f(K) \qquad (3.1)$$

where Q represents innovation for a spatial unit of observation and K is knowledge inputs (usually industrial R&D and university research). As was explained in Chapter Two, the knowledge production function assumes that knowledge is automatically commercialized, or $K = K^c$. However, as we pointed out, this assumption that knowledge spills over and is commercialized is inconsistent with Arrow's (1962) observation that not all knowledge becomes economic knowledge,

$$K - K^c > 0. \qquad (3.2)$$

As Arrow emphasized, due to the high levels of uncertainty and asymmetry that are inherent in new knowledge, incumbent enterprises are constrained in their ability to transform knowledge into economic knowledge, resulting in a commercialization rate by incumbent enterprises of θ. Theta could be interpreted as reflecting the commercialization capabilities of incumbent enterprises.

A large literature has emerged focusing on what has become known as the appropriability problem (Cohen and Levin, 1989). The underlying issue revolves around how firms that invest in the creation of new economic knowledge can best appropriate the economic returns from the knowledge (Arrow 1962). Audretsch (1995b, 26) proposed

> shifting the unit of observation away from exogenously assumed firms to individuals (agents) with endowments of new economic knowledge.... But when the lens is shifted away from focusing on the firm as the relevant unit of observation to individuals, the relevant question becomes, how can economic agents with a given endowment of new knowledge best appropriate the returns from that knowledge?

A Knowledge Spillover Theory of Entrepreneurship

Knowledge not commercialized by incumbent enterprises creates the opportunity set for potential entrepreneurs to transform that knowledge through commercialization by starting a new firm. Such a new firm formation constitutes a knowledge spillover, which is the basis of the knowledge spillover theory of entrepreneurship (Acs et al., 2005). The decision to exploit an opportunity through the creation of a new firm has been examined in the occupational choice literature in labor economics, which offers an explanation of the decision to exploit opportunities at the level of the individual, based on monetary criteria as well as psychological characteristics. Models of occupational choice have been developed by Evans and Jovanovic (1989) and David Blanchflower and Andrew Oswald (1998), building on the earlier work of Knight (1921), Lucas (1979), and Jovanovic (1982).

The intertemporal choice between becoming an entrepreneur or remaining an employee depends on the expected payoff accruing to the respective alternatives. The individual who chooses to remain an employee will receive a wage with certainty, which we will refer to as the agent's expected utility from remaining an employee. If, on the other hand, the agent chooses to become an entrepreneur, his expected utility is dependent on the probability of success and the expected payoff

(π). For an individual to engage in entrepreneurial activities, his or her expected net payoff from entrepreneurial activities must be larger than the expected net payoff from remaining an employee, to compensate for the higher risk of entrepreneurship. If $\pi > w$, then there exists a probability such that the choice of being an entrepreneur is optimal for the individual. Assuming that there exists a $\pi > w$, some agents will shift from employment to being entrepreneurs, thereby commercializing part of their given aggregate knowledge stock. The formation of a new firm is based on the equation reflecting occupational choice:

$$E_{srt} = \gamma(\pi^* - w) \tag{3.3}$$

where E reflects the decision to become an entrepreneur (generally stated in terms of probabilities), π^* is the profits expected to be earned from entering into entrepreneurship, and w is the wage that would be earned from employment in an incumbent enterprise; s stands for sector, r is region, and t is time.

Once an opportunity (new or unexploited knowledge) is discovered, the decision to exploit the opportunity is determined by cultural considerations as well as profit opportunities. An entrepreneurial culture is defined as a social context where entrepreneurial behavior is encouraged (Johannisson, 1984). This culture includes two interrelated aspects: first, the entrepreneurial orientation of the local population, and second, the distribution of entrepreneurial characteristics among local institutions, such as the community/regional political leadership, financial institutions, and educational institutions. Various authors have emphasized that the strength of local entrepreneurial culture varies spatially, although empirical testing of the relationship between local cultural and entrepreneurial activity is difficult, and interpretations of the causes of such variations differ.

An interpretation of the effect of local culture on entrepreneurial activity is provided by Sven Illeris (1986), who draws upon the work of Danish ethnologists. He suggests that at least three contrasting "life modes" can be identified: self-employment, "career" and "wage-work." These life-modes are culturally and socially determined, and they influence the propensity of individuals to create new businesses. In the self-employment life-mode, the dominant job-related motivation is to own the means of production and control the production process. This cultural tradition is carried over from generation to generation. This lifestyle is most frequently found in rural areas characterized by independent and self-reliant small-scale farmers, ranchers' artisans, and small business owners. It is rare in areas dominated by large-scale operations.

The dominant value of the "wage earner" life-mode is the sale of one's labor at the highest possible price in order to maximize the utility of one's leisure time. Such individuals are therefore unlikely to set up new businesses, except possibly if they were unemployed and unable to find alternative paid employment. This life-mode is likely to be most common in localities and regions characterized by a narrow industrial base and dominated by large externally owned firms. The local dominance of large firms and secondary branch locations of firms should have a negative effect on the regional formation rate.

The dominant value of individuals with a career life-mode is the advancement of their career. They are likely to be well educated and working in large hierarchical private or public sector organizations. They will start their own businesses if this becomes the best way in which to benefit from their skills, knowledge, and expertise. These businesses are often technologically advanced, innovative, and with good marketing capabilities. Career-mode entrepreneurs are often concentrated in large metropolitan areas and smaller attractive cities (Savage, Dickens, and Fielding, 1988). In fact, the 1990s saw a high incidence of highly educated individuals starting new businesses, especially in the technologically advanced sectors of the economy, like computers, biotechnology, and Internet start-ups (Sweeney, 1987, 1991, 1996).

Since the expected profit opportunity accruing from entrepreneurship is the result of knowledge not commercialized by the incumbent firm, entrepreneurial opportunities will be shaped by the magnitude of new knowledge but constrained by the commercialization capabilities and preferences of incumbent firms,

$$E_{srt} = \gamma(\pi^*(K, \theta, C) - w) \qquad (3.4)$$

where K is the aggregate stock of knowledge and θ ($0 < \theta < 1$) refers to the share of knowledge not exploited by incumbents (or spillover potential), and the extent of an entrepreneurial culture is represented by C. Studies of new firm formation from the 1980s often examined the role of industrial restructuring, which has been associated with (1) the shift from manufacturing to service businesses, (2) a reduction in both firm and plant size, and (3) a shift to higher levels of technology. The shift from manufacturing to services, which are usually less capital intensive than manufacturing, could increase the rate of new firm formation. Regions that are dominated by large branch plants or firms will tend to have less new firm formation (Mason, 1994). Most new firm founders have either managerial or skilled labor backgrounds. Consequently, the occupational structure of a city or region might also be expected to influence the supply of new firm founders. The spatial division of labor within multisite enterprises has resulted in many peripheral areas being dominated by externally-owned branch plants performing routine assembly and production services.

Another important difference that impacts new firm formation is local variation in agglomeration effects. These contribute to new firm formation either through demand effects, such as increases in population, or from regional spillovers, such as labor market characteristics. Krugman's (1991a and 1991b) theory links firm formation rates to three types of spillovers within a region. The first emanates from the observation by Marshall (1890) that a pooled labor market yields increasing returns at a spatial level. Second, agglomerations are conducive to a greater provision of nontraded inputs. Such inputs are provided both in greater variety and at lower cost in larger economies. The third source of convexities emanates from what Acs, Audretsch, and Feldman (1992 and 1994) termed economies of information flows. Thus, the formation rate for each industry sector should increase with the existing local density of establishments in that sector, or with the sector specialization.

Equation 3.4 implicitly assumes away any institutional or individual barriers to entrepreneurship. Yet a rich literature suggests that there is a compelling array of financial, institutional and individual barriers to entrepreneurship, which results in a modification of the entrepreneurial choice equation:

$$E_{srt} = \gamma(\pi^*(K, \theta, C) - w)1/\beta \qquad (3.5)$$

where β represents those institutional and individual barriers to entrepreneurship, spanning factors such as risk aversion, financial constraints, and legal and regulatory restrictions. The existence of such barriers explains why economic agents might choose not to enter into entrepreneurship, even when confronted with knowledge that would otherwise generate a potentially profitable opportunity. Thus, this chapter focuses on a reduced model to show how local differences in knowledge stocks, the presence of large firms as deterrents to knowledge exploitation, and an entrepreneurial culture might explain regional variations in the rates of entrepreneurial activity,

$$E_{srt} = (K, \theta, C). \tag{3.6}$$

Variables Used for Analysis of the Formation Model

From the previous discussion it should be clear that the major hypotheses concerning the regional variation in firm formation rates are that (1) higher formation rates are promoted by knowledge; (2) industrial restructuring away from manufacturing and toward smaller businesses should promote new firm formation; and (3) the existence of an entrepreneurial culture should promote start-up activity. To test these hypotheses, we estimate a regression model where the dependent variable is the 1995 + 1996 average annual firm formation rate divided by the labor force (in thousands). This is analogous to the method used by David Keeble and S. Walker (1994) and P. Davidsson, L. Lindmark, and C. Olofsson, (1994). The entrepreneur starting a new business is assumed to live in the same LMA as the new firm, and to have benefited from spillovers within that region. This approach to standardizing the formation rate has the added advantage of a clear lower bound of 0.00 (for no new businesses), and a theoretical upper bound of 1,000, which would represent the extreme case where every worker within a region started a new business during a year.

There are two important qualifications to be noted concerning this firm formation rate. The first has to do with the timing of the recognition of the new firm. While firms enter the regional economy on a continuous basis, the LEEM file annually reports only the first-quarter employment of each establishment and firm, representing their number of employees during their March 15 pay period each year. If an establishment hires its first employee after March, we do not count the new firm as active until the following year. Therefore, the new firms that we count have had employees for an average of six months by the time the LEEM file records their "first" employment (Acs and Armington, 1998). Second, the average time between an entrepreneur's decision to create a new organization and the initial operation of the business has been found to be about two years (*Global Entrepreneurship Monitor*, 2002). Therefore, much of the entrepreneurial activity has taken place two to three years earlier than the first appearance of the firm's employment in the LEEM file.

The counts of firm formations, along with numbers of establishments and employees, were tabulated by LMA, industry sector, and year from the LEEM file at the U.S. Bureau of the Census, Center for Economic Studies, in suburban Washington DC. All other variables were tabulated from county-level data collected (often from other agencies) on a compact disk called "USA Counties 1998" by the U.S. Census Bureau.

The primary explanatory (independent or exogenous) variables include the share of college graduates and high school dropouts in the adult population as proxies for the stock of knowledge, sector specialization as proxy for knowledge spillover potential, and the share of proprietors and average establishment size as proxies for entrepreneurial culture. In addition, we control for regional differences in unemployment, population growth, and income growth.

To measure the level of knowledge in the economy, we use two correlated, but distinct, measures of educational attainment in each region. The first is the share of adults who are *high school dropouts*, defined as the number of adults without a high school degree in 1990, divided by the total number of adults (population 25 years or older).[10] The lack of a high school degree should be a good proxy for the proportion of unskilled and semiskilled labor, and should be negatively related to the formation rate. In fact, as shown in Table 3.3, the simple correlation between the percentage of the population without a high school degree and the formation rate is −0.19. The mean percentage of the U.S. population without a high school degree is 27%. These summary statistics are shown in Tables 3.3 and 3.4 for this variable and all other independent variables used in this chapter.

---

[10] Available data on educational attainment at the county level, which were aggregated to the LMA level, were limited to Decennial Census data from 1990. It is regrettable that the update from the 2000 Decennial Census was still not available at the county level in 2002, but it would surely have shown great increases in educational attainment levels in most regions.

Table 3.3. *Correlations of firm formation rates and associated regional characteristics*

	Formations/LF	Establ. Size	Specialization	High School Dropout	College Grads	Popul. Growth	Income Growth	Proprietor Share
1995 + 1996 firm formations/1,000 '94 labor force	1.00							
Establishment size '94 empl./'94 establ.	−0.42	1.00						
Business specialization '94 establ./population	0.53	−0.31	1.00					
High school dropouts '90 adults < hs/adults (25+)	−0.19	−0.05	−0.52	1.00				
College graduates '90 adult grads/adults	0.29	0.22	0.37	−0.70	1.00			
Population growth sqrt ('94 pop/'92 pop)	0.54	−0.02	0.04	−0.12	0.23	1.00		
Income growth per cap. sqrt ('94 pers. inc/'92 pers. inc)	0.36	0.19	0.001	0.04	0.06	0.70	1.00	
Proprietor share '94 proprietors/labor force	0.30	−0.63	0.46	−0.19	−0.05	0.005	−0.19	1.00
Unemployment rate '94 unempl./'94 labor force	−0.03	−0.27	−0.37	0.29	−0.32	−0.001	−0.18	0.20

Note: Pearson Coefficients, smaller than .12 are not significant at the .02 level.

Table 3.4. *Summary statistics for LMA-level variables*

	Mean	Std. dev.	Min.	Max.
Firm formations/LF = avg '95 + '96 formations/'94 LF (1,000s)				
All sectors	3.740	0.938	2.06	10.18
Local market	1.790	0.499	*	*
Retail trade	0.872	0.215	*	*
Manufactures	0.187	0.079	*	*
Distribution	0.425	0.140	*	*
Business services	0.368	0.181	*	*
Extractive	0.096	0.057	*	*
Establishment size = '94 sector employment/'94 sector establishments**				
All sectors	15.1	2.9	8.3	21.2
Local market	11.2	2.4	7.1	25.4
Retail trade	13.2	2.1	8.3	20.1
Manufactures	55.2	21.6	10.7	139.0
Distribution	13.5	3.7	6.9	26.5
Business services	13.9	6.9	4.1	79.9
Extractive	11.1	8.0	3.9	77.6
Sector specialization = '94 sector establishments/'94 population (1,000s)				
All sectors (business specialization)	21.4	3.40	10.8	45.1
Local market	10.11	1.84	4.70	22.50
Retail trade	5.77	0.91	2.49	13.30
Manufactures	1.35	0.46	0.38	4.09
Distribution	2.73	0.73	1.23	5.42
Business services	1.39	0.57	0.49	3.98
Extractive	0.49	0.34	0.15	2.87
High school dropouts = '90 adults < hs/ adults (25+)	0.279	0.080	0.117	0.541
College graduates = '90 adult college grads/adults	0.159	0.050	0.069	0.320
Population growth = sqrt ('94 population/'92 pop)	1.011	0.0103	0.980	1.062
Income growth = sqrt ('94 pers. inc. per cap./'92 p. inc. p. c.)	1.051	0.0157	1.008	1.104
Proprietor share = '94 proprietors/'94 labor force	0.206	0.058	0.099	0.448
Unemployment rate = '94 unempl. /'94 labor force	0.062	0.0246	0.020	0.293

*Data suppressed to maintain confidentiality.
**1994 employment estimated as average of 1991 and 1996 employment by LMA and sector.

The share of *college graduates* is defined as the number of adults with college degrees in 1990 divided by the total number of adults. This is a proxy measure of both technical skills needed in the economy – for example, engineers and scientists – and skills needed to start and build a business, like finance and marketing and complex reasoning. In 1990, an average of 15.9% of the adult population had a college degree. The simple correlation of college graduate share with regional formation rates is positive, with a coefficient of .29, and we expect it to be positively related to the birth rate, even after controlling for other important factors (Simon and Nardinelli, 2002; Glaeser, Scheinkman, and Shleifer, 1995; Rauch, 1993). Prior U.S. empirical work has presented rather convincing evidence at the individual level that, other things being equal, educational attainment levels are positively associated with new business formation (Bates, 1991; Evans and Leighton, 1990).

We do not use measures of university and industrial research and development expenditures as indicators of regional differences in the levels of knowledge. These expenditure data, generally based on National Science Foundation surveys, are limited to formal research in large institutions and businesses, and virtually exclude most research and development investments by smaller firms and individuals. In addition, Bruce Kirchhoff and colleagues (2002) found that at the LMA level, the university R&D expenditures were correlated .70 with the regional share of adults with college degrees. They found (p. 14) that inclusion of R&D expenditures in similar regression analyses of formation rates did not increase the explanatory power of the model, although the estimated coefficients were generally significant, but tiny (standardized coefficient of .02 when the college graduates variable is included, and .07 without college graduates). This suggests that the "official" R&D data fail to incorporate the regional differences in new knowledge development that we would like to measure.

The entrepreneurial culture is measured primarily by the *share of proprietors* already in the economy. It is calculated as the number of proprietors in 1994 divided by the 1994 labor force. Proprietors are members of the labor force who are also business owners. This measure averages 20.5% nationally, and varies from a low of 9.9% to a high of 44.8% across LMAs. It includes both the self-employed who have no employees and the owners of unincorporated businesses that have employees. The simple correlation between the regional formation rate and the share of proprietors is 0.30, indicating a moderately strong relationship between these variables.

In order to assess the potential for positive effects from spillovers, many studies have measured density using the square root of the regional population, or population per square mile. Such measures, however, do not indicate the extent of pooled labor markets, or the probability of social networks among relevant knowledge workers, since they tell us nothing about the density of similar establishments in the region. They are more indicative of physical crowding than of communication opportunities for knowledge spillovers. Therefore, we introduce a new measure that captures the density of establishments in a region relative to its population. Sector *specialization* is the number of establishments in the industry sector and region in 1994 divided by the region's 1994 population. The greater the number of establishments relative to the population, the more spillovers that should be facilitated (Ciccone and Hall, 1996). Because this measure will be standardized by the national average, it may be thought of as either the local supply of each sector's establishments per 1,000 population relative to the national supply, or as the region's share of all establishments in that sector nationally relative to the region's share of U.S. population. This makes clearer its function as a rough measure of the probable frequency of exposure of the populace to the knowledgeable management and technical personnel working in a sector. However, when all industry sectors are pooled together, the sector specialization measure becomes *business specialization*, an indicator of the relative supply of private sector businesses in the region. This would tend to be low in regions dominated by agricultural production (farms and ranches), by government activities, and possibly by retirement communities.

Establishment size is a proxy for the structure of industry in the region. It is measured as 1994 employment divided by the number of establishments in 1994 in the region. It should be negatively related to regional formation rate since larger average establishment size indicates greater dominance by large firms or branch plants and greater large firm commercialization of knowledge, leaving less potential for spillovers to outsiders. As noted earlier, large establishments also tend to result in a smaller share of employees with managerial experience and a lower level of local competition. They may also tend to resist change, due to higher sunk capital and rigid bureaucracies, among other factors. Thus, establishment size is expected to have a negative effect on new firm formation. Edward Glaeser and colleagues (1992) interpreted the inverse of establishment size (establishments per worker) as a measure of local competition, which they considered the best measure of the regional culture of entrepreneurship.

In most studies of new firm formation in the 1980s, there was a heavy emphasis on the explanatory power of unemployment (Storey, 1991; Evans and Leighton, 1990). Unemployment increased significantly in several countries and stayed at very high levels over an extended period. It was suggested that when workers are unemployed, they might be more likely to start their own businesses. The formation of new firms, in turn, may reduce the unemployment rate, as the new firms employ not only the owner but also others. However, this relationship is more complicated. Higher levels of unemployment might also indicate a reduction in aggregate demand throughout a regional economy, thereby putting downward pressure on the rate of new firm formation (Storey and Johnson, 1987). Audretsch and Michael Fritsch (1994), and Catherine Armington and Acs (2002) have found conflicting results for this variable – it is not clear whether, or when, the impact of local differences in unemployment rates is negative or positive. David Storey (1991, 177) found that, generally speaking, time series analyses point to unemployment being positively associated with new firm formation, whereas cross-sectional or pooled cross-sectional studies appear to indicate the reverse. This apparent inconsistency may be due to differences in sectoral requirements for start-ups, with the industry sectors that require relatively small amounts of capital being more suitable for start-ups in periods of higher unemployment. It may also reflect missing variables that might indicate other aspects of labor demand.

The *unemployment rate* is the traditional calculation for the year prior to our formation measurement period – the average number of unemployed in 1994 divided by the 1994 labor force. It is expected to be negatively related to formations overall, but probably positively related to new firm formation rates in industries with low capital requirements, and negatively related to those with high capital requirements. The simple correlation between the unemployment rate and the firm formation rate is close to zero, and is not statistically significant.

Finally, *population growth* is the average annual rate of increase in the region's population in the previous two-year period (calculating, for example, the compound growth ratio from 1992 to1994 from the square root of the ratio of the 1994 population to the 1992 population). It serves as a proxy for the attractiveness of the region for both living and doing business, in place of the many other partial indicators of attractiveness (parks, highways, taxes, schools, universities, crime, etc.) that have been used for this purpose. Population growth may function as both a supply and a demand variable. A growing population increases the supply of potential founders of new businesses, and it increases the demand for consumer services. It captures the extent to which cities are relatively attractive to both migrants and immigrants, for living and for doing business. Population growth in a region stimulates growth in both the quantity and variety of businesses supplying that region's consumers. This business growth usually takes place by a combination of expansion of existing businesses and formation of new businesses.

Income growth is similarly calculated as the average annual rate of increase of personal per capita income in the region in the prior two years. Income growth in excess of population growth captures local growth in labor productivity, and concomitant increases in local average quality of life. There are several mechanisms by which faster-growing incomes might contribute to higher rates of new firm formation. Increasing per capita income is likely to increase disposable income, leading to greater demand for a wider range of income-elastic goods and services. In addition, higher income growth rates may enable potential new business founders to raise local capital more easily at lower cost, thereby facilitating new firm formation.

Of course, some of these variables may in fact be partially endogenous, or correlated with other variables. Although income and population growth were measured for a previous two-year period, their regional differences are likely to persist over time, and future growth differences certainly result from current differences in formation rates. The share of proprietors and the agglomeration effects measured by sector or business specialization may also be the result of more firm formations in the recent past, as well as contributing factors to future formations. In fact, much of the economic geography literature today is concerned with cumulative growth mechanisms in which cause and effect are simultaneous. Our regression results should be interpreted carefully, and do not necessarily imply causality.[11]

Empirical Results from Estimation of the Formation Model

Table 3.5 shows the results of least squares regression on the 1995 + 1996 average annual firm formation rates for all industries together, and for each of the six industry sectors, based on the 394 Labor Market Areas.[12] We present standardized beta coefficients, so that each parameter indicates the sensitivity of formation rate variation to normalized variation in the corresponding independent variable. The t-ratios shown for each were calculated from the simple estimated standard errors. These were recalculated later with a correction for heteroscedasticity, and those were very similar to the uncorrected standard errors. The estimated coefficients are generally consistent with our expectations, but with several important exceptions. The explanatory and control variables together explained about two-thirds of the regional differences in firm formation rates, but much less for distributive services, and much more (.86) for business services.

Sector specialization is the strongest explanatory variable. With a coefficient of .46 for all sectors together, and .50 or higher for each of the six sectors, it is estimated that a region whose existing specialization is one standard deviation higher than the national average (around 20% higher) will have a firm formation rate that is half a standard deviation (around 25%, or 13% for half) higher. The effects of sector specialization are particularly strong for business services, for which the coefficient is .86.

---

[11] We have also abstained from considering financial variables and such regional knowledge factors as local research and development expenditures. The availability of adequate financial resources to fund new firms is an important determinant of new firm formation, which we hope to take into account in subsequent research. Both university-based and industrial R&D activity may be important contributors to regional new firm start-up rates, but they are not easily measured, and are also highly correlated with college degree shares.

[12] Although we have 10 years of annual firm formation data, we have chosen not to use pooled cross-section time series regressions. Most of the independent variables describing the characteristics of the LMAs change very little over time, and the errors from omitted variables will be nearly identical for each LMA from year to year, and so the diagnostic statistics from such an analysis would be very misleading.

Table 3.5. *Regression coefficients for firm formation rates of LMAs by sector (standardized beta coefficients, with t-ratios below, bold if significant at .05 level)*

Avg. 1995 + 1996 Formations/LF	All Sectors	Local Markets	Retail Trade	Manufactures	Distribution	Business Services	Extractive
Adj. R sqrd	0.67	0.65	0.64	0.63	0.49	0.86	0.67
Establishment size	**-0.36**	**-0.15**	**-0.22**	**-0.22**	**-0.15**	-0.02	-0.01
	(-7.08)	-3.43	-4.04	-5.48	-3.01	-0.82	-0.37)
Sector specialization	**0.46**	**0.53**	**0.50**	**0.76**	**0.64**	**0.86**	**0.79**
	(11.03	12.2	11.99	22.8	14.8	25.2	23.6)
Share of proprietors	-0.01	**0.11**	**0.21**	**0.13**	-0.05	0.03	-0.01
	(-0.29)	2.66	4.73	3.34	-0.90	1.14	-0.20)
High school dropout	**0.23**	**0.19**	**0.20**	**0.15**	**0.38**	0.03	**0.17**
	(5.09)	3.83	3.90	3.11	6.85	1.05	3.84)
College graduates	**0.29**	**0.24**	**0.22**	0.08	**0.25**	0.01	**0.11**
	(6.36)	4.82	4.44	1.58	4.30	0.33	2.46)
Population growth	**0.37**	**0.40**	**0.32**	**0.15**	**0.27**	**0.17**	**0.18**
	(7.81)	8.39	6.61	2.92	4.61	5.69	3.76)
Income growth	**0.16**	**0.15**	0.09	0.03	0.08	**0.07**	0.01
	(3.31)	3.14	1.75	0.68	1.44	2.33	0.25)
Unemployment rate	0.08	**0.17**	**0.18**	**0.14**	**0.16**	**0.06**	0.07
	(1.91)	4.47	4.65	3.34	3.51	2.48	1.85)

Number of observations is 394 (LMAs) in each sector.
Note: See Table 3.4 for specification of variables.

The next strongest explanatory variable is population growth, which is also strongly positive and statistically significant. This is not telling us merely that new firm formations tend to keep up with the growth in the size of the regional economy but that the formation *rate*, in terms of new firms per 1,000 potential workers in the LMA, is higher in regions that are growing faster than average. However, the coefficient on income growth, while also positive and significant, is quite small, and only barely significant at the .05 level for all sectors together. These results on sector specialization, population growth, and income growth are consistent with those found by Reynolds (1994), Keeble and Walker (1994), and Audretsch and Fritsch (1994). But when analyzing separately for each of the industry sectors, we find that the positive parameters on income growth are only significant for business services and the local market sector.

The coefficient for human capital measured by share of college graduates is positive and statistically significant, suggesting that regions that have higher levels of education will have higher start-up rates. This is consistent with M. Savage, P. Dickens, and T. Felding (1988) and Anselin, Varga, and Acs (1997, 2000), who found that in technologically advanced industry, individuals with greater skills, knowledge, and expertise are more likely to start businesses. However, for both business services and manufacturing, this coefficient is only barely positive, and not statistically significant. Reynolds (1994) had previously found a negative and statistically significant relationship between college education and the new firm formation rate in manufacturing. The results do suggest that manufacturing firms may behave differently than other sectors of the economy.

The positive and statistically significant coefficient for the share of the adult population without a high school degree (high school dropouts) is at first surprising, but it is easily explained. As shown in Table 3.3, the correlation between the high school dropout share and the new firm formation rate has a negative coefficient, as noted earlier. However, it is much more strongly negatively correlated with college education, with a coefficient of −0.70. After controlling for the share of adults with college degrees, the additional effect of a greater share of less educated workers is to facilitate the start-up process by providing cheap labor for the new firms. Even the most sophisticated businesses need some workers who are less educated to do the manual labor. This positive impact of "high school dropout" after controlling for "college degree" is consistent across most of the industry sectors, except for business services, where neither of the educational attainment variables was significant.

The coefficient for establishment size is negative and statistically significant, as expected. Regions with predominately smaller establishments have a higher firm formation rate than regions with more large establishments. This supports the thesis that regions that have already restructured away from large manufacturing dominance have a higher formation rate than regions that have not. These results are consistent with the findings of Audretsch and Fritsch (1994).

The coefficient for the unemployment rate is positive, although it is tiny and not statistically significant at the all-industry level. This result is surprising, given that previous cross-sectional studies have generally found a consistently negative result (Audretsch and Fritsch, 1994, and Storey, 1991). Furthermore, the coefficients on unemployment were positive for all of the six sectors, and significantly so for all but the extractive industries. Perhaps the exceptionally low levels of unemployment and even shortages of labor in the United States in the 1990s account for the prevailingly positive relationship between unemployment and new firm formations in this period. The implication here is that as workers shift from being employed to unemployed, the overall entry rate in the region tends to go up slightly, although there is no evidence that it is necessarily the unemployed who are starting the new firms.

The coefficient on the share of proprietors in the region is negative and statistically insignificant for the all-industry equation, perhaps because the share of proprietors is strongly negatively correlated with establishment size, −0.63. As the average establishment size in a region increases, there are fewer opportunities for self-employment, and a smaller proportion of the labor force is made up of owners. When we drop establishment size from the estimated regression, the coefficient on self-employment becomes positive and statistically significant, while the other variables remain virtually unchanged. Within several of the industry sectors – local market, manufacturing, and retail – the share of proprietors is significantly positively related to firm formation rates. The separate regressions for the six industry sectors are not very sensitive to the presence of the establishment size variable. It has positive and statistically significant coefficients for local market, manufacturing, and retail, but its presence somewhat reduces the t-statistics on other variables.

Table 3.6 shows regression results for individual years from 1991 to 1999. The equations are almost identical to those presented in Table 3.5, with the exception that we have dropped the share of proprietors because of its multicollinearity with firm size and lack of significance in the earlier regressions. The results are robust with respect to each of the different years, and remarkably similar during periods of contraction and expansion. The strong negative and statistically significant coefficient for establishment size shows that smaller establishment size was consistently associated with higher levels of firm formations. Business specialization continued to have a positive effect on new firm formations throughout the decade. Population growth continues to be much more important than income growth. The coefficient on the unemployment rate is generally small and not statistically significant. This suggests that new firm formation was not influenced by the unemployment rate in the 1990s, with perhaps the exception of 1990. Both human capital variables are also consistent over time and show very little variation.

Table 3.7 continues to explore the educational attainment variables, to investigate the effects separately in order to analyze the impact of their collinearity on our prior analyses. We estimate these equations again for each of three periods – 1991, 1995, and 1999 – and then alternatively drop the high school dropout variable and then the college graduate variable. The estimated coefficients for all of the other variables remain substantially the same when either of the education variables is dropped. The coefficients on the remaining educational attainment variable become weaker, suggesting that the two variables play a different role in explaining new firm formation.

Conclusions

This chapter has reexamined the issue of new firm formation in light of recent theoretical developments in economic geography and new growth theory. Using a new longitudinal microdata source, we constructed annual data on firm formations for 394 labor market areas, between 1991 and 1999, and for six industrial sectors for the average of 1995 and 1996 firm formations. We find considerable variation in the

Table 3.6. *Effects of regional characteristics on annual firm formation rates of LMAs from 1991 through 1999 (estimated standardized beta coefficients, with t-ratios below, bold if significant at .05 level)*

Formations(t)/LaborForce(t−1)	1991	1992	1993	1994	1995	1996	1997	1998	1999
Adj. R sqrd	0.61	0.64	0.61	0.63	0.67	0.67	0.63	0.66	0.61
Establ. size	**−0.37**	**−0.35**	**−0.33**	**−0.29**	**−0.33**	**−0.35**	**−0.33**	**−0.36**	**−0.33**
empl. (t−1)/establ. (t−1)	(−9.41)	−9.28	−8.52	−7.67	−8.64	−9.05	−8.72	−9.68	−7.91
Business specialization	**0.45**	**0.45**	**0.49**	**0.48**	**0.49**	**0.43**	**0.38**	**0.45**	**0.44**
establ. (t−1)/population (t−1)	(10.25	10.66	10.98	11.20	11.72	10.52	8.71	10.96	9.85)
High school dropouts (1990)	**0.23**	**0.22**	**0.26**	**0.22**	**0.26**	**0.22**	**0.20**	**0.26**	**0.23**
adults < hs/adults (25+yrs)	(4.66	4.41	5.06	4.44	5.65	4.77	4.09	5.44	4.67)
College grads (1990)	**0.22**	**0.19**	**0.20**	**0.18**	**0.26**	**0.27**	**0.27**	**0.27**	**0.26**
adult grads/adults (25+yrs)	(4.49	3.96	4.26	3.88	5.97	6.21	5.86	6.03	5.32)
Population growth	**0.31**	**0.32**	**0.32**	**0.37**	**0.36**	**0.43**	**0.46**	**0.50**	**0.46**
sqrt (pop (t−1)/pop (t−3))	(7.20	7.86	7.50	7.88	7.92	11.47	10.43	12.89	11.87)
Income growth (per capita)	**0.16**	**0.23**	**0.24**	**0.20**	**0.18**	**0.13**	0.07	0.02	**0.09**
sqrt (pers. inc (t−1)/pers. inc (t−3))	(4.06	5.91	5.83	4.35	3.87	3.20	1.44	0.45	2.39)
Unemployment rate	**0.10**	−0.01	−0.04	0.01	**0.07**	0.06	0.03	0.04	0.08
unempl. (t−1)/labor force (t−1)	(2.25	−0.23	−0.88	0.27	1.99	1.61	0.70	0.97	1.86)

Number of observations is 394 (LMAs) in each year.

Table 3.7. *Effects of alternative specifications of educational attainment on models of firm formation rates for 1991, 1995, and 1999 (estimated standardized beta coefficients, with t-ratios below, bold if significant at .05 level)*

| | Firm Formations per Prior Year Labor Force in Thousands | | | | | | | | |
| | 1991 | | | 1995 | | | 1999 | | |
Firm formations(t)/LabForce(t−1)	Both	No HS	Coll	Both	No HS	Coll	Both	No HS	Coll
Adj. R sqrd	0.61	0.59	0.59	0.67	0.64	0.65	0.61	0.59	0.59
Establ. size	**−0.37**	**−0.33**	**−0.36**	**−0.33**	**−0.26**	**−0.33**	**−0.33**	**−0.28**	**−0.33**
empl. (t−1)/establ. (t−1)	(−9.41)	−8.32	−8.84	−8.64	−6.89	−8.40	−7.91	−6.68	−7.60
Business specialization	**0.45**	**0.48**	**0.40**	**0.49**	**0.53**	**0.42**	**0.44**	**0.48**	**0.39**
establ. (t−1)/population (t−1)	(10.25	10.79	9.14	11.72	12.31	10.10	9.85	10.42	8.68
High school dropouts (1990)	**0.23**	**0.12**	–	**0.26**	**0.11**	–	**0.23**	0.08	–
adults < hs/adults (25 + yrs)	(4.66	2.66	–	5.65	2.67	–	4.67	1.83	(–)
College grads (1990)	**0.22**	–	**0.10**	**0.26**	–	**0.12**	**0.26**	–	**0.12**
adult grads/adults (25 + yrs)	(4.49	–	2.36	5.97	–	3.27	5.32	–	3.09
Population growth	**0.31**	**0.33**	**0.28**	**0.36**	**0.42**	**0.33**	**0.46**	**0.49**	**0.48**
sqrt (pop (t−1)/pop (t−3))	(7.20	7.67	6.52	7.92	9.28	7.09	11.87	12.48	12.00
Income growth per capita	**0.16**	**0.18**	**0.18**	**0.18**	**0.14**	**0.22**	**0.09**	**0.12**	**0.10**
sqrt (pers. inc (t−1)/pers. inc (t−3))	(4.06	4.29	4.29	3.87	2.92	4.74	2.39	3.01	2.47
Unemployment rate	**0.10**	0.08	**0.15**	**0.07**	**0.08**	**0.11**	0.08	**0.09**	**0.11**
unempl. (t−1)/labor force (t−1)	(2.25	1.88	3.47	1.99	2.02	2.95	1.86	2.01	2.68

Number of observations is 394 (LMAs) for each model alternative.

74

new firm formation rates across regions, but little variation over time. The data show substantial differences in new firm formation rates, from the generally low rates in the industrial Northeast to the much more dynamic South and West. As hypothesized in the model, the regression analysis shows that variations in the new firm formation rates are substantially explained by regional differences, human capital, sector or business specialization, population growth rates, and the average size of existing businesses.

The strong negative relationship between new firm formation rates and establishment size indicates that regions that have already restructured toward smaller businesses (usually away from large manufacturing, toward services and more local competition) have higher rates of new firm formation than regions that have not. We find significant evidence of the importance of human capital on new firm formation rates. People in regions that have a high percentage of college graduates are much more likely to start businesses than those in regions with high concentrations of less skilled workers. After taking into account the share of college graduates, higher shares of high school dropouts also contribute to high rates of new firm formation.

We find strong support for the importance of specialization on new firm formation. These results are some of the strongest and are consistent across regions, sectors, and time. Population growth rates are strongly positively related to new firm formation, and income growth rates also contribute positively, but with small impact compared to population growth. We find a little support for a positive impact of unemployment on new firm formation rates. This is explained in part by the fact that in the 1990s unemployment problems were replaced by a labor shortage in the United States. Also, the share of proprietors has no detectable impact on the new firm formation rate, after controlling for the other factors we included. These results strongly support the new generation of growth models that suggest that knowledge is an important determinant of new firm formation and economic growth.

CHAPTER FOUR

Human Capital and Entrepreneurship

Introduction

This chapter extends research reported in the previous chapter, which focused on firm formation in six sectors: distributive, manufacturing, business services, extractive, retail trade, and local market. The current chapter focuses on the rapidly growing service sector and subsectors of service industries, which are defined by their founders' educational requirements and their primary markets.

Since the mid eighties, the role of education and human capital externalities has been recognized as a key variable in theories of economic growth. Lucas (1988) emphasizes that the economies of metropolitan areas are a natural context in which to understand the mechanics of economic growth, and an important factor contributing to this growth is the catalytic role of human capital externalities within the cities. While the benefits of human capital to individuals have been extensively studied, economists are now realizing that individuals do not capture all of the benefits from their own human capital. Some benefits spill over to their colleagues and observers – through discussion, example, publications, and positive attitudes toward change, risk, and new knowledge.

Several interesting findings provide some groundwork for this chapter. First, Rauch (1993) finds that cities with higher average levels of human capital also have higher wages and land rents. Second, Glaeser, Scheinkman, and A. Shleifer (1995) find that for a cross section of cities, a key economic determinant of growth is level of schooling, just as has previously been found for countries. They suggest that higher education levels influence later growth, not through increased savings but by promoting higher rates of growth of technology through spillovers. Finally, Simon and Nardinelli (1996, 2002) find historical evidence for both the United States and the United Kingdom that cities with more knowledgeable people grow faster in the long run because (a) knowledge spillovers are geographically limited to the city and (b) knowledge is more productive in the city within which it is acquired.

However, none of these studies asks the question "What type of activity do agents pursue that leads to faster economic growth?" This question is important because if we wish to explain how growth occurs, we need to identify the transmission mechanism from human capital to growth. Jovanovic and R. Rob (1989) develop a model where individual agents augment their knowledge through pairwise meetings at which they exchange ideas. In each time period, each individual (or economic agent) seeking to augment his or her knowledge meets another agent chosen randomly from a distribution of agents. The higher the average level of human capital of the agents, the more "luck" the agents will have with their meetings and the more rapid will be the diffusion and growth of knowledge. If this knowledge contributes to technical innovations, new products, processes, or markets, we have a microeconomic foundation, not only for the impact of human capital externalities on total factor productivity but also for making those external effects dependent on both the average level of human capital and the local concentration of businesses with employees with relevant knowledge or examples to share.

We empirically investigate how the new firm formation rates for various subsectors of service industries are influenced by human capital differences in 394 Labor Market Areas, while controlling for other regional characteristics that are also likely to affect firm formation rates. After discussing measurement of the service firm formation rate, we examine how and why the new firm formation rates vary across geographic regions. We present an empirical model and discuss the basic results of estimating this model for the service sector as a whole. To clarify some of these results, we define nine subsectors of services and reestimate the model using these subsectors. We conclude that the extent of human capital already in a region has a significant effect on the new service firm formation rate. The service firm formation rate is even more sensitive to how specialized with similar businesses (establishments per 1,000 people) the local area already is, compared to the national average. The greater this specialization is, the more probable the relevant knowledge spillovers are and the more likely that the resulting new ideas will lead to new firm formations.

Measurement of New Firm Formation Rate

The Sector of Inquiry

This chapter focuses on the service sector of the U.S. economy. Why do we feel that the service sector is preferable to manufacturing for analysis of new firm formation? First, there has been widespread concern among economists and policymakers alike about the dynamics of the service sector. The slowness of productivity growth in services, together with its rising share in nominal GNP and in employment, have been blamed for exerting a major drag on the productivity growth of the overall economy and its competitive performance. Second, the service sector has been growing much faster than other sectors, increasing its share of private employment from 28.3% in 1990 to 32.8% in 1998. Third, the broad range of firms in the service sector employ workers with a wide variety of skills, and they tend to be more labor-intensive than capital-intensive, so that area differences in human capital may have a stronger impact on the service sector than on more capital-intensive sectors. Fourth, new firm formation rates are much higher in the service sector than in the manufacturing sector (Acs and Armington, 2004b). Indeed, cities with high concentrations of manufacturing have typically been the slowest-growing cities over the past 20 years. Fifth, the persistence of new jobs in services and manufacturing was very similar, despite differences in capital intensity, demand shocks, and labor relationships (Armington and Acs, 2004). Finally, much of the growth in service jobs has been in new firms. While some of these new firms merely replace older establishments that have closed, many others serve new markets, provide new services, or apply innovative techniques to compete with older businesses.

The local economic impact of the formation of a new service firm is much broader than the immediate impact we can measure from the number of new jobs it creates in its first year. New service firms may be providing the local market with services that were not previously available, or competing with existing providers to drive down prices or improve services. If their services are exportable, the new businesses may be generating income from outside the region, and perhaps contributing to a local specialized cluster that will attract yet more businesses and employees. And, of course, the new firms will buy products and other services from local businesses.

The Firm Formation Rate

Firm formation rates are calculated for each of the 394 LMAs, based on the number of new service firm formations during each of three recent time periods – 1990 through 1992, 1993 through 1995, and 1996 through 1998. Services are defined narrowly – not including trade or financial services.[1] Because the Labor Market Areas vary greatly in size, the absolute numbers of new firm formations must be standardized by some measure of the LMA size before it is meaningful to compare them across areas. When dealing with the whole service sector, firm formation rates are calculated as the number of new firms per 1,000 members of the labor force in the LMA in the prior year (Evans and Jovanovic, 1989). A worker starts each new business, and the labor market approach implicitly assumes that the entrepreneur starts the new business in the labor market where he or she lives and previously worked.

When comparing new firm formation rates for different subsectors of the service industry, we need to standardize for the differences in sizes of both areas and subsectors. For this purpose, we express new firm formation rates in terms of the number of new firms relative to the number of establishments already in existence in that subsector and LMA. This could be termed the ecological approach because it considers the amount of start-up activity relative to the size of the existing population of businesses.

Variations in Regional New Firm Formation Rates in the 1990s

Table 4.1 shows annual variations in the numbers of new firm formations and the formation rates for service firms in the United States. Gross service firm formations were increasing fairly steadily during the 1990s, to just under 195,000 in 1997. These service firm formations account for nearly two-fifths of all nonfarm employer-firm formations. Net service firm

---

[1] Services were defined to include all establishments with primary Standard Industrial Classification codes ranging from 7000 to 8999 in any year in which they had employees.

Table 4.1. *Gross and net formations of service firms by year, 1990 to 1998, and service firm formation and employment as a share of all sectors*

Year	Service Firm Formations		Gross Formation Rates	Service Share of All Sectors	
	Gross	Net	per 1,000 LF	Formation	Employment
1990	170,345	24,521	1.375	35.1%	28.3%
1991	173,475	24,928	1.378	37.1%	29.2%
1992	167,266	20,140	1.324	37.0%	29.8%
1993	174,884	28,546	1.365	36.7%	30.6%
1994	177,743	27,481	1.376	36.7%	30.9%
1995	186,050	33,220	1.421	36.9%	31.1%
1996	192,018	31,812	1.452	37.9%	31.4%
1997	194,916	19,936	1.452	39.0%	32.1%
1998	191,911	n.a.	1.445	38.4%	32.8%

n.a. = not available.

Note: Gross formation includes all new service firm formations in each year. Net formations are the excess of firm formations over firm closures each year.

formations, defined as annual firm formations minus firm closures during the same year, average only about 25,000 during the 1990s, and vary widely. Net firm formations in services accounted for about two-thirds of the net firm formations in all industries in most of these years (not shown). The rate of new service firm formation per 1,000 workers in the labor force was remarkably constant, increasing only from 1.375 in 1990 to 1.452 in 1997, and falling slightly in 1992 and again in 1998. Services accounted for 35.1% of all firm formations in 1990, and increased their share to 38.4% of all firm formations in 1998. At the same time, employment in services increased from 28.3% to 32.8% of total private sector nonfarm employment.

Table 4.2 looks at some of the regional variation across LMAs in the new firm formation rates, again using the number of new service firm formations per 1,000 workers in the labor force. The top 20 LMAs ranked by formation rate had an average annual service firm formation rate of 2.26 per 1,000 of labor force, while the lowest 20 LMAs averaged only a third as many new service firm formations, 0.77 per 1,000 of labor force. The LMAs with the highest formation rates appear to be almost evenly divided between very large LMAs and relatively small LMAs, but all the LMAs

Table 4.2. *Regional variation in LMA sizes and service firm formation rates, 1996–1998, highest and lowest formation rates (annual average service firm formations per 1,000 1995 labor force)*

LMA	Largest Place	Avg 1996–1998 Formation Rate	Service Firms '95	1995 Labor Force	1995 Population
Top 20 LMAs by formation rates					
287	Laramie, WY	3.276	2,250	90,242	157,260
71	West Palm Beach, FL	2.790	12,791	602,263	1,320,841
72	Cape Coral, FL	2.598	4,845	251,563	555,042
70	Miami, FL	2.517	36,811	1,794,995	3,559,134
393	Bellingham, WA	2.362	2,244	114,745	248,175
69	Sarasota, FL	2.316	5,704	280,316	677,113
344	Bozeman, MT	2.280	2,255	113,581	214,480
376	Reno, NV	2.260	4,421	254,723	489,925
345	Missoula, MT	2.211	2,398	126,036	255,454
91	Atlanta, GA	2.188	26,826	1,746,367	3,159,274
352	Grand Junction, CO	2.140	1,628	92,686	180,242
289	Denver, CO	2.135	20,972	1,241,321	2,116,579
359	St. George, UT	2.105	1,037	82,660	185,658
353	Farmington, NM	2.076	1,137	73,850	145,934
354	Flagstaff, AZ	2.065	2,173	139,112	288,115
379	Las Vegas, NV	2.060	7,083	613,097	1,178,223
75	Daytona Beach, FL	2.025	3,614	217,087	517,867
74	Orlando, FL	2.014	11,732	763,432	1,423,362
67	Tampa, FL	2.007	18,150	1,090,154	2,174,602
392	Bend, OR	1.991	1,492	95,114	187,506
AVERAGE OF TOP 20 LMAS		2.26			
Bottom 20 LMAs by formation rates					
151	Lorain, OH	0.803	2,505	211,001	417,376
139	Kokomo, IN	0.800	1,153	95,821	183,584
133	Findlay, OH	0.794	1,553	128,032	245,284
225	Appleton, WI	0.793	3,497	316,960	518,380
224	Sheboygan, WI	0.785	1,147	106,522	190,707
183	Watertown, NY	0.777	1,248	105,549	257,062
227	Wausau, WI	0.773	2,178	195,815	359,420
187	Sunbury, PA	0.773	1,135	89,741	192,916
181	Elmira, NY	0.772	2,149	167,177	350,349
128	Greensburg, IN	0.767	658	69,562	130,547
182	Olean, NY	0.767	1,378	112,608	241,924
134	Lima, OH	0.764	1,679	132,715	261,596

(*continued*)

Table 4.2 (*continued*)

LMA	Largest Place	Avg 1996–1998 Formation Rate	Service Firms '95	1995 Labor Force	1995 Population
6	North Wilkesboro, NC	0.757	766	74,383	144,671
185	Amsterdam, NY	0.757	652	53,750	111,218
154	Zanesville, OH	0.756	1,033	85,927	184,493
237	Galesburg, IL	0.734	878	70,347	147,675
219	Marshalltown, IA	0.708	725	59,299	110,541
178	Oneonta, NY	0.673	996	75,827	160,694
218	Mason City, IA	0.672	1,156	81,392	150,274
126	Richmond, IN	0.662	713	55,891	105,835
AVERAGE OF BOTTOM 20 LMAS		0.77			

in the lowest birth rate group were relatively small. Why do some of the smallest have the highest formation rates, while many others in their size group exemplify "small and sleepy"?

Table 4.3 lists the LMAs with the largest and smallest populations in 1995. There is considerable variation in the birth rates of the large LMAs, varying from Miami FL with a birth rate of 2.52 new service firms per 1,000 of labor force down to Bridgeport CT with only 1.24. These 15 largest LMAs had an average new firm formation rate of 1.67, with an average corresponding three-year increase in employment of 4.68%. At the same time, the smallest 15 LMAs averaged only 1.00 new service firm formation per 1,000 of labor force, with only half the rate of growth in employment. This raises the question, which we will address later, of whether larger places typically have other characteristics that account for their higher service firm formation rates and higher growth rates, or whether it is the larger size of these economic areas that contributes to their higher average rates of new service firm formation and growth.

Why Do Firm Formation Rates Vary Across Economic Areas?

It is clear from the previous section that the service firm formation rates vary greatly across local economic areas. Recently, a growing literature has sought the determinants of such local variation in rates of new firm formation, and has identified a number of factors that contribute to these differences. The agglomeration effects that contribute to new firm formation can come both from demand effects associated with increased

Table 4.3. *Regional variation in LMA sizes and service firm formation rates, 1996–1998, largest and smallest populations (formation rates in average annual service firm formations per 1,000 1995 labor force)*

	Largest Place	1995 Population	Avg 1996–1998 Formation Rate	Avg 1995–1998 Employment Change	1995 Firms
Largest 15 LMAs					
383	Los Angeles, CA	15,273,490	1.61	4.91%	109,555
194	New York, NY	10,974,248	1.85	3.75%	93,034
243	Chicago, IL	7,687,064	1.45	3.91%	58,924
113	ArlngtnWashBalt, VA	5,738,252	1.61	4.82%	59,517
196	Newark, NJ	5,488,581	1.79	4.09%	50,249
197	Philadelphia, PA	5,424,998	1.35	3.05%	41,508
116	Detroit, MI	5,258,367	1.26	3.65%	36,185
205	Boston, MA	4,727,659	1.53	3.21%	40,779
378	San Francisco, CA	4,335,465	1.88	6.06%	39,967
320	Houston, TX	4,007,275	1.61	5.44%	28,919
70	Miami, FL	3,559,134	2.52	4.00%	36,811
394	Seattle, WA	3,470,732	1.79	5.47%	28,764
209	Bridgeport, CT	3,432,869	1.24	3.54%	30,209
91	Atlanta, GA	3,159,274	2.19	6.78%	26,826
331	Dallas, TX	2,861,201	1.88	7.44%	23,953
	AVERAGE OF 15 LARGEST		1.67	4.68%	
Smallest 15 LMAs					
148	Vincennes, IN	112,611	0.99	2.89%	782
253	Union City, KY	112,257	0.90	3.91%	651
283	North Platte, NE	111,929	1.11	2.24%	1,002
273	Fairmont, MN	111,436	0.95	1.09%	977
185	Amsterdam, NY	111,218	0.76	1.82%	652
219	Marshalltown, IA	110,541	0.71	−0.70%	725
266	Aberdeen, SD	109,103	1.17	0.64%	968
327	Brownwood, TX	107,861	1.20	3.79%	751
126	Richmond, IN	105,835	0.66	−0.40%	713
291	Salina, KS	105,237	1.14	1.48%	920
258	Blytheville, AR	105,214	0.98	8.95%	524
245	FortLeonardWood, MO	104,561	1.36	2.84%	673
101	Thomasville, GA	104,131	1.19	8.29%	641
324	Big Spring, TX	103,279	1.07	3.07%	657
212	Hutchinson, MN	103,042	0.97	−5.04%	742
	AVERAGE OF 15 SMALLEST		1.00	2.32%	

local population, income, and business activity and from supply factors related to the quality of the local labor market and business climate.

Among areas with broadly similar regional demand and business climate characteristics, there are further differences in rates of new firm formation and economic growth that are associated with the specific qualities of their human capital, as well as the propensity of locally available knowledge to spill over and stimulate innovative activity, which culminates in new firm formations. First, highly educated populations provide the human capital embodied in their general and specific skills for implementing new ideas for creating new businesses (Glaeser, Scheinkman, and Shleifer, 1995). Second, they also create an environment rich in local knowledge spillovers, which support another mechanism by which new firm start-ups are initiated and sustained (Reynolds, Miller, and Maki, 1994). Third, to the extent that new firms use skilled labor intensively, they are more likely to be located in cities with concentrations of highly educated labor in order to reduce the costs of hiring a crucial input (Rauch, 1993). Thus, regions that are richer in educated people should have more start-up activity. Variation in local new firm formation rates should be positively related to local educational attainment rates. Furthermore, areas that already have relatively intense development of service businesses will have higher rates of new service firm formations, resulting in large part from spillovers of relevant specialized knowledge (Littunen, 2000). We would expect that areas with relatively high shares of high school dropouts would have lower rates of new firm formation.

Eduard Lazear (2002) has contributed insights into one mechanism that contributes to the higher firm formation rates in larger cities, based on the presence of higher levels of individuals with a "career" life-mode and a college education. Because their dominant value is the advancement of their career, though they are most likely to be working in large hierarchical private or public sector organizations, they will start their own businesses if this becomes the best way in which to benefit from their skills, knowledge, and expertise. Individuals can be expected to choose self-employment only if $\pi^* > w$. These businesses are often technologically advanced, innovative, and with good marketing capabilities. Career-mode entrepreneurs are often concentrated in large metropolitan areas and smaller attractive cities.

In fact, the 1990s saw an increase in the incidence of highly educated individuals starting new businesses, especially in the technologically advanced sectors of the economy, like computers, biotechnology, and Internet-dependent businesses (Acs, FitzRoy, and Smith, 2002). However, there was also an increase in formations of many service businesses using relatively unskilled labor for such services as building cleaning, security, detective, and secretarial. These may be started by career-oriented individuals who have recognized opportunities or developed new ideas to allow them to compete favorably in these markets, on the basis of their own experiences or on spillovers from others.

New firm formations should be positively associated with higher levels of local human capital (including relevant knowledge spillovers):

$$\text{Firm Birth Rate}_{srt+2} = \alpha_r + \beta \, \text{Human Capital}_{srt} + \gamma \, [X]_{srt} + e_r$$

$$(4.1)$$

where X is a vector of control variables, the subscript r indexes LMAs, t refers to time, and e is stochastic disturbance. The conditioning information set is a vector of exogenous population and business variables specific to each Labor Market Area r.

In a world of perfect information, employed agents confronted with new economic knowledge would not face a choice between developing the innovation as employees within their existing firm, or taking the idea outside by starting up their own firm. However, the asymmetry of such knowledge leads to a host of agency problems spanning incentive structures, monitoring, and transaction costs. The existence of such agency costs and the resistance of bureaucracies to change provide an incentive for agents with new ideas to form their own new firms. (The potential profit that might accrue to the entrepreneur in excess of a salary, if any, provides a further incentive to take the risks of self-employment.) And further, this same asymmetric nature of information causes the rate of new firm start-ups to vary from city to city, depending on the underlying knowledge conditions in each (Audretsch, 1995b).

Similarly, the equilibrium distribution of labor (people) and capital (firms) across cities was constantly changing during this period in which rapid changes in technology and relative demand for outputs caused some industries to become unprofitable and others more profitable (Jorgenson, 2001). Across cities, the local entrepreneurial response to these changes in supply and demand varied greatly, leading to variations in the firm formation rate and in the proportion of entrepreneurs.

Empirical Model of Services Formations

Following from the previous discussion, our major hypotheses concerning the regional variation in service firm formation rates deal with differences in levels of human capital and opportunities for spillovers, while controlling for local differences in a set of other regional characteristics that are likely to affect new firm formation rates. To test the basic hypothesis that the new firm formation rates are positively related to the level of human capital in a region, we estimate a regression model where the dependent variable is the average annual new service firm formation rate (dividing gross formations by the labor force in thousands) for 1996–1998. This is analogous to the method previously used for other industries by Keeble and Walker (1994) and Armington and Acs (2002). The explanatory (independent or exogenous) variables include both the human capital variables discussed in the following subsection and the regional control factors discussed later.

Human Capital Variables

To measure the level of human capital in each local economy, we use two measures of educational attainment in each region, as well as a measure of the relative intensity of similar businesses in the same sector or subsector, or service specialization. The first measure of educational attainment is the share of college graduates, identical to that used in Chapter Three.

The second measure of educational attainment is the high school dropout rate, defined slightly differently than in Chapter Three. It is calculated as the percentage of adults (population 25 years or older) without college degrees who did not have high school degrees in 1990. We used only the adults without college degrees as the base for this calculation, rather than all adults, in order to reduce the negative correlation of the high school dropout rate with the share of adults with college degrees. College share of adults is correlated −.70 with high school dropout share of adults, but this falls to −.59 when we calculate only the high school dropout share of noncollege adults. Nationally, 33% of noncollege adults were high school dropouts in 1990, and this varied from 17% to 60% across LMAs. As before, we expect the high school dropout rate to be negatively related to the formation rate for most types of service firms.

Formal education itself does not usually provide either the skills or the inspiration to start a new business. But higher education trains individuals to rationally assess information and to seek new ideas. Therefore, higher-educated people are more likely to acquire useful local knowledge spillovers from others who are involved in research or in managing some service business. The quantity or probability of potentially useful knowledge spillovers is expected to be a function of both the amount of knowledge in the region and the number of similar business establishments, relative to the population of the economic area. *Service-sector specialization* is a similar concept to that used in Chapter Three, here defined as the number of service establishments in the region divided by the region's population in thousands. The greater the number of establishments relative to the population, the more spillovers should be facilitated due to density of, and competition between, similar establishments in that industry (Ciccone and Hall, 1996).

Regional Control Variables

The human capital variables whose impact we are analyzing are not the only explanation for differences among LMAs in new firm formation rates. We control for differences in a number of other regional characteristics that are commonly thought to influence the rates at which new firms are formed. Summary statistics are provided in Table 4.4 for the new firm formation rates, and for all of the regional socioeconomic variables that are used in the models estimated here.

Population growth and *income growth* are both defined as in Chapter Three, with appropriate period adjustments to represent the period immediately prior to that of the formations being analyzed. Higher growth rates of population and per capita income during the preceding period are both expected to promote higher service firm formation rates.

We control for agglomeration effects in each region primarily by including the log of *population* as a control variable, since we expect proportional differences in population to impact the new firm formation

Table 4.4. *Summary statistics on variables for services regressions (observations are 394 Labor Market Areas, covering entire United States)*

	Mean	Std Dev.	Minimum	Maximum
Average Annual service firm formations per 1,000 labor force				
1996–1998	1.269	0.371	0.662	3.276
1993–1995	1.275	0.352	0.688	3.327
1990–1992	1.233	0.337	0.692	2.785
Human capital				
College degrees, % of adults, 1990	0.159	0.050	0.069	0.320
High school dropouts, % of noncollege adults, 1990	0.329	0.082	0.167	0.598
Sector specialization, service estab/population (000), 1995	7.620	1.400	3.755	15.548
Regional characteristics in prior period, Population growth ratio,				
1993–1995 avg	1.010	0.010	0.989	1.059
Per capita income growth ratio,				
1993–1995 avg	1.040	0.013	0.969	1.084
Log of population, 1995	12.801	0.940	11.543	16.542
Unemployment rate, 1994–1995 avg	0.060	0.024	0.020	0.290
Avg employment per establ., all-industry, 1994	15.097	2.881	8.266	21.237
Business specialization, establ./popul. (000), all-ind., 1994	21.834	3.584	10.774	45.105

rates, rather than simple differences in numbers of people. Agglomeration effects are expected to have a positive impact on the start-up rate. Lucas (1993) asserts that the only compelling reason for the existence of cities would be the presence of increasing returns to agglomeration of resources, which make these locations more productive. However, agglomeration effects may be more complex and may have effects that vary across different types of service subsectors.

The *unemployment rate* is similar to that in Chapter Three, but is calculated for the two-year period prior to our start-up measurement period – for example, for 1996–1998 formations, we use the average number of unemployed in 1994 and 1995 divided by the labor force in 1994. The positive effect of unemployment increasing the supply of entrepreneurs may dominate in the service industries, with its generally lower capital requirements.

Business specialization is the total number of private sector establishments in the region divided by the region's population, as was used for the all-industry analyses in Chapter Three. However, since this analysis of service firm formation also takes into consideration the local specialization in the service sector, we expect that the greater the general business specialization, the higher the local costs of land and labor, and the lower the service firm formation rate will be (Acs, FitzRoy, and Smith, 2002). However, if knowledge spillovers from other industries are more important than those from similar industries (Glaeser et al., 1992), this general business specialization variable might be positively related to formation rates of new service firms.

Establishment size is a proxy for the broad structure of business in the region. It is measured for 1996–1998 formations as the total area employment in 1994 in all industries divided by the number of all-industry establishments in 1994 in the area. A local business structure with no dominant large firms may offer fewer barriers to entry of new firms and more opportunities for knowledge spillovers. Furthermore, where small firms predominate in a geographical area, there is a much broader population of business owners, and more individuals may visualize their own careers as leading to the founding of independent new firms. Thus, the average size of area establishments should be negatively related to the new firm formation rates, since larger average size indicates greater dominance by large firms or branch plants (Armington and Acs, 2002). Because nearly all young businesses are small, and most large establishments are considerably older than average, differences in the average size of establishments may also be a proxy for the differences in the average age of local business establishments. In fact, over time, a high rate of new firm formation will generally lead to lower average establishment size in an area.

As with the independent variables in Chapter Three, it must be pointed out that many are correlated with each other, and some may be partially endogenous to others. Because many regional differences persist over time, the use of prior period characteristics is only partially successful in building a case for service firm formations as an effect, rather than a cause. The general agglomeration variable, log of area population, is only correlated .35 with the formation rate, but it is correlated .61 with the college degree share of adults and .51 with the average size of area establishments in all industries. Future differences in area rates of growth in population and income certainly result from current differences in area firm formation rates. Spatial differences in unemployment are influenced by local variations in industry mix, demographics (including educational attainment), and other relatively stable factors (such as local unemployment insurance regulations), in addition to the relative health of the local economy and tightness in the labor market, for which we use it as an indicator.[2] This study only attempts to sort out a few new details in this complex of interrelationships.

Empirical Results for All Services Together

Table 4.5 shows the results of least squares regression on the 1990–1992, 1993–1995, and 1996–1998 average annual firm formation rates for the service sector for 394 Labor Market Areas. We present standardized beta coefficients,[3] so that each parameter indicates the sensitivity of formation

---

[2] The use of deviations from long-term averages of each area's unemployment rate in future work might facilitate isolating the long-term structural causes of local unemployment from shorter-term variations, but both contribute to the spatial differences in the relative tightness in the labor market and the health of the local economy. In addition, the long and uncertain lags in the timing of new business formations (between the original formation decision and the registering of employees that triggers recognition of the start-up) preclude the usefulness of time series analysis until much more is understood about both the theory and the facts.

[3] These can be calculated from the ordinary coefficients, but it is more illuminating to view them as being estimated from standardized variables. In this case, rather than using the levels, ratios, and percents whose means and deviations are shown in Table 4.4, we would transform each variable by subtracting its mean value (calculated from all 394 LMA values) and then divide this adjusted value by the standard deviation of all 394 values. These transformed values will have a mean of zero and a standard deviation of one, and each value represents the deviation of that particular LMA from the mean. Since the 394 LMAs constitute the universe at a point in time (rather than a sample of areas), it is apparent that the resulting standardized beta coefficients can be interpreted quite simply as measures of the impact of a standard deviation difference in the independent variable on the standardized dependent variable. For example, using standardized variables, if we estimate that $x = 0.1y + 0.5z$, then we can say that each standard deviation in the value of y is associated with 0.1 of a standard deviation of x, and each standard deviation of z is associated with half of a standard deviation of x. Obviously, it follows that x is five times more sensitive to z than to y.

Table 4.5. *Regression coefficients for service firm formation rates in Labor Market Areas during three consecutive time periods (standardized betas with t-ratios below, bold if significant at .05 level)*

	1996–1998	1993–1995	1990–1992
Adj. R sqd	.718	.658	.625
Human capital			
College degree/adults '90	**0.16**	**0.10**	**0.19**
	3.39	1.79	3.40
High school dropouts/noncollege adults '90	**0.16**	**0.21**	**0.14**
	4.21	4.86	3.20
Sector specialization, service establ./population	**0.63**	**0.60**	**0.47**
	6.53	5.63	4.26
Regional characteristics			
Population growth	**0.51**	**0.46**	**0.41**
	18.05	14.44	11.46
Per capita income growth	**0.09**	**0.19**	**0.13**
	3.03	5.62	3.77
Population (logarithm)	**0.22**	**0.16**	**0.18**
	4.92	3.25	3.6
Unemployment rate	**0.06**	**− 0.09**	**0.17**
	1.64	−2.32	4.08
Avg size of all establ. (employment)	**− 0.34**	**− 0.33**	**− 0.32**
	−8.06	−8.13	7.30
Business specialization, all establ./population	**− 0.21**	−0.07	−0.03
	−2.42	−0.71	−0.31
Number of observations (LMAs)	394	394	394

Note: Formation rates are three-year average formations per 1,000 labor force in prior year. Undated exogenous variables represent prior year, or prior two-year averages.

rate variation to normalized variation in the corresponding independent variable. The t-ratios shown for each were calculated from the simple estimated standard errors. These were also calculated with a correction for heteroscedasticity, with results that were very similar to the uncorrected standard errors. The estimated coefficients are generally consistent with our expectations, but with several important exceptions. The explanatory and control variables together explain about two-thirds of the regional differences in new service firm formation rates.

Only two of the three human capital variables showed the hypothesized relationships. For human capital measured by share of college graduates, the coefficients are positive and statistically significant for all except the 1993–1995 period, confirming that regions with higher shares of college-educated adults generally have higher firm formation rates. This positive result on human capital is consistent with previous research (Storey, 1991). The 1993–1995 period was one of recovery from the short recession in 1991, which had resulted in a fall in service firm formations in 1992. It appears that the service firm formation rate is less sensitive to the areas' educational attainment levels during such a recovery period.

The positive and statistically significant coefficient for high school dropouts as a share of the noncollege adult population is at first surprising – however, it is consistent with our earlier results for the whole economy (Armington and Acs, 2002). There, we suggested that after controlling for the proportion of adults with college degrees,[4] the additional effect of a greater share of less-educated workers is to facilitate the start-up process by providing cheap labor for the new firms. Even the most sophisticated businesses need some relatively uneducated workers to do the manual labor. Thus, the relationship between educational attainment and new firm start-ups at the regional level may be U-shaped, with both low levels and high levels of education conducive to firm formation and growth. We will examine this issue in greater depth when we analyze subsector data for services formations, distinguishing by educational requirements for founders.

The coefficient on intensity of service establishments is positive and statistically significant, suggesting that regions that already have a relatively strong supply of service establishments will have higher rates of new service firm formation, as predicted by the theory of regional

---

[4] Note that when estimated for 1996–1998 without the high school dropout rate, the coefficient for college degree falls to .10, and when estimated without college, the coefficient on high school dropout falls to .12, while other coefficients remain substantially the same.

spillovers (Jovanovic and Rob, 1989). Indeed, this factor has the strongest relationship of any of our independent variables. The 0.63 value estimated for 1996–1998 for the standardized coefficient indicates that a locality with a service establishment intensity that is one standard deviation more intense than the mean (i.e., 9.0 rather than the mean of 7.6 establishments per 1,000 population) will be likely to have firm start-up rates that are 0.63 of a standard deviation higher than the mean (i.e., 1.50 rather than the mean of 1.27 per 1,000 labor force). When we tried replacing this measure of service establishment intensity with the share of employment in services, the estimates were much weaker, and so we conclude that it is important that the local service sector have many business establishments, rather than many employees with service experience.

Furthermore, once we control for the intensity of service establishments, the additional intensity of all establishments is negatively related to service firm formation in 1996–1998, and insignificant in earlier periods. This suggests that start-ups are facilitated by spillovers from clusters of similar establishments, but that a relatively high intensity of other types of establishments may actually discourage new service firm formation. Business crowding, in general, apparently does not lead to higher rates of service firm start-ups. These results shed additional light on the debate between diversity and specialization (Glaeser et al., 1992), supporting the view that spillovers have important positive effects within broad industry sectors, but do not play an important positive role across sectors. This finding is consistent with that of Acs, Felix FitzRoy, and Ian Smith (2002), who found no spillovers across unrelated industries. We could better distinguish the separate effects of the specialization of related and unrelated industries in the area, and avoid the inflation of the parameter on service specialization by its inclusion in general business specialization, if we used nonservice business specialization, rather that general business specialization. This substitution was made in exploratory work on 1996–1998 formations, which showed that the parameter on service specialization fell somewhat, but not dramatically, and the estimates for the other parameters in the model remained similar. However, because it was not feasible to use this formulation consistently for the subsequent analysis of subsectors of services, and only limited results could be released in accord with Census confidentiality restrictions, we chose to use the broader business specialization model consistently throughout this research.

While the results for the three time periods shown in Table 4.5 are broadly similar, there is one additional difference to be noted. The estimated coefficient on the unemployment rate is positive and statistically significant for 1990–1992, when the economy was undergoing a small recession, but it is negative and barely significant during 1993–1995 and insignificant during 1996–1998, suggesting that this positive effect disappears as the economy improves, or as mean unemployment falls. These results are inconsistent with some previous research (Storey, 1991) that generally found a negative relationship between unemployment and formations in cross-sectional analyses. Our results raise the possibility that during recessions, more workers turn to entrepreneurship, as the competition for positions as employees is stiffer. Although higher relative unemployment rates were associated with higher relative service formation rates in the subsequent period, there is no evidence that the formerly unemployed workers were the ones starting the new businesses. Moreover, the service firm formation rate actually fell, nationally, during the 1991 recession (as measured in the year ending in March 1992). The unemployment rate may have served as a proxy for omitted variables in the previous research cited, while those effects were more precisely attributed to the additional variables we have controlled for in this study, robbing the unemployment variable of its apparent effect.

The signs on the other control variables are as expected. Local population growth differences had a very strong positive influence on new service firm formation rates. When local labor force growth was substituted for population growth, its estimated parameter was much lower, suggesting that this local growth variable is functioning more as an indicator of growth in demand for services than as an indicator of the supply of either entrepreneurs or labor. Regions that have higher per capita income growth and those with higher levels of agglomeration (of population) have higher rates of service firm formation. The average size of all local business establishments has a strong negative relationship to service firm formation rates -- local dominance by large businesses appears to inhibit the formation of new businesses, while the presence of many smaller businesses may serve both to stimulate competition and to facilitate knowledge spillovers.

Subsectors Within the Service Industry

The service sector narrowly defined by the Standard Industrial Classification (SIC) system still incorporates a huge variety of diverse businesses. Our capacity to disaggregate this sector was severely limited by data disclosure constraints, which allowed it to be divided into no more than nine subsectors. Our first priority was to better distinguish the relationship of our human capital variables to the formation rates of various types of service activities, hypothesizing that an important aspect of this linkage is the supply of educationally qualified potential entrepreneurs. Therefore, our primary classification of the 150 4-digit SIC service industries was based on the educational requirements expected of the founders of most new firms in each industry code, using three categories for this dimension. The second important industry characteristic to control is its target market, so that we can better account for the effect of local differences in the demand for various types of services. We categorized the market segment served by each of the service industry codes using three categories. Together, these defined nine service subsectors, within which the service activities are fairly homogeneous with respect to these two dimensions – educational requirement and market segment.

A major factor affecting the supply of new service firms is the availability of individuals with the qualifications generally needed to recognize the opportunities; identify new services, markets, or delivery systems; organize the new firm; and hire the first employees. We therefore expected that the sensitivity of service firm formation rates to the relative supply of adults with various levels of education would differ across service subsectors distinguished by typical educational requirements of their founders. We distinguish activities that are most frequently started by people who do not have college degrees (called "high school" level for simplicity) from those generally requiring an "advanced" (graduate, postgraduate, or professional) degree, and assigned the remainder to "college." These allocations were based on subjective judgments, using our general knowledge of service industries, supplemented by the detailed descriptions of the 4-digit SIC classes in the 1987 *Standard Industrial Classification Manual* (U.S. Office of Management and Budget, 1987).[5]

---

[5] We originally hoped to base this classification on the Bureau of Labon Statistics occupational distribution data for each three-digit industry group, and to use subjective

An obvious reason for variation across locales in their rates of service firm formation is variation in local demand for services, and so we distinguished three general markets – local consumers, local businesses, and nonlocal (broader regional, national, or export) markets. Each 4-digit SIC code was assigned to one of these market segment categories, based on close reading of the descriptions of the activities within the definition of the code. It was expected that a substantial portion of the variation in formations of local consumer service firms would be associated with differences in population growth. Similarly, it was expected that locales with stronger general business specialization relative to the population would be associated with higher rates of local business service firm formations. New service firms serving a broader, nonlocal market should be considerably less sensitive to these local market differences. Thus, this dimension was expected to improve the control of local variation in demand for new service firms.

The resulting subsector classifications for each of the 4-digit SIC are listed in Appendix C, where they are ordered by SIC code within each subsector. Data on the number of establishments and employees in each 4-digit SIC in 1995 are included, so that it is easy to pick out the larger industry codes dominating each subsector. This Appendix also shows the net growth rates for numbers of establishments and their employment between 1995 and 1998, as well as the number of new firm formations during 1996 through 1998 per 100 (1995) establishments for each industry code.[6] Table 4.6 provides a summary of the diverse firm formation rates and relative sizes (shares of total service employment) for these nine services subsectors defined according to their market segments

judgment only to distinguish among the 4-digit codes within each 3-digit group. However, we found that many activities requiring academic skills or advanced training for leadership positions reported occupational distributions very heavily weighted toward semiskilled and unskilled workers. Hospitals and hotels were extreme examples of this contrast between educational requirements for workers and those for the individuals responsible for starting the businesses. Similarly, classification of self-employed workers by SIC was not at all representative of the qualifications of the owners or managers of new employee firms in that SIC. Many self-employed workers serve under contract to large firms, and few need to deal with the management or financial challenges of employee businesses.

[6] The Appendix C entries do not sum to the national totals for each subsector because of the infrequent occurrence of establishments that were never classified to the 4-digit level. These were generally assigned to the 4-digit code that had the most establishments reported within the SIC classification provided, but are not included in the aggregate 4-digit data in this Appendix.

Table 4.6. *1996–1998 firm formation rates and relative size of service subsectors defined by market segments and founder's education requirement*

Education Requirement and Market Segment	Average Annual* Formations per 100 Establ. in Subsector		Share of Services 1995 Employment	
All services	8.84		100.0%	
All education classes				
Local business market		10.66		26.1%
Local consumer market		7.18		54.9%
Nonlocal markets		12.66		19.0%
High school				
All markets	9.29		30.4%	
Local business		12.22		9.3%
Local consumers		8.42		15.9%
Nonlocal markets		7.86		5.2%
College degree				
All markets	9.25		26.1%	
Local business		8.60		10.2%
Local consumers		9.08		13.6%
Nonlocal markets		10.72		2.3%
Advanced degree				
All markets	8.33		43.5%	
Local business		10.31		6.6%
Local consumers		5.31		25.4%
Nonlocal markets		14.78		11.5%

* The sum of firm formations in 1996, 1997, and 1998 is divided by 3, and then divided by the number of establishments in 1995, and then multiplied by 100.

and founders' education requirements. Looking first at how the new firm formation rates differ by education requirement, note that they are quite similar for all three categories, ranging only from 8.33 formations per 100 existing establishments in the advanced degrees category, up to 9.29 for the category of service businesses that are probably founded by individuals with only a high school education. But when we categorize the service sector by primary market, we find that the firm formation rate for service businesses that focus on local consumer markets (which account for about 55% of employment in services) is only 7.18 new firms per 100 establishments in that market category. At the other extreme, the services that cater to nonlocal markets showed formations at nearly twice that rate – 12.66 new firms per 100 existing establishments – but those services account for only 19% of employment in services.

For the nine subsectors defined by the education requirement and the market segment together, the firm formation rate was highest, at 14.78, for businesses in nonlocal markets with founders normally having advanced degrees. The largest industry groups in this subsector are engineering and management consulting and computer programming services, all of which are subject to rapid innovation and turnover. The subsector requiring the same advanced degree for founders, but serving primarily the local consumer market, had only 5.31 new firms for each 100 existing establishments, and medical offices and religious organizations dominate this subsector. Businesses that normally require a college degree for their founder had formation rates that were quite similar across all three of the market segments. Businesses commonly founded by those with no more than a high school degree also showed great variation across market segments, with high formation rates for the nonlocal market (primarily the hotel and motel group), and low ones for the local consumer market (including various repair, cleaning, and beauty services and child day care).

The first subsector regression model reported in Table 4.7 is a simple pooled regression on average new firm formation rates for 1996 through 1998, where each observation is a subsector in an LMA. Thus, there are 3,546 observations, from each of the nine subsectors in each of the 394 LMAs. If we use r to indicate LMA and em to indicate subsectors distinguished by education and market, we can specify this model as follows:

$$\text{Formation rate}_{rem} = f\,(\text{Coll}_r, \text{HighSch Drop}_r, \text{Subsector specialization}_{rem},$$
$$\text{Pop gro}_r, \text{Incomegro}_r, \text{Poplog}_r, \text{Unempl}_r, \text{EstablSize}_r,$$
$$\text{Business specialization}_r). \qquad (4.2)$$

Most coefficients fall somewhat relative to the all-service model results shown in Table 4.5, suggesting that the independent variables are not equally important to all of the subsectors. The coefficient on business specialization, which had been somewhat elevated as a result of some collinearity between it and the sector specialization, falls somewhat in this pooled subsector regression, because there is little multicollinearity between it and the individual service subsector specialization levels. However, at 0.54 the subsector specialization remains by far the strongest influence on the formation rates. The adjusted R-squared is lower in this subsector model because some of the additional variation in formation rates across subsectors is not as well explained.

Obviously, this simple pooled subsector model estimates only a single coefficient to represent an average of how all subsectors relate to each exogenous variable. But when we discussed the reasons for defining those subsectors, we focused on expected differences in their coefficients with some of these variables. If we estimated each subsector model separately, we could not easily restrict the coefficients on the locality variables that should be unaffected by subsector differences. Alternatively, we could estimate the model separately for each of the dimensions – education and markets. But that fails to make use of the information we have on how these LMAs differ on both dimensions simultaneously, and so the results would be subject to aggregation errors, which could be avoided by making use of both dimensions simultaneously.

In order to allow for variation in the estimated coefficients of variables that should be sensitive to our subsector dimensions, while controlling consistently for other regional characteristics, we expand the independent variables to be subsector-specific for the dimensions we want to test. Naturally, we expected the educational attainment variables to be sensitive to the education requirement dimension. We also wanted to investigate how the subsector specialization affected the rate of new firm formation in different market segments. We anticipated that subsectors that differed in education requirement might also differ in their relationship to income growth rates and unemployment rates. Market segment was expected to affect how the formation rate varied with population growth, the average size of local establishments, and the business specialization in the locality. Since little is known about the residual agglomeration effect that is represented by the logarithm of population, we did not try to anticipate whether it would be sensitive to either the market segment or the educational requirement, and we therefore tested it with both dimensions.

Table 4.7. *Regression coefficients for service subsector firm formation rates in Labor Market Areas during 1996–1998, with subsectors defined by education requirement and market segment (standardized betas with t-ratios below, bold if significant at .05 level)*

	Pooled 9 Subsectors	Pooled, with Dummy-Distinguished Exogenous Variables					
		Educational Requirement			Market Segment		
		High School	College Degree	Advanc'd Degree	Local Business	Local Consumer	Nonlocal
Adj. R sqd	.566			.660			
Human capital							
College degree/adults '90	**0.14**	0.01	**0.21**	**0.11**			
	7.47	0.41	8.09	4.02			
High school dropout/ noncollege adults '90	**0.09**	0.03	0.04	**0.16**			
	5.77	1.26	1.91	6.85			
Sector specialization, establishments/popul.	**0.54**				**0.53**	**0.25**	**0.77**
	36.40				18.55	9.25	32.05
Regional characteristics							
Population growth	**0.36**				**0.35**	**0.44**	**0.20**
	32.09				19.43	22.83	11.19

	(1)	(2)	(3)	(4)	(5)	(6)	(7)
Per capita income growth	**0.07** (5.96)	**0.06** (3.35)	**0.08** (4.44)	**0.06** (3.28)			
Population (logarithm)	**0.16** (9.18)	**−0.06** (−2.35)		**0.06** (2.18)	**0.23** (7.81)	**0.20** (7.50)	
Unemployment rate	**0.05** (3.23)	0.01 (0.47)	**0.05** (2.54)	0.02 (1.15)			
Avg size of all establ. (Employment)	**−0.26** (−16.04)				**−0.17** (−6.87)	**−0.47** (−19.79)	**−0.14** (−6.36)
Business specialization, Establishments/popul.	**−0.06** (−3.59)				−0.01 (−0.22)	−0.02 (−0.74)	**−0.07** (−2.96)
Number of observations	3,546			3,546			

Note: All variables are expressed as deviations from mean values for all LMAs within each subsector. Subsector firm formation rates are three-year average formations per 1,000 labor force in 1995.

Using the previous notation, this more detailed pooled estimation model has the following form:

$$\text{Formation rate}_{\text{rem}} = f\,(\text{Coll}_r^*\,\text{Dum}_e,\ \text{HighSch Drop}_r^*\,\text{Dum}_e,\ \text{Subsector}$$
$$\text{specialization}_r^*\,\text{Dum}_m,\ \text{Pop gro}_r^*\,\text{Dum}_m,\ \text{Income gro}_r^*$$
$$\text{Dum}_e,\ \text{Pop log}_r^*\text{Dum}_e^*\,\text{Dum}_m,\ \text{Unempl}_r^*\,\text{Dum}_e,$$
$$\text{Establ Size}_r^*\,\text{Dum}_m,\ \text{Business specialization}_r^*\,\text{Dum}_m).$$
$$(4.3)$$

Each of the exogenous variables is now in the form of cross products with dummies for the education requirement (Dum_e) or/and the market segment (Dum_m). The three dummies for each dimension take the usual form of a dummy variable, with a value of zero unless the observation is for the segment specified for that dummy variable. We first standardized all of the nine exogenous variables and the endogenous variable to have a mean of zero and a standard deviation of one within each of the nine subsectors. Therefore, each standardized variable represents a relative measure for the LMA within the subsector. Then we created dummy variables for each of the three values for each of the subsector dimensions – market and education. Finally, we multiplied each exogenous variable times the appropriate three dummies to create three specialized exogenous variables for each of the relevant dimensions of the subsectors. Thus, the original 9 exogenous variables in the pooled subsector model expand to 30 variables – since log of population has been multiplied by each of three education dummies and each of three market dummies, and each of the other variables has been multiplied by each of three dummies of one type. This allows us to estimate the model as a single equation across all subsectors simultaneously, while distinguishing among the dimensions we wanted to test for differences in estimated coefficients.

The results of the estimation of this model are shown in the last six columns of Table 4.7. Looking first at the human capital variables in this estimated model, we see that the relationship between an area's share of adults with college degrees and its service firm formation rate is stronger for the subsectors generally requiring a college education, but tiny and not significant for the formation rate of service businesses requiring only a high school education for the founder. There is also a significant positive relationship between the share of adults with college degrees and the formation rates of service businesses normally requiring an advanced degree for the founder, since there is substantial similarity between the distribution of college degrees and that of advanced degrees.

The positive and statistically significant coefficient for the relationship of shares of high school dropouts to formation of new service firms that require advanced degrees might suggest that such businesses are more dependent on having a large pool of unskilled labor. The statistically insignificant coefficients for the impact of the share of high school dropouts on formation rates in the subsectors of services that require only high school or college degrees suggests that such businesses are not as sensitive to the supply of unskilled labor. However, having found that higher shares of high school dropouts are not strongly positively associated with higher formation rates for service businesses requiring less than college education for their founders, but are positive for those requiring advanced degrees, we conclude that the explanation of the positive coefficients on high school dropout share is a mystery that needs further focused research.

The subsector specialization is a significant explanatory variable for all market segments, but the formation of new firms serving nonlocal markets is particularly sensitive to the prior specialization in similar businesses. An area whose subsector specialization in services for nonlocal markets is one standard deviation above average will tend to have formation rates for similar firms that are .77 of a standard deviation above average. This corroborates the many prior case study analyses that addressed the spillover effects of certain rapidly growing local industry clusters (usually of high-technology firms with nonlocal markets), and suggests that these spillover effects are particularly important for businesses that are not focusing on local markets. However, there is also a strong clustering effect for local business services, and a smaller but very significant one for local consumer services.

Most of the estimated coefficients for regional characteristics crossed with education or market dummies were similar to those estimated without such distinctions. However, the differences that appeared are quite illuminating. The population variable was crossed with all six dummies, since we did not have a clear concept of the additional agglomeration effect that was being captured by population, only that it was needed to prevent systematic underestimation of formation rates in large

Labor Market Areas. The estimated parameters on population for all the subsectors of services defined by their founders' education requirement were tiny and either barely significant or insignificant.[7] Formation rates for services to local markets, both consumers and businesses, are sensitive to the size of the local economic area, even after controlling for both the local population growth rate and the local business specialization. In contrast, that for nonlocal markets was not only under .02 and insignificant, but it also weakened the other parameter estimates so badly that we dropped it from the model. Perhaps the high coefficient on subsector specialization for nonlocal services has captured all of the relevant agglomeration effects for that subsector.

When we distinguish the impact of population on formation rates by the education requirement for founders, it appears that larger population contributes a tiny bit to the formation rate of service firms requiring advanced degrees, but it slightly reduces the formation rate of firms normally started by high school dropouts. This might be interpreted as additional evidence of the positive effects from greater volumes of knowledge spillovers for highly educated potential entrepreneurs, versus the negative effect of greater competition in larger markets for services provided by less-educated entrepreneurs.

The coefficient on unemployment is positive and statistically significant only for service firms normally started by college graduates. This provides some clarification of the conflicting results found in previous studies of the effects of unemployment levels on new firm formation rates. Apparently, after controlling for regional differences in income growth rates, areas with higher unemployment tend to have higher new firm formation of services requiring founders with college degrees, but not those normally founded by high school dropouts or those with advanced degrees.

Finally, the negative coefficient on average size of local businesses is strongest for formation of new firms serving local consumer markets, suggesting that areas dominated by large businesses are less likely to have

---

[7] These were later omitted, which had the effect of very slightly strengthening a few of the remaining estimates. Unfortunately, disclosure constraints prevented our showing both sets of results.

a dynamic local consumer service subsector. The coefficient on business specialization is both tiny and insignificant for formations of firms serving either local businesses or local consumers, contrary to our expectations that a higher business specialization would lead to higher formation rates for business services. It has a significant negative impact only for formation of new firms serving nonlocal markets, and that impact is quite small.

These results suggest that the regional differences in new firm formation rates do indeed depend to a large degree on the educational requirements and the market served by the newly formed firms. In particular, the local levels of educational attainment impact primarily the firm formation rates of the types of firms that are normally founded by better-educated entrepreneurs, and do not affect formation rates for those normally founded by individuals with less than a college degree. While formation rates of all service businesses are higher in areas with greater specialization in similar service establishments, new formations of firms serving nonlocal markets are three times more sensitive to this subsector specialization than those serving local consumer markets, and those serving local business markets are twice as sensitive as those serving local consumers.

Conclusions

Many of the most interesting explanations for the connection between growth and human capital levels have focused on productive externalities generated by human capital. The potential for these externalities differs greatly across economic areas in the United States, depending both on the levels of education of their workforce and on the strength of the presence of existing businesses in the same industry sector. It appears that an important mechanism by which these externalities contribute to economic growth in cities is through their impact on the level of entrepreneurship. And entrepreneurship provides the catalyst for increasing productivity, as well as increasing diversity and volume of goods and services produced in an area.

This chapter has modeled the geographic variation in formation rates of service firms, focusing on their relationship to local human capital and the potential for knowledge spillovers from existing similar businesses. A key variable for the firm formation rate is the educational attainment of the labor force. Although the actual knowledge acquired with a college degree seldom suffices as the basis for a successful new business, the analytical methods learned in college facilitate both future acquisition of knowledge and openness to new ideas received as spillovers from other activities in the area. Indeed, after controlling for basic differences in the underlying rates of population growth, the strongest factor accounting for differences in new firm formation rates was the local specialization in similar businesses in the area. These results suggest that higher education influences later growth through the increased discovery and implementation of innovative ideas, resulting in more new firm formations.

In addition to the positive impact on rates of new firm formation of higher proportions of adults with college degrees, we also found an additional positive impact of higher proportions of high school dropouts among the non-college-educated portion of the adult population. This suggests that positive effect of educational attainment is limited to college education. Although the high school graduate share is strongly positively correlated with the formation rate, after allowing for the effect of differences in the local share of college graduates, we found that the additional impact of higher shares of high school graduates is negative, since higher shares of high school dropouts were positively associated with formation rates. In a few subsectors of services, this unexpected relationship was weak and not significant – for the business services subsector, and for the subsectors of service business that are likely to be started by workers without college degrees. This effect may be partially explained by the function of high school dropouts in supplying cheap labor to both old and new businesses. The high school dropout rate may also be interacting in a complex way with unemployment, with which it is fairly strongly correlated – regions with higher shares of high school dropouts also tend to have higher unemployment rates.

Our results have two important implications for theory. First, our results support our earlier conclusions in Chapter Three that specialization promotes knowledge spillovers, and they relate to innovation and entrepreneurship. Apparently, new firm formations are facilitated by spillovers from clusters of similar establishments, but a relatively high overall business specialization (other types of establishments) may actually discourage new service firm formations.

Second, the results suggest that human capital does in fact play an important role in the rate of new firm formation and economic growth. The results offer very little support for the large literature on unemployment and entrepreneurship. The relationship between low levels of education and unemployment may indeed be much more complicated than simple models suggest.

CHAPTER FIVE

Entrepreneurship and Employment Growth

Introduction

As we showed in Chapter Two, neoclassical growth theory had no mechanism to explain the relationship between entrepreneurial activity and economic growth (Solow, 1956). Because scale economies operate at the establishment level, in the traditional Solow model economic growth relied on physical capital investment in larger establishments. However, capital accumulation can explain only a small amount of the variation in economic growth across regions (Ciccone and Hall, 1996).

Recent theories of economic growth focus on the importance of knowledge and view knowledge externalities, as opposed to scale economies, as the primary engine of economic growth (Romer, 1986). This suggests that if the domestic economy is endogenously growing, and if we believe in competitive markets, then knowledge spillovers must feature in the economic landscape. This concept of spillovers solves the technical problem in economic theory of reconciling increasing returns (which are generally needed to generate endogenous growth) with competitive markets.

The concept of knowledge spillovers leads to several theoretical issues. First, a large body of recently emerged literature has been studying the spatial extent of knowledge spillovers with particular attention to spillovers from industrial and academic research. At different levels of spatial aggregation (such as states, metropolitan areas, counties) in different countries (e.g., the United States, France, Germany, Italy, Austria), and with the application of different econometric methodologies (e.g., various spatial or aspatial methods), many of these studies conclude that geographical proximity to the knowledge source significantly amplifies spillovers between research and innovating firms. Strong evidence is provided both for the United States (e.g. Acs, Anselin, and Varga, 2002; Varga, 1998; Anselin, Varga, and Acs, 1997; Audretsch and Feldman, 1996; Jaffe, Trajtenberg, and Henderson, 1993) and for Europe (e.g., Fischer and Varga, 2003; Autant-Bernard, 2001) that knowledge flows are bounded within a relatively narrow geographical range. Although certain industrial differences exist (e.g., for innovation in the microelectronics, instruments, or biotechnology sectors, proximity is more significant than for new technology development in the chemicals or machinery sectors), the hypothesis that spatial proximity is an important factor in innovation is strongly supported in the literature.

Second, not all types of industrial structure promote knowledge spillovers equally. It is shown, for instance, by Glaeser and colleagues (1992) that economic growth in U.S. cities is directly related to localized intersectoral knowledge flows.

Third, knowledge spillovers do not appear to be constant over time, and they affect mature and young industry sectors differently. The empirical and theoretical literature suggests that knowledge spillovers are more important in the early stages of the industry life cycle, when young firms flourish (Utterback, 1994), but little attention has been directed to analysis of the mechanics by which local spillovers are associated with industry growth. One potential interpretation of this stronger association between knowledge spillovers and younger industries is that cities that are endogenously growing may have higher levels of entrepreneurial activity. Organization ecology supports the latter, suggesting that typically, entrepreneurs enter the local economy through a new organization that involves some degree of local knowledge spillovers, and these new businesses benefit from local network externalities (Hannan and Freeman, 1989).[1]

The purpose of this chapter is to examine variations in regional employment growth rates in the context of an endogenous growth model

---

[1] Broad local differences in entrepreneurial activity have historically contributed to variation in regional growth rates. Between 1960 and 1983, for example, the number of corporations and partnerships in the United States more than doubled (from 2.0 million to 4.5 million), but this growth was not at all evenly distributed geographically. The regional differences in business formation rates, in turn, reflect regional differences in a number of other local economic factors, such as quantities of knowledge spillovers, rates of return on investment, productivity, unit labor costs, and levels of competition (Acs, 2002).

with a particular emphasis on knowledge spillovers and the new firm formations they lead to. The major changes in employment usually are associated with the early stages of a new industry life cycle, when competition is fiercer and technology is more fluid (Jovanovic, 2001).[2] The 1990s were a period when several industries were in their early stages – semiconductors, computers, and communications equipment and software, components of the Information Age (Jorgenson, 2001) – and these resulted in substantial product and process changes in many other sectors of the economy (Bresnahan, Gambardella, and Saxenian, 2001).

We test the hypothesis that increased entrepreneurial activity that takes advantage of knowledge spillovers leads to higher overall growth rates of regional economies. The next section of this chapter further examines some of the theories explaining variation in growth rates across local economies. After discussing the measurement of employment growth rates for Labor Market Areas, we examine the aggregate data showing the contribution of new firms to economic growth. We then present the regression model and the empirical results from our estimation of it. We find that higher levels of employment growth rates are strongly positively associated with entrepreneurial activity, and weakly positively associated with human capital. After taking account of the impact of entrepreneurial activity, they are negatively associated with agglomeration effects (business specialization and density) in all sectors of the economy except manufacturing.

Why Do Local Employment Growth Rates Vary?

The growth of cities and regions has many facets, and we focus on continuing the search for an understanding of why some areas persistently show much higher growth than others. We will build on three literatures that have been found to have an important impact on variation in regional growth. First, several papers in the last decade have confirmed the connection between the initial level of human capital in an area and the more rapid employment growth of that area (Rauch, 1993;

---

[2] According to Jovanovic, we are entering the era of the young firm. The average age of all companies in the stock market is shrinking. The younger firm will thus resume a role that, in its importance, is greater than it has been at any time in the last 70 years or so.

Glaeser, Scheinkman, and Shleifer, 1995), demonstrating the link between human capital (knowledge) and employment growth. Second, knowledge spillovers play an important role in economic growth (Romer, 1990). Finally, no matter how richly endowed an economic environment is with intellectual, social, human, and financial resources, some person has to be entrepreneurial to organize these resources to pursue market opportunities (Baumol, 1993, 2003, 2004).

Recent theoretical work has identified human capital as a key variable in explaining economic growth (Lucas, 1988 and 1993). Human capital in these Lucas models is an unobservable force or magnitude, not much different than having a society imbued with the Protestant ethic, according to Lucas. However, one aspect of these aggregate models is their focus on the external unobservable effects of human capital. This is quite different from the internal effects that human capital models focused on before. Lucas suggests that there are individual interactions that are central to individual productivity and typical of the activities that are usually found in cities. On purely economic grounds, there is no other reason to keep cities from flying apart. As Lucas (1988, 39) points out, "What can people be paying Manhattan or downtown Chicago rents for, if not for being near other people?"

In two influential papers, Simon and Nardinelli (1996 and 2002) observed the simple fact that modern economic growth almost always accompanies the growth of cities. While many attribute this relationship to the demands of the growing factories or the supply of modern transportation systems, Lucas has attributed it to the external effects of human capital. In this model of growth (1988), the amount of human capital in a society affects the productivity of each worker, apart from the worker's individual human capital. The acquisition of human capital by individual workers generates external effects, or spillovers of knowledge. The spillovers increase with the concentration of human capital. It is plausible that such external economies are strongest within a city because the costs of acquiring the exchanged information – particularly small bits of information – are lower in cities. If human capital generates external economies, those economies whose industries use human capital more intensively should grow faster, other things being equal.

Studying English cities in 1861–1911, Simon and Nardinelli tell a story about city growth involving people exchanging information within certain occupations and industries. Focusing on business profession-als, they found that in addition to such concentrated sources of growth as ports, new textiles, and other manufacturing, human capital played an important role in the long run. The providers of information did not include a large proportion of city population, but their presence may have made the difference between fast growth and stagnation. The knowledge transferred in face-to-face meetings of people with high levels of human capital, rather than through printed materials or large-scale manufacturing experience, may well be the driving force behind the typ-ical city's long-run growth. In a second study looking at human capital and the rise of American cities between 1900 and 1990, they found that American cities with proportionately more individuals with high levels of human capital in 1900 grew more rapidly over the next 86 years. They also found considerable persistence of the effects of geographic differ-ences in human capital, with the distribution of human capital in the first decade of the twentieth century still playing a role in later decades.

One implication of the Lucas (1988) model is that individuals do not capture all of the benefits from their ownership of human capital. Given the existence of human capital externalities, economically identical work-ers will tend to earn higher wages in areas that are richer in human capital, compared to areas that are poorer in human capital. While it is clearly not valid to infer causation from this relationship among countries at different levels of development, this constraint can be avoided by ana-lyzing differences in cities within a country. In a country with a well-developed communications system, the cost of capital and the level of disembodied technological knowledge will presumably be similar in most of its cities. Rauch (1993), using Standard Metropolitan Statistical Areas, finds support for the Lucas thesis, estimating that one additional year of average educational attainment will raise local total factor productivity by 2.8%.

Glaeser, Scheinkman, and Schleifer (1995) examine the relationship between economic growth and years of schooling for a cross section of 203 U.S. cities between 1960 and 1990, looking at initial educational attain-ment and subsequent population growth. The median years of schooling exert a positive and significant influence on the subsequent population growth, using standard controls. A closer inspection of schooling shows that the percentage of the population with high school degrees or some college is more important than the percentage of the population with college degrees. This result suggests the importance of a well-educated labor force, rather than just a larger share at the top of the education distribution. The results for income are similar, with higher initial educational attainment associated with higher incomes. They conclude that the growth of cities is similar to that of countries. Since cities' differences are not created by different savings rates or different labor force endowments, it is suggested that the higher education levels influence later growth not through savings but through influencing the rate of innovation.

Finally, Jones (2002) examines the impact of increases in human capital on the U.S. economy between 1950 and 1993. The research is motivated by the fact that formal education, which is a human capital investment, has increased substantially. As of 1940, less than 25% of adults in the United States had completed high school and only about 5% had college degrees. By 1993, more than 80% had completed high school, and more than 20% had college degrees, raising mean educational attainment by four years. Jones (1995b) suggested that this large increase in human capital would generate temporarily high growth rates as well as long-run effects. He finds that each additional year of education leads to a 7% rise in output per worker, and so the four-year rise in average educational attainment raised output per hour worked by about 28% over this 53-year period, or by an annualized amount of about 0.5% per year, accounting for just under a third of the growth during this period. The remaining two-thirds of growth is attributed to a rise in the stock of knowledge.

Despite the general consensus that knowledge spillovers within a given location stimulate employment growth, there is little consensus as to exactly how this occurs. What type of economic activity will promote positive externalities leading to more economic growth? This question is important, given the debate in the literature about the nature of economic activity and how it affects economic growth. Knowledge spillovers may occur between individuals working in the same or different industries, and there has been considerable debate about whether specialization or diversity is more conducive to growth through spillovers. The Marshall-Arrow-Romer (MAR) externality concerns knowledge spillovers between firms within an industry. Arrow (1962) presented an early formalization; the paper by Romer (1986) is a recent and influential statement. Applied to cities by Marshall (1890), this view says that the concentration of an industry in a city facilitates knowledge spillovers between firms and, therefore, the growth of that industry.

The MAR model formalizes the insight that the concentration of an industry in a city promotes knowledge spillovers between firms and, therefore, facilitates employment growth in a city industry. An important assumption is that knowledge externalities with respect to firms do exist, but only for firms within the same industry. Thus, the relevant unit of observation is extended from the firm to the region in the theoretical tradition of the MAR model and in subsequent empirical studies, but spillovers are limited to occur within the relevant industry. The transmission of knowledge spillovers across industries is assumed to be nonexistent, or at least trivial.

These theories of externalities are extremely appealing because they try to explain simultaneously how cities form and why they grow. MAR, in particular, predict that industries cluster geographically to absorb the knowledge spilling over between firms. In addition, they predict that regionally specialized industries grow faster because neighboring firms can learn from each other much better than can geographically isolated firms.

A very different position is espoused by Jane Jacobs (1969), who perceives information spillovers between industry clusters to be more important than within-industry information flows. She argues that new ideas are formed by combining older ideas (see also Weizman, 1998, for a formalization). Heterogeneity, not specialization, is seen as the most important regional growth factor, and so Jacobs's theory predicts that growth should be faster in areas that are highly industrially diversified. She asserts that the crucial externality in cities is cross fertilization of ideas across different lines of work and industries. For example, New York grain and cotton merchants saw the need for national and international financial transactions, and so the financial services industry was born. Nathan Rosenberg (1963) also discusses the spread of machine tools across industries and describes how ideas are transmitted from one industry to another. Because cities bring people together from different walks of life, they foster such transmission of ideas. Lucas (1993) emphasizes metropolitan areas as the most natural context in which the compact nature of geographic growth facilitates personal interchange, communication, and knowledge spillovers, both within and across industries. In Jacobs's view, a shared scientific base facilitates the exchange of existing ideas and generation of new ones across different, but complementary, industries. Thus, industry diversity rather than specialization may be the operative mechanism of economic growth.

Glaeser and colleagues (1992) analyze the six largest industries in each of 170 U.S. cities to investigate the relative impact of diversity and specialization, and their results are consistent with the presence of Jacobs-type externalities. They find that industries grow sluggishly in cities with high degrees of specialization. Feldman and Audretsch (1999) also test whether diversity or specialization of economic activity better promotes technological change and subsequent economic growth. They find support for the diversity thesis but little support for the specialization thesis.

Acs, FitzRoy, and Smith (2002) also test the MAR hypothesis that industrial R&D spills over across regional industry clusters, using 36 cities and six separate industry clusters over four years. Estimating a model that looks at the impact of university knowledge on high technology employment growth, they find that university research and development spills over across narrowly defined 3-digit industries, supporting the heterogeneity hypothesis. These results suggest that risk pooling, shared infrastructure, and thick labor markets are more important sources of agglomerations than knowledge spillovers, which they find to be of greater value when they come from firms engaged in similar activities.

However, as Duranton and Puga (1999) point out in their survey of this issue, the results may depend on the sector concerned. In fact, the aforementioned studies looked at spillovers within various narrowly defined industrial sectors, and they might not have controlled sufficiently for differences in industry life cycles, or for dominance by large old firms. For the moment, the role of specialization and diversity does not seem to have been resolved by the literature. Different time periods and different samples give different results that suggest that there is no universal truth on the topic.

Where do market opportunities come from? They come from the information and knowledge that accumulates in every local economy. In the new growth theory, at the microlevel, profit-maximizing firms produce knowledge – just like any other good – that is, knowledge production is endogenized. At the macrolevel, the production of knowledge carries obvious implications for growth. It is channeled into growth mainly through two mechanisms: First, firms run their businesses more efficiently, and second, knowledge spills over across firms, acting as a shift factor in their production functions. Both effects tend to increase firm-level productivity. However, in the new growth theory the opportunity to exploit knowledge spillovers accruing from aggregate knowledge investment is not adequately explained. In essence, these models assume that knowledge – defined as both codified and tacit R&D findings – automatically transforms into commercial activity. However, the imposition of this assumption lacks intuitive as well as empirical backing. Acs and Varga (2002, 2005) and Acs and colleagues (2004) argue that it is one thing for technological opportunities to exist, but an entirely different matter for them to be discovered, exploited, and commercialized.

One of the key features of an urban economy is the partitioning of knowledge among individuals. Even if the total stock of knowledge were freely available, spatially and temporally unbounded, knowledge about the existence of any particular information would still be limited (Hayek, 1945). Because of asymmetric information, knowledge is not uniformly at everyone's disposal, and no two individuals share the identical scope of knowledge or information about the economy. Thus, only a few people may know about a new invention, a particular scarcity, or resources lying fallow. It is this specific knowledge, frequently obtained through knowledge spillovers, that may lead to profit-making opportunity.

However, many more opportunities are recognized than are actively pursued. Bringing new products and services into existence usually involves considerable risk. By definition, entrepreneurship requires the making of investments today without assurance of what the returns will be tomorrow. Despite the absence of current markets for future goods and services, and in spite of the moral hazard when dealing with investors, suppliers, and customer markets for future goods and services, many individuals do succeed in creating new businesses. The ability to overcome these barriers to entrepreneurship varies among individuals, and such skill is not evenly distributed across economic areas. The market dynamics associated with entrepreneurship are not, it appears, so much those associated with changes in the number of businesses or products in the market as they are those associated with changes in the characteristics of firms or products. At least in some, if not most, cases, entry represents an *agent of change* in the market (Geroski, 1995, 431).

Thus, we propose to model local economic growth as a function of the various information externalities present in the regional knowledge base – the set of technical and nontechnical information inputs, knowledge, and capabilities about new technologies and processes. We estimate a model that explains differences in regional employment growth rates as a function of the regional levels of entrepreneurial activity, agglomeration effects, and human capital:

employment growth$_{srt+1}$

$$= f(\text{entrepreneurial activity}_{srt}, \text{agglomeration effects}_{srt}, \text{humancapital}_{rt})$$

$$(5.1)$$

where s stands for industrial sector, r stands for regions, and t stands for time.

While our model suggests that causation runs from entrepreneurial activity to economic growth, several authors have suggested that causation might run the other way, with economic growth causing new firm formation. However, in neither the Solow model (1956) nor the Romer model (1990) is new firm formation the outcome of economic growth. In fact, in the Solow model, you can argue that existing firms, through expansion by formations of new secondary establishments, will accommodate all new growth with no need for new firms. In the Romer model, even though the number of firms, formation rates, and the scale of operation cannot be determined in the model, the number of firms is fixed (equal to the number of individuals), no entry occurs (labor being constant) and all firms operate at the same level. In principle, these models typically assume what amounts to a "representative firm," which is supposed to capture microeconomic behavior.

Strictly speaking, the concept of entrepreneurship operates at the individual level. While requiring skills and other resources, entrepreneurship essentially requires people taking certain actions – entrepreneurial behavior. Entrepreneurial action, or the pursuit of opportunity, takes us from the individual to the firm level. A new business, in which the entrepreneur has a controlling interest and strictly protected property rights, provides a vehicle transforming personal skills, knowledge, and ambitions into economic actions. Underlying the start-up of each new organization is an entrepreneur who acquired the knowledge to recognize and pursue a good business opportunity (Lazear, 2002). Firms create output (and jobs as a by-product), and entrepreneurs create firms. Framing the challenge this way sheds light on new firm formations and the entrepreneurs that create them, providing a new focus for addressing an old question – where growth comes from in local economies (Hart, 2002).

Regional Employment Growth Rates

Employment Growth Data

Two slightly different sources of data on employment are used in this chapter. For the five-year period from 1991 to 1996, all establishments in the LEEM in 1991 or 1996 were tabulated, classified by their Labor Market Area and their industry sector in the first of those years that they had positive employment. This analysis uses the same six industry sectors that were defined for the study of firm formation rates in Chapter Three. The employment growth rates for 1991 to 1996 were calculated as the change in employment over that period divided by the mean of beginning and ending employment, for each class of establishments. For calculating the gross change rates, each establishment's employment change over the five-year period was further classified according to the type of employment change – expansion or shrinkage of an establishment with some employment in both years, and formation or closure if employment was zero in one of the years.[3] In addition, for those establishments classified as expanding, if they expanded by a minimum of five employees during the five-year period and averaged at least 15% growth per year (or a total of 101% over the original level), they were counted as "high-growth" establishments and their employment changes were summed up to calculate the growth rate from high-growth establishments.

Employment and growth calculations for all other periods are based on aggregate employment data from County Business Patterns, which has the same source in the Census Bureau as the LEEM. The county-level CBP aggregate employment data were classified by LMA and tabulated for use

---

[3] Thus, all firms that were formed and subsequently closed within the five-year period are omitted from this table and from the analysis of the 1991–1996 growth rates.

in calculating average establishment sizes and average annual employment change rates for LMAs for 1990 to 1993, 1993 to 1996, and 1996 to
1999. These average compounded annual growth rates were calculated
from the cube root of the ratios of the relevant employment levels in the
beginning and ending years, less 1. Using this growth rate calculation, the
resulting growth rate can be applied to the starting employment level and
compounded over three years to produce the ending employment
level.

Variation in Growth of Local Economic Areas

Employment in an area tends to keep pace with the growth of population
in that area, other things being equal, and so it is useful to examine both
the rate of increase in employment and how it differs from the rate of
increase in population. It is not clear whether the growing economy is
attracting the increasing population or the growing population is simply
causing the economy to expand to keep up with local demand and supply.
Table 5.1 focuses on the LMAs whose employment growth rates from 1991
to 1996 were among the highest or lowest in the country. Further, the
last column shows the extent to which each of these areas' employment
growth exceeded its population growth rate. For the LMA growth-rate
comparisons in Tables 5.1 and 5.2, rates of change of both employment
and population are expressed as the five-year change divided by the 1991
level.

There is considerable variation in regional growth rates during this
period. Employment change ranged from a low of −5.9% for the LMA
containing Hilo HI to a high of 47.1% for St. George UT. The highest
excess of employment growth over population growth was the 35.2%
in Kankakee IL, followed by Laurel MS with 30.9%. There were many
cases where employment change did not appear to be closely related to
population change. About 50 LMAs had lower growth in employment
than in population in the first half of the 1990s. The poor employment
growth of the Hilo LMA, already noted, was accompanied by population
growth of 9.7%, so that its relative employment growth was −15.7%
over the five-year period. Note that 2 of the 10 LMAs with the highest
employment growth had relatively low population growth, while only
3 of the 10 LMAs with the highest rates of employment loss also had
population losses.

Table 5.1. *Five-year growth rates from 1991 to 1996 for Labor Market Areas with highest and lowest employment growth rates (growth measured as five-year change divided by 1991 level)*

LMA	Biggest Place	1991 Employment	Employment Growth	Population Growth	Empgr-Popgr*
Highest 10 LMAs by empl. growth					
359	St. George, UT	34,400	47.1%	24.0%	23.0%
298	Monett, MO	27,362	39.9%	18.6%	21.4%
312	Austin, TX	321,222	38.8%	18.5%	20.3%
242	Kankakee, IL	41,609	38.8%	3.6%	35.2%
360	Provo, UT	87,500	37.2%	18.1%	19.1%
379	Los Vegas, NV	391,494	35.9%	28.1%	7.8%
284	Colorado Springs, CO	138,892	35.8%	18.9%	16.9%
352	Grand Junction, CO	45,682	34.5%	15.0%	19.5%
354	Flagstaff, AZ	60,529	34.4%	18.5%	15.9%
28	Laurel, MS	24,645	32.9%	2.0%	30.9%
Lowest 10 LMAs by empl. growth					
177	Syracuse, NY	401,336	−1.5%	−2.0%	0.5%
383	Los Angeles, CA	5,639,265	−1.6%	3.9%	−5.5%
208	Springfield, MA	241,400	−2.0%	−1.4%	−0.6%
187	Sunbury, PA	60,697	−2.5%	3.0%	−5.6%
371	Bakersfield, CA	138,692	−3.1%	8.5%	−11.6%
183	Watertown, NY	60,656	−3.5%	1.3%	−4.8%
179	Binghamton, NY	103,907	−3.6%	−3.4%	−0.1%
347	Honolulu, HI	400,509	−3.8%	4.3%	−8.1%
193	Poughkeepsie, NY	238,525	−5.8%	1.6%	−7.4%
356	Hilo, HI	41,089	−5.9%	9.7%	−15.7%

* Empgr-Popgr represents the rate at which employment increased in excess of the overall growth rate of the population.

Table 5.2 shows the five-year growth rates for the 10 largest and smallest LMAs, based on their employment in 1991. Employment growth rates were substantially higher in the smallest LMAs, averaging 19.6%, compared to the 3.9% average of the largest LMAs. In the 10 largest LMAs, employment growth just barely kept up with population growth, and so their five-year relative employment growth was a mere 0.6%. The population growth rates of the largest and smallest LMAs were quite similar, and so even after controlling for population growth, the smallest LMAs had significantly higher relative employment growth.

Table 5.2. *Five-year growth rates for 1991–1996 for largest and smallest Labor Market Areas (growth measured as five-year change divided by 1991 level)*

			1991 Employment	Employment Growth	Population Growth	Empgr-Popgr*
Largest LMA's						
383	Los Angeles	CA	5,639,265	−1.6%	3.9%	−5.5%
194	New York	NY	4,290,264	0.6%	1.1%	−0.5%
243	Chicago IL	IL	3,302,354	7.0%	4.5%	2.5%
113	ArlngtnWashBalt	VA	2,639,292	7.4%	3.8%	3.6%
196	Newark	NJ	2,359,911	3.1%	2.4%	0.7%
197	Philadelphia	PA	2,154,296	2.5%	0.4%	2.0%
205	Boston	MA	2,143,471	7.1%	1.9%	5.1%
116	Detroit	MI	1,921,754	13.0%	3.6%	9.4%
378	San Francisco	CA	1,772,575	3.1%	3.6%	−0.5%
320	Houston	TX	1,567,212	8.2%	9.8%	−1.5%
AVG OF 10 LARGEST LMAs				3.9%	3.3%	0.6%
Smallest LMAs						
77	Lake City	FL	27,522	15.1%	11.7%	3.4%
298	Monett	MO	27,362	39.9%	18.6%	21.4%
158	Athens	OH	26,508	10.7%	3.2%	7.6%
337	Ardmore	OK	26,068	16.4%	3.5%	12.9%
258	Blytheville	AR	25,229	19.9%	−5.8%	25.7%
283	North Platte	NE	24,722	15.9%	1.5%	14.4%
28	Laurel	MS	24,645	32.9%	2.0%	30.9%
327	Brownwood	TX	23,711	19.6%	5.4%	14.2%
324	Big Spring	TX	21,698	10.7%	1.9%	8.8%
245	FortLeonardWood	MO	19,895	11.9%	−1.0%	12.9%
AVG OF 10 SMALLEST LMAs				19.6%	4.4%	15.2%

* Empgr-Popgr represents the rate at which employment increased in excess of the overall growth rate of the population.

Employment Growth from Newly Formed Establishments

It is evident from Table 5.3 that the employment growth derived from newly formed establishments plays a far more important role in the economy than has previously been generally recognized. There are four important findings we note in summary. First, for the economy as a whole, over the five-year period of the early nineties, employment in 1996 of the new establishments that started up after 1991 (formations)

Table 5.3. *Establishment employment, net and gross employment change rates for 1991–1996, by firm type, and by industry sector*

Establ. Class	Employment		Empl. Change 1991–1996 as % of Mean Empl. in Class					High-Growth*Establ.	
	1991	1996	Net	Formations	Expansions	Shrinkers	Deaths	Empl. Chg.	Establ. Share
All	92,265,576	102,149,281	10.2%	26.3%	17.8%	−13.5%	−20.5%	8.9%	4.68%
Firm type									
Single unit	38,532,294	44,811,609	15.1%	31.3%	20.1%	−11.1%	−25.3%	9.8%	n.a.
Multiunit	53,731,429	57,324,994	6.5%	22.6%	16.0%	−15.3%	−16.9%	8.3%	n.a.
Industry Sector									
Local market	33,434,183	37,773,144	12.2%	25.8%	17.9%	−12.8%	−18.7%	9.4%	4.45%
Retail trade	19,443,520	21,477,074	9.9%	33.3%	13.4%	−12.3%	−24.4%	8.0%	3.48%
Manufactures	18,450,502	18,556,546	0.6%	13.3%	17.0%	−14.2%	−15.5%	9.4%	7.03%
Distribution	11,887,375	12,719,155	6.8%	23.4%	20.0%	−14.8%	−21.7%	9.4%	5.57%
Bus. services	7,780,445	10,385,762	28.7%	43.6%	25.2%	−14.6%	−25.5%	7.4%	6.20%
Extractive	1,269,551	1,237,600	−2.5%	24.5%	19.4%	−18.5%	−27.9%	8.6%	5.69%

Employment change rates are based on the mean of 1991 and 1996 employment for the class of establishments. Employment change attributable to formations is the 1996 employment of all establishments formed since 1991 that survived to 1996, divided by the mean of 1991 and 1996 employment for the class of establishments.

Firm type = multi if establishment was part of multiunit firm in either year; otherwise single (or independent).

* High-growth establishments expanded by an average of at least 15% per year (adding at least 5 empl.).

n.a. = not available.

represented 26.3% of the mean employment over that period. This was by far the largest source of employment change. The growth from expanding establishments that existed in 1991 was only 17.8%, and this increase was offset by the loss of 13.5% of their employment from shrinking establishments, and another 20.5% loss from the deaths of some of those 1991 establishments. The net effect of all these gross changes in employment of establishments between 1991 and 1996 was an increase of only 10.2% over the five years, or roughly 2% annually.

Second, when we distinguish formations by the type of establishment – whether the establishment is a single-unit firm or a new location under the ownership or control of a multiunit firm – the employment growth rate of 31.3% from new single-unit firms is much greater than the 22.6% growth from the new secondary locations or branch plants of multiunit firms. This same 9% difference is maintained between the net[4] employment growth rates of 15.1% for single-unit firms versus 6.5% for establishments in multilocation firms. These differences strongly suggest that the role of externalities leading to new firms and plants is greater than that of scale economies of existing firms as a driving factor behind growth.

Third, most of the six sectors had similar patterns of gross employment change rates, but the sector differences in employment gains from formations were much more varied than any of the other components of gross employment changes. These differences in gains from establishment formations accounted for most of the differences across sectors in rates of net employment change. The exceptionally low rate of increase from establishment formations in manufacturing (13.3%) supports P. Geroski's (1995) earlier analysis showing that new formations do not appear to play an important role in manufacturing.

Fourth, these data allow us to evaluate the frequent claim that the majority of new jobs are created by expansion of a relatively small number of rapidly growing establishments (Bhide, 2000; Birch, 1987). The right-hand column shows that less than 5% of the establishments in 1991 had high average growth rates to 1996 (averaging at least 15% per year for five years, and increasing by at least five employees). If this assessment were

---

[4] Net employment growth rates are calculated as the difference between the rates of employment gains from formations and expansions of establishments and employment losses from shrinkage and closures of establishments.

limited to gross job growth from expansion of existing establishments, then it is true that this small number of high-growth establishments created marginally more jobs than the much larger number of low-growth establishments – increases of 8.9% from high growth account for just over half of the 17.8% growth from all expanding establishments. However, this job growth from high-growth establishments totals only a third of the gains from new establishments, again suggesting that the impact on employment growth from innovations resulting in new firms and secondary establishments is much greater than that from scaling up the size of existing businesses. These patterns are fairly consistent across industry sectors and firm types. Manufacturing did have a higher share of high-growth establishments, but these still contributed just over half of the growth from expanding establishments in that sector.

Data on the shares of high-growth establishments in each LMA are provided in Appendix D. This table also provides each LMA's data for employment, numbers of establishments, and population in 1991, as well as the growth rates from 1991 to 1996 for employment and population, and their employment growth in excess of their population growth rate for that five-year period. Employment in the United States grew 10.7% during those five years, while population grew only 5.2%, so that employment grew 5.5% relative to population. Note that there are many cases of both extremely high population growth and population losses, and the growth rate of employment appears to be fairly independent of these population growth extremes. Furthermore, the share of local establishments classified as high growth (popularly called gazelles, following Birch, 1987) is fairly constant across LMAs, and does not appear to be closely correlated with the employment growth rate.[5]

It has been widely assumed that the areas with high rates of employment growth also typically have bigger shares of high-growth establishments and higher rates of new firm formation. To test this assumption for the 394 Labor Market Areas in the United States, we calculated Pearson correlation coefficients for each pair of these three variables (using firm formation averages from 1994 through 1996 only). The local employment growth rates are correlated 0.62 with the high-growth share of establishments during this period, but their correlation with the firm formation

---

[5] The data printed in this Appendix, as well as firm formation rates from Appendix B, are also available for downloading from Zoltan Acs's Web site.

rates is only 0.42. Firm formation rates were correlated 0.43 with the local high-growth shares. Thus, it is clear that there are many other important factors influencing overall employment change rates, in addition to the impact of local differences in firm formation rates and the relative size of the tiny share of local businesses that are enjoying high growth. We will try to identify some of them in the next section.

Exogenous Variables for Analyzing the Local Growth Model

From the discussion earlier, it should be clear that the major hypotheses concerning the regional variation in growth rates are related to dynamic externalities, and that one way to capture the extent of these spillovers is to examine how growth rates vary across regions. The literature suggests that higher employment growth rates should be associated with higher rates of entrepreneurial activity, increased industry diversity, and higher levels of human capital. The detailed definitions of these explanatory (independent or exogenous) variables follow.

We include two measures of entrepreneurial activity. The flow of entrepreneurial activity is measured as the *new firm formation rate*, which was the dependent variable of the models in Chapters Three and Four. These firm formation rates are calculated from LEEM data for various time periods for each of the 394 LMAs, for the same six industry sectors as in Chapter Three, and for the total private sector (all-industry). The number of new firms is divided by the size of the local labor force (in thousands) in the year prior to the time span, and so the formation rates represent the number of new firms per 1,000 of labor force in each LMA. Higher rates of entrepreneurial activity in an area are expected to be associated with higher employment growth in that area.

Our second measure of entrepreneurial activity is the *share of proprietors* in the area's labor force. This measure has been used in several European studies, including that of S. Wennekers and R. Thurik (1999). It measures not current entrepreneurial activity but the cumulative effects of past activity, and so it serves more as a measure of the local popularity of owning one's business. Proprietors are members of the labor force who are also business owners, including both those with employees and the self-employed who have no paid employees. The share of proprietors is defined for each LMA and year as the number of proprietors divided by the labor force in the same year, just as in Chapter Three. This share averaged 20.5% nationally, and varied from a low of 10.6% to a high of 40.4% across LMAs in 1996.

We include two measures of agglomeration effects that characterize local economies. We measure *sector specialization* as the number of establishments in each industry sector and region divided by the region's population in thousands. After standardizing by the national average, this measure is almost identical to the specialization measure used by Glaeser and colleagues (1992). Sector specialization will be positively related to employment growth if specialization contributes to regional growth. A negative relationship would suggest that the competitive effects of specialization are stronger than its contribution to growth through more diverse knowledge spillovers. When dealing with all industries together, this variable represents *business specialization* – the intensity of local business development per capita. In Chapter Three, we found that this relative specialization contributed strongly to the new firm formation rate, both by sector and for all businesses. However, in Chapter Four we found that greater sector specialization contributed to higher formation rates, but that the additional impact of greater business specialization (primarily other sectors) reduced formation rates.

To control for the vast differences in the physical density of economic activity in various LMAs, we use *business density*, defined as the number of establishments per square mile in that industry and region. If firms in cities or other areas with high concentrations of businesses benefit from the closeness of other businesses in the same sector, then higher establishment densities should contribute to employment growth. Since the regression analysis uses each area's relative levels of business density in each industry, rather than absolute levels, there is no need to correct for differences in national industry presence or demand. Establishment density should be positively related to local growth rates if agglomerations drive demand or increase network externalities (Ciccone and Hall, 1996). However, higher densities are also likely to be indicative of the extent of physical crowding of businesses, which leads to higher costs of doing business, and perhaps therefore less growth.

We include two measures of human capital that have been found to have a positive impact on regional growth in previous studies (Simon and Nardinelli, 2002). The first is the share of adults with at least a *high school degree*, with adults defined as persons 25 years or older. Those adults without high school degrees are the principal supply of unskilled and semiskilled labor for work in manufacturing branch plants and retail or unskilled service establishments. Higher shares of high school graduates indicate a generally higher level of human capital in the area.

The second measure of educational attainment is the share of *college graduates*, defined as the number of adults with college degrees in 1990 divided by the total number of adults, just as in Chapters Three and Four. This serves as a proxy for both the technical skills needed in the economy and the skills needed to start and build a business. Naturally, the number of college degree holders is included in the number of high school degree holders, so that these two measures will suffer from collinearity, and we will test them separately. We expect that employment growth will be positively related to higher average levels of education, at both the high school and the college level (Glaeser, Scheinkman, and Shleifer, 1995).

To control for differences in the size distribution of businesses in each industry and region, we include average local *establishment* size, measured for each industry sector and economic area as in Chapter Three (employees per establishment). Mean establishment sizes vary nationally from 11 employees for the local market sector up to 55 for manufacturing. Regions that are dominated by large branch plants or firms are likely to be less competitive and slower growing than those with many smaller establishments.

As discussed earlier, the complex interrelationships among these variables suggest a need for care in analysis and caution in interpretation. Share of regional adult population with high school degrees is highly correlated with the share holding college degrees. Certainly, the average size of establishments is smaller when the share of proprietors is higher, as confirmed by their simple correlation of -0.63. Both the industry specialization and the establishment density are partially the effect of firm formation rates in the past, as well as contributing factors during the period under study. We will control for some of these econometrically by estimating alternative models with subsets of these variables, to isolate the effects of multicollinearity.

Table 5.4 presents summary statistics for all variables, and a correlation matrix showing how the pairs of variables relate to each other is provided in Table 5.5. The correlation coefficients show the correlation of the variables used for regression analysis for the first and third of the

Table 5.4. *Summary statistics for LMA-level variables in the growth model*

	Mean	Std. dev.	Min.	Max.
Employment growth rate (3-year avg) $((e(t+3)/e(t)*1/3)-1$				
1990 to 1993	0.0188	0.0196	−0.0278	0.1390
1993 to 1996	0.0273	0.0149	−0.0243	0.0902
1996 to 1999	0.0214	0.0150	−0.0207	0.0989
Firm formation rate (3-year avg) $(f(t+1)+f(t+2)+f(t+3))/3/LF(t)*1000$				
1990	3.605	0.872	2.192	9.239
1993	3.710	0.932	2.060	9.870
1996	3.477	0.876	1.984	9.876
1990 Human capital (share of adults 25+yrs)				
High school degree share	0.721	0.080	0.459	0.883
College degree share	0.159	0.050	0.069	0.320
Business specialization Establishments(t)/popul.(t) *1000				
1990	2.146	0.332	1.151	4.123
1993	2.176	0.347	1.155	4.464
1996	2.214	0.364	1.131	4.728
Establishment size Employment(t)/establishments(t)				
1990	14.93	2.97	8.14	21.51
1993	15.05	2.87	8.19	21.03
1996	15.58	2.90	8.25	22.67
Business density ln(establishments(t)/sq. miles)				
1990	0.352	1.168	−3.82	4.80
1993	0.397	1.159	−3.73	4.78
1996	0.441	1.157	−3.67	4.82
Share of proprietors Proprietors(t)/labor force (t)				
1990	0.205	0.058	0.106	0.390
1993	0.203	0.055	0.099	0.389
1996	0.212	0.057	0.106	0.404

Table 5.5. *Correlations of employment growth rates and regional characteristics for 394 Labor Market Areas for 1990–1993 and for 1996–1999*

	Employm't Growth	Firm Formation	College Degree Share	High School Degree Share	Business Specializ'n	Establish. Size	Business Density
Empl. growth rate (3-year avg)							
1990–1993	1.00						
1996–1999	1.00						
Firm formation rate (3-year avg)							
1990–1993	0.37	1.00					
1996–1999	0.41	1.00					
College graduate share (1990)							
1990–1993	−0.11	0.25	1.00				
1996–1999	0.38	0.31	1.00				
High school degr. share (1990)							
1990–1993	−0.02	0.18	0.70	1.00			
1996–1999	0.29	0.18	0.70	1.00			
Business specialization							
1990–1993	0.10	0.54	0.43	0.55	1.00		
1996–1999	0.10	0.50	0.40	0.55	1.00		
Establishment size							
1990–1993	−0.32	−0.43	0.25	0.07	−0.28	1.00	
1996–1999	0.06	−0.38	0.19	0.04	−0.31	1.00	
Business density							
1990–1993	−0.50	−0.21	0.36	0.13	−0.04	0.68	1.00
1996–1999	0.15	−0.13	0.37	0.14	−0.09	0.63	1.00
Proprietor share							
1990–1993	0.37	0.31	−0.13	0.13	0.44	−0.65	−0.61
1996–1999	−0.01	0.27	−0.05	0.21	0.50	−0.64	−0.60

Note: Pearson coefficients smaller than .10 are not significant at the .05 level.

three-year periods, so that we can see the range of changes in those that changed their relationships over time. The most important column in Table 5.5 is the first, which shows correlations with employment growth rates. Their correlations with the educational attainment/human capital variables were tiny and negative in the period from 1990 to 1993, but by 1996–1999, they had become substantial and positive, as the economy was transformed into more knowledge-based businesses.

Additional correlations (not shown) looked at how growth rates and formation rates for consecutive periods correlated over time, and how the relationship of educational attainment rates to growth rates changed over time. First, we found that firm formation rates are highly correlated over time −.96 between consecutive three-year periods. Second, the correlations of employment growth rates between the same consecutive periods are 0.31 and 0.18, respectively. Indeed, from year to year there is very little correlation between consecutive annual employment growth rates in LMAs. Third, the correlation between human capital and employment growth increased over the decade for both college and high school degree shares, suggesting that employment growth has been increasing its sensitivity to educational attainment, as the economy shifts to more knowledge-based activities.

Empirical Results of Estimating the Growth Rate Model

We estimate several regression models to attempt to explain differences in LMA employment growth rates during the 1990s. All variables are used in the regressions in their standardized form, so that the national mean is subtracted from each, and the resulting relative rate is divided by its standard deviation across all LMAs. Thus, each standardized variable measures how the area differs from the national average, in terms of the standard deviation of that variable. Standardizing their distribution over LMAs so that each has a mean of zero and a standard deviation of one allows us to make direct comparisons of the estimated standardized beta coefficients for different industry sectors. Each coefficient can then be interpreted as the share of the independent variable's standard deviation that is reflected in the local deviation of the employment change rate from average rates. The regression results are therefore recorded as standardized beta coefficients, along with their t-scores.

Table 5.6. *Analysis of factors associated with differences in employment growth rates in LMAs by three-year period (estimated standardized beta coefficients, with t-ratios below, bold if significant at 0.05 level)*

3-Year Empl. Change Rate (t to $t + 3$)	1990–1993	1993–1996	1996–1999
Adjusted R squared	0.40	0.30	0.32
Firm formation rates per LF	**0.50**	**0.64**	**0.56**
Avg annl. $t + 1$ to $t + 3$ formation rate	9.47	11.4	10.1
College degree share 1990	−0.06	−0.12	0.10
College degr./adults (25+yrs)	−0.88	−1.60	1.41
High school degree share 1990	**0.14**	**0.21**	**0.29**
High sch. degr./adults (25+yrs)	2.32	3.03	4.32
Establishment size	**0.26**	**0.43**	**0.14**
Employment (t)/establishments(t)	4.00	6.59	2.25
Business specialization	**−0.38**	**−0.20**	**−0.39**
Establ.(t)/population(t)	−6.17	−3.00	−6.14
Business density	**−0.41**	**−0.24**	0.09
ln (estab.(t)/sq miles)	−6.76	3.79	1.50
Share of proprietors	**0.27**	0.08	0.12
Proprietors(t)/labor force(t)	4.44	1.26	1.84
Number of observations (LMAs)	394	394	394

In Table 5.6, we show the results of this estimation for annual growth rates averaged over each of three three-year periods for 394 LMAs for all industries together. There are several important results in these estimates. First, the coefficient on the firm birth rate is always positive, large, and statistically significant, as hypothesized. To interpret these coefficients, we use the summary statistics in Table 5.4 to determine that the standard deviation of growth is about 1.5%, and the standard deviation of firm formation rates is about 0.9 new firms per 1,000 in the labor force. Therefore, the estimated standardized coefficient of entrepreneurial activity of about 0.55 indicates that a difference of one firm formation per 1,000 in the labor force in a region's average is associated with a difference of about eight-tenths of a point in the region's growth rate.[6] Our findings of

---

[6] More precisely, if a region's firm formation rate were higher by 0.9 (one standard deviation in formation rates), the coefficient of .55 indicates that we should expect the

positive relationships between firm birth and local economic growth rate differences are inconsistent with Fritsch (1997), who found no relationship between firm formations and employment growth in Germany, but they are consistent with Reynolds (1999), who found a similar positive relationship.

Human capital appears important for employment growth, even beyond its impact on firm formation rates. The high school level of educational attainment appears to be much more important for growth than the college graduate level. The greater the proportion of the area's adults with a high school degree, the higher the employment growth rates. The strength of this positive relationship was increasing throughout the 1990s. The additional impact of higher shares of college degrees was insignificant throughout the decade. These results are consistent with Glaeser, Scheinkman, and Shleifer (1995) and Simon and Nardinelli (2002).

The average size of establishments in an area is positively related to growth, after allowing for the strong positive impact of new firm formation rates, which, we found earlier, were strongly negatively related to establishment size. This tendency for greater growth in areas with larger businesses is surprising, as it conflicts with the popular image of large old businesses reducing their employment while smaller younger ones are growing.

When we aggregate all industries together, the business specialization variable degenerates from a measure of industry specialization in the region to a measure of the local density of businesses relative to the local density of people. Therefore, the negative and statistically significant coefficient on business specialization suggests that areas with more businesses relative to their population tend to have less growth, rather than greater growth. These results are consistent throughout the decade.

The negative and statistically significant coefficients on establishment density suggest that when other factors are the same, employment growth will be greater in regions that have less physical crowding in their industry. Thus, when measured by the number of establishments per square mile,

region's growth rate to be .55 times 1.5% (one standard deviation in growth rates) = 0.8 percentage points higher growth.

the agglomeration effect on growth seems to be negative for Labor Market Areas, after allowing for the impact of the formation rate differences. This is in contrast with the findings of Glaeser and colleagues (1992) and C. Ciccone and R. E. Hall (1996), who used growth in other industries in each area as an indication of the size of the agglomeration effect, and found a positive relationship with growth. Indeed, it contrasts with much of the theoretical literature on agglomerations (Krugman, 1991a). Perhaps these older studies' inability to adequately measure the impact of differences in the level of competition resulted in their agglomeration variables serving as proxies for competition instead. Or perhaps the primary impact of agglomeration effects is on formation rates, so that our negative coefficient represents only the higher costs of physical crowding.

The coefficient on the share of proprietors is positive and statistically significant for 1990; however, it is insignificant for the latter two time periods, perhaps suggesting that larger shares of proprietors were associated with higher growth only in recession years. It may also indicate that the demonstration effect of the older proprietors has recently been supplanted by the differences in human capital or other variables. The coefficient for the share of proprietors is barely one-tenth of that for entrepreneurial activity, indicating that it is not so much the accumulated stock of entrepreneurial activity but the flow that is important for economic growth. This result suggests that it is younger firms (age and not smaller size per se) that are more important for promoting growth and productivity. These results are inconsistent with Martin Carree and colleagues (2002). The importance of regional differences in the share of proprietors and the importance of business density both appeared to be falling during the nineties, while the importance of human capital was increasing.

Little is known about the typical rates of growth of employment in the first few years of newly formed businesses, and so we had no solid basis for determining the most suitable lag between the formation and the growth variables. Because of the limited amount of data available and the very high serial correlation of formation rates, we were not able to use standard statistical tools to estimate the lags. In spite of these constraints, we attempted to test whether estimates for lagged growth rates would

Table 5.7. *Analysis of factors associated with differences in lagged employment growth rates in LMAs (estimated standardized beta coefficients, with t-ratios below, bold if significant at 0.05 level)*

3-Year Empl. Change Rate	1990–1993	1993–1996	1996–1999
Adjusted R squared	0.40	0.22	0.28
Firm formation rate per labor force	**0.50**	**0.54**	**0.52**
Avg annl. formation rate 1991–1993	9.47	8.92	9.00
College degree share 1990	−0.06	−0.12	**0.18**
College degr./adults (25+yrs)	−0.88	−0.32	2.53
High school degree share 1990	**0.14**	**0.17**	**0.24**
High sch. degr./adults (25+yrs)	2.32	2.39	3.46
Establishment size 1990	**0.26**	**0.35**	**0.15**
Employment/establishments	4.00	4.77	2.10
Business specialization 1990	**−0.38**	**−0.22**	**−0.35**
Establishments/population	−6.17	−3.07	−5.13
Business density 1990	**−0.41**	**−0.24**	0.08
ln (estabishments/sq miles)	−6.76	3.51	1.15
Share of proprietors 1990	**0.27**	0.08	0.08
Proprietors/labor force	4.44	1.15	1.19
Number of observations (LMAs)	394	394	394

better explain their regional differences. Table 5.7 shows the results of using the regional characteristics at the beginning of the 1990s to explain regional growth rates with no lags, with three-year lags, and with six-year lags. We have also averaged growth rates over three years to control for any business cycle effects (i.e., positive intertemporal correlation between regional growth rates that often exists) that may be erroneously captured by the firm formation rate resulting from positive correlation between growth and subsequent firm formation rates. The first column of Table 5.7 repeats the result in Table 5.6 for growth during the period from 1990 to 1993. The adjusted R squared falls as we increase the lag between the independent variables and the resulting growth rates, indicating that these relationships are better explained without use of lags. Of course, because the formation rates in LMAs are very highly correlated across consecutive time periods, we did not expect use of lags to substantially improve the estimates.

Table 5.8 presents results estimated for growth in each of our six industry sectors during the period from 1991 to 1996.[7] The coefficient on formation rates is positive and statistically significant for five of our six industry sectors, with the exception of manufacturing, where it was insignificant. This exception may explain the prior findings of industrial organization economists that new firm start-ups are not important for employment growth in manufacturing (e.g., Geroski, 1995). These results also do not support some of the recent research on the relationship between economic development and industrial clusters (Rocha, 2004). Much of the research in industrial organization, labor economics, and regional science has been limited to analysis of data from the manufacturing sector, and those conclusions have been generalized to the whole economy. While these generalizations from the behavior of manufacturing firms are not always valid in other sectors, they may be valid for other sectors that are also dominated by large plants. Certain aspects of our results are consistent with Audretsch and Fritsch (2002) and with Glaeser and colleagues (1992), who found the impact of competition on growth stronger outside of manufacturing than in manufacturing.[8]

In these industry-specific estimations, the sector specialization variable actually measures the relative specialization of each region in each industry sector. The negative and statistically significant coefficients on industry sector specialization indicate that greater geographic specialization in a sector leads to less growth in that sector, rather than greater growth, again with the exception of manufacturing. Although manufacturing has a positive coefficient, it is not significantly different from zero.

---

[7] The average birth rates for the period from 1991 to 1996 were calculated from the average of the number of births in 1992, 1993, 1995, and 1996, divided by the labor force in 1993 in thousands. The number of firm births by LMA and sector in 1994 was not easily available, but had been shown consistent with the previous and subsequent years for more aggregated annual birth data.

[8] Formation rates measure a different kind of competition than Glaeser et al. (1992) referred to. Relative formation rate measures focus on competition between and/or induced by new firm formation (associated with the relative strength of barriers to entry), and do not take account of the potentially strong competition among incumbent firms.

Table 5.8. *Analysis of factors associated with differences in employment growth rates during 1991–1996 in LMAs by industry sector (estimated standardized beta coefficients, with t-ratios below, bold if significant at 0.05 level)*

Empl. Change rate 1991–1996	All Industry	Local Mkt.	Retail	Manuf.	Distribut.	Bus. Serv.	Extract.
R sqrd	0.33	0.44	0.25	0.14	0.13	0.10	0.31
Firm formation rate 1991–1996	**0.62**	**0.54**	**0.54**	−0.04	**0.41**	**0.57**	**0.42**
Avg annl. '91–'96 formations/'93LF	11.3	11.3	8.98	−0.59	6.86	4.96	5.19
College degree share	−0.11	0.10	0.02	**0.15**	0.06	−0.03	0.13
'90 college degr./adults	−1.66	1.51	0.22	−2.02	0.73	−0.34	1.87
High school degree share	**0.14**	−0.08	−0.04	0.06	**0.16**	0.12	0.03
'90 high sch. degr./adults (25+)	2.02	−1.23	−0.56	0.87	2.06	1.61	0.40
Sector specialization	**−0.30**	**−0.50**	**−0.34**	0.14	**−0.28**	**−0.57**	**−0.53**
'91 sector establ./population	−4.78	−8.40	−5.19	1.92	−4.10	−3.97	−6.30
Establishment size	**0.20**	**−0.25**	0.07	−0.09	−0.07	**−0.17**	**−0.41**
'91 sector empl./sector establ.	3.26	−4.55	0.96	−1.61	−1.03	−3.02	−9.30
Business density	**−0.22**	**−0.13**	**−0.23**	**−0.15**	**−0.11**	−0.05	**−0.14**
ln ('91 sector establ./sq mile)	−4.61	−2.91	−4.78	−2.75	−1.97	−0.91	−2.84
Share of proprietors	**0.16**	0.03	0.02	**0.21**	0.01	**−0.14**	0.01
'91 proprietors/labor force	2.81	0.61	0.34	3.79	0.10	−2.54	0.09
Number of observations per sector	394	394	394	394	394	394	394

Employment change rate is the 1991 to 1996 net change in employment of establishments in LMA and sector, divided by mean of 1991 and 1996 employment in LMA and sector.
Firm formation rate is the average of new firm formations in 1992, 1993, 1995, and 1996, divided by 1993 labor force. Comparable data on 1994 formations were not available by sector.

This suggests that after allowing for the higher formation rates associated with it, greater sector specialization does not generally lead to the higher levels of technological externalities or other knowledge spillovers that promote growth in that sector. This is consistent with the findings of Glaeser and colleagues (1992), Feldman and Audretsch (1999), and Acs, FitzRoy, and Smith (2002).

The coefficients estimated at the industry-sector level for most of the other variables were smaller and weaker, but generally similar to those discussed earlier for all industries together for the period from 1990 to1993.

The alternative model formulations shown in Table 5.9 for employment growth rates during 1996 to 1999 reveal the importance of the formation rates and human capital variables in explaining differences in growth rates. Model A replicates the full model shown in the last column of Table 5.6, in which the adjusted R-squared indicates that 32% of the regional variation in growth rates was explained by the full set of independent variables. Models B and C show that we can explain virtually the same amount of this variation without the help of the establishment size, business density, or share of proprietors. The coefficients on the remaining independent variables maintain their values and signs, and that for college degree share becomes somewhat larger and statistically significant. Thus, it appears that our control variables that represent the existing structure, beyond the relative level of business specialization, do not contribute much to the explanation of growth differences across regions.

Model D shows the effect of dropping the high school degree share. The estimated coefficient on college degree share is doubled, and the explained variation falls slightly, to 27%. Dropping the business specialization variable in Model E reduces the coefficients on the remaining two – formation rates and college degree shares – and further reduces the explained variation to 23%. Model F uses only the firm formation rate, and its coefficient is higher, because it no longer has to share the positive effects of education with any education variable. However, Model F only explains 16% of the variation in growth rates, which is just half of the explanatory value of the full model.

Because we were curious about the weak coefficients estimated for most of the business structure variables that we had included in the original model to control for local characteristics expected to influence growth

Table 5.9. *Alternative models of LMA employment growth rates during 1996–1999 for all industries (estimated standardized beta coefficients, with t-ratios below, bold if significant at 0.05 level)*

1996–1999 Empl. Change Rate	A	B	C	D	E	F	G	H
Adjusted R sqrd	0.32	0.32	0.31	0.27	0.23	0.16	0.03	0.14
Firm formation rate per LF	**0.56**	**0.54**	**0.49**	**0.43**	**0.32**	**0.41**	–	–
Avg '92–'96 formation rates	10.10	9.96	9.59	8.53	6.89	8.81	–	–
College degree share 1990	0.10	0.11	**0.17**	**0.34**	**0.27**	–	–	**0.35**
90 college degr./adults	1.41	1.65	2.75	7.27	5.91	–	–	4.80
High school degree share 1990	**0.29**	**0.30**	**0.29**	–	–	–	–	0.11
'90 hs degr./adults (25+)	4.32	4.50	4.31	–	–	–	–	1.47
Business specialization 1991	**−0.39**	**−0.35**	**−0.38**	**−0.26**	–	–	0.08	**−0.13**
'91 establ./'91 population	−6.14	−5.85	−6.50	−4.94	–	–	1.38	−2.04
Establishment size 1991	**0.14**	**0.13**	–	–	–	–	0.01	−0.06
'91 empl/'91 establ.	2.25	2.60	–	–	–	–	0.10	−0.81
Business density 1991	0.09						**0.19**	0.05
ln ('91 establ./sq mile)	1.50						2.61	0.76
Share of proprietors 1991	0.12						0.06	0.04
'91 proprietors/91 labor force	1.84						0.78	0.56
Number of observations	394	394	394	394	394	394	394	394

rates, in Model G we tried dropping formation rates and both educational attainment variables to see if the impacts of the business structure variables could be better measured without the interference of formation and education rates. Only business density acquired significance in this model, but it explained only 3% of the variation in growth rates, and so it hardly matters.

While new firm formation rate seems to be the best available measure of the relative levels of competition (low barriers to entry) within industries and areas, formations also involve new employment in the new firms, adding directly to the growth of the region. In equation H we estimate equation A without the firm formation rate. The results are unequivocal – without the new firm formation rate the equation loses most of its explanatory power. In addition, without the influence of the formation rate, variable college degree share becomes significantly positive, while high school share loses significance and the negative coefficient on business specialization falls by two-thirds of its prior value. Regional growth rate variation is closely associated with the regional variation in new firm formation rates.

International Comparisons

Are the results obtained in this chapter consistent with studies from other countries? Recently, Acs and Storey (2004) have examined the results of research on the effects of new firm formation on employment growth in several countries. Table 5.10 provides a summary of the results obtained from four papers that examine the link between new firm formation – our measure of entrepreneurship – and economic development in the United States and Europe (Audretsch and Keilbach, 2004). The studies cover four different countries over four very different time periods, and their diversity needs to be stressed. Their measures of "economic development" are radically different, covering both employment change and productivity. Three of the studies cover all industry sectors, but the Braunerhjelm and Benny Borgman (2004) study covers only manufacturing. Finally, and perhaps most important of all, the "controls" vary markedly from one study to another.

Nevertheless, despite this diversity, there appears to be some evidence that geographical areas that experience a rise in new firm formation

Table 5.10. *Studies linking entrepreneurship with economic development at the regional level*

Authors	Acs/Armington	Van Stel/Storey	Audretsch/Keilbach	Braunerhjelm/Borgman
Country	United States	United Kingdom	Germany	Sweden
Time period	1991–1999	1980–1998	1989–1992	1975–1999
Dependent variable	Employment change	Employment change	Gross value added	Value added per employee
Sectors	All private sectors	All private sectors paying VAT	All private sectors	Production industries
Independent variables				
New firm formation rate	+	+/−/0	+	+
Specialization	−			+
Population density	− /0	− /0		
Education attainment	+/0			0
Establishment size	+/−			0
Wage rates		0/ +		
R&D			+	
Capital stock			+	

+ indicates significant positive relationship found.
− indicates significant negative relationship found.
0 indicates variable tested and found not significant.
Blank indicates relationship not tested.

also then experience economic development. This is the clear positive outcome in three of the four studies and would seem to imply that entrepreneurship can play an important and consistent role in facilitating economic development.

Conclusions

Recent theories of economic growth view local externalities, as opposed to scale economies, as the primary engine in generating growth in cities and their closely integrated surrounding counties (Labor Market Areas). While scale economies operate at the plant level, externalities operate at the level of the individual or the firm, primarily through entrepreneurial activity. We investigated the impact of some of these externalities on regional economic growth from an entrepreneurial perspective by examining the relationship of local employment growth to local entrepreneurial activity. Using data on 394 local economic areas and six industrial sectors, covering the entire (nonfarm) private sector economy of the United States during the 1990s, we found that higher rates of entrepreneurial activity were strongly associated with faster growth of local economies.

Our analysis suggests that new organizations play an important role in taking advantage of knowledge externalities within a region, and that entrepreneurship may be the vehicle by which these spillovers contribute to economic growth. Local differences in firm formation rates have the strongest impact on employment growth rates of any of our independent variables. This is probably not a direct effect of the new employment in new firms but a reflection of the impact of innovation and competition generated by the new firms, and of the same local environment that helped determine the level of entrepreneurship. More than half of the explained variation in growth rates was attributable to the local variation in new firm formation rates.

Both of the educational attainment variables have contrary effects on formation and on growth. After allowing for the strong effect of formation rates on growth rates, the share of adults with high school degrees has a significantly positive impact on growth rates, while the measured impact of college degree share is not significantly different from zero. This result is consistent with other recent research indicating that it is the general level of education that is important for development, not higher levels of education for a small segment of the population.

The physical density of businesses per square mile has a negative impact on growth. We had expected that denser agglomerations of businesses would increase both local demand for products and services and local supply of inputs, while also increasing network externalities among similar businesses. However, apparently the negative effects on growth of the greater competition among similar businesses within a dense area are stronger than the potential positive effects alluded to here. Similarly, sector specialization has a negative impact on employment growth, after allowing for its positive impact through formation rates.

Several qualifiers are in order for these results. Perhaps most importantly, employment growth is not the same as economic growth, and so the issue of accounting for productivity growth is still unanswered. While the aggregate direct impact of new firms on employment may be small, nevertheless the survivors play an important role in employment creation. These results, while preliminary, suggest that scholars interested in theories of growth should study entrepreneurship to better understand the impacts of knowledge spillovers and greater competition. Recently, Acs and Varga (2005) found that both entrepreneurial activity and agglomeration effects increased the level of technological change through knowledge spillovers.

Finally, our results have important implications for theory. They help fill the gap in our understanding of the connection between entrepreneurship and economic growth. These results support not only the new growth theory but also those theories that suggest that knowledge spillovers and the resulting increase in entrepreneurship are important contributors to economic growth (Acs and Varga, 2005; Acs et al., 2005; Acs and Storey, 2004; Michelacci, 2003). Without adequate entrepreneurship, growth will be lower, because knowledge spillovers will be less effective.

CHAPTER SIX

Summary and Theoretical Insights

The efficiency of transforming knowledge into economic applications is a crucial factor in explaining macroeconomic growth. New growth theory treats this factor as *exogenous*. The theory offers no insight into what role, if any, entrepreneurship and agglomeration play in the spillover of tacit knowledge. The answer to this question can be pursued through the lens of the "new economic geography" and the newest wave of entrepreneurship research. This book has pursued a better understanding of both the relationship between geography and technological change and that between entrepreneurship and technological change, because these lines of research may prove fruitful in better explaining variations in economic growth rates.

New growth theory emphasizes the crucial role of knowledge spillovers in macroeconomic growth, but it leaves out the regional dimension, although substantial evidence has been provided in the recent empirical economics literature that a significant share of knowledge spillovers is localized. The new economic geography extends this framework by pointing to both the interplay between spillovers and agglomeration and the resulting cumulative regional growth, but it leaves out the macroeconomic dimension. The theory of entrepreneurship focuses on the role of new firm formation and offers a knowledge spillover theory of entrepreneurship as one mechanism by which these spillovers affect regional growth. We first present findings on new firm formation and then on employment growth, followed by an outline of theoretical issues.

Table 6.1. *Summary of impacts of regional variables on entrepreneurial activity and employment growth rates in LMAs in the mid-1990s*

Independent Variables	Firm Formation Rates	Employment Growth
Firm formation rate		+
Establishment size	−	+
Sector specialization	+	−
Business density		−
High school degree*	−	+
College degree	+	0
Population growth	+	
Income growth	+	
Share of proprietors	0	0
Unemployment rate	0	

+ indicates significant positive relationship generally found.
− indicates significant negative relationship generally found.
0 indicates variable tested and found not generally significant.
  Blank indicates relationship not tested.
* The coefficient on high school degree is the negative of that on high school dropout share.

Statistical Findings on New Firm Formation

In the introduction to this book, we suggested that local variations in entrepreneurial activity could be the result of different efficiencies in knowledge spillovers, and ultimately the source of differences in economic growth. The analyses reported in Chapters Three and Four have examined some of the important factors explaining geographic differences in entrepreneurial activity. During the 1990s, there were large variations in firm formation rates across LMAs, but the formation rate in each LMA was fairly stable. The correlations between consecutive pairs of annual firm formation rates for LMAs were generally about 0.96, suggesting that these rates are primarily a function of local socioeconomic characteristics that change only slowly.

In Table 6.1, the first column summarizes the consistent significant relationships supported by our regression-based modeling of these differences in firm formation rates across LMAs at various periods during the 1990s. The second column summarizes the results for employment growth. A quick glance at these reveals that many of the regional characteristics we are investigating have apparently contradictory impacts on firm formation rates and employment growth rates. These contradictions provide a key to much of the confusion and apparently conflicting results found in previous analyses of geographic differences in growth rates and entrepreneurship, many of which suffered from data limitations or restricted sectoral scope, such that their variables failed to reflect the concepts the investigators were attempting to measure.

The strongest explanatory variable for entrepreneurial activity is the relative specialization rates of existing businesses – the higher the supply of local establishments per capita, the higher the rate of new firm formation. Examining this relationship for each of the six industry sectors defined for the analysis in Chapter Three, we see that the influence of this factor is much stronger when limited to the impact of the relative concentration of existing businesses within a sector on new firm formations in that sector. When dealing in Chapter Four with market subsectors of the service sector, we found that the impact of specialization was particularly strong for service businesses that generally focus on nonlocal markets. When we added a measure of each region's overall business specialization, in addition to the service sector specialization, we found that a greater regional specialization in other sectors (above-average numbers of businesses relative to the regional population) led to lower new firm formation rates.

These findings give strong statistical support to the popular media attention to the leveraging effect of regional growth clusters of new businesses in such sectors as information technology, biotechnology research, and higher education. The spillover of relevant knowledge and trained skilled employees, and the presence of a supporting network of services for any specific sector, all contribute to an increase in the frequency of entrepreneurial activity in that sector.

The theory of knowledge spillovers predicts the consistent negative relationship we found between the new firm formation rate and the size of incumbent businesses. Larger average employment of establishments in a region leads to lower expected rates of new firm formation. Areas that are dominated by large businesses are less likely to foster entrepreneurial activity, as C. Mason (1994) had previously shown. Large establishment size is also frequently associated with manufacturing dominance, while regions that have restructured toward services have higher formation rates, according to Audretsch and Fritsch (1994). Employees of large businesses may also be less inclined to network and socialize outside the circle of their fellow employees, and so they have less potential for spillovers. They may even strongly resist change in the community, to minimize competition for markets or labor or other resources and to keep local costs down.

When we examine the effect of relative differences in local human capital, we find the expected positive effect of higher educational levels in a region leading to higher rates of entrepreneurial activity in both the regional private economies as a whole (Chapter Three) and in the service sectors of these Labor Market Areas (Chapter Four). Higher shares of adults with college degrees are associated with higher rates of new firm formation, as was found also by Anselin, Varga, and Acs (1997). However, for both manufacturing and business services, this effect was not significant.

We also found a positive relationship between the percentage of the population without a high school degree and new firm formation. This was further examined in Chapter Four, where we looked in detail at subsectors of service firms. A major factor affecting the supply of new service firms is the availability of individuals with the qualifications generally needed to recognize the opportunities; identify new services, markets, or delivery systems; organize the new firm; and hire the first employees. We therefore expected that the sensitivity of service firm formation rates to the relative supply of adults with various levels of education would differ across service subsectors distinguished by typical educational requirements of their founders.

The positive coefficient for the relationship of shares of high school dropouts to formation of new service firms that require advanced degrees might suggest that such businesses are more dependent on having a large pool of unskilled labor. However, having found that higher shares of high school dropouts are not strongly positively associated with higher formation rates for service businesses requiring less than college education for their founders, but are positive for those requiring advanced degrees, we conclude that the explanation of the positive coefficients on high school dropout share needs further research.

The share of proprietors was not significantly associated with the rate of new firm formation, after taking into consideration all of the other factors. We had expected that it would serve as an indicator of the strength of the local "entrepreneurial culture," and that higher levels would lead to a greater tendency for others to choose to form their own businesses. It is fairly strongly negatively correlated with establishment size, and so establishment size may have absorbed the expected positive effect. After allowing for the higher firm formation rates associated with lower average establishment size in a region, we found that there was no measurable additional impact from higher shares of proprietors.

Both population growth and income growth contribute to the rate of new firm formation, as expected. These variables were introduced to control for the effects of many unmeasured local differences across regions. Population growth serves as a proxy for the general attractiveness of a region, as well as an indicator of the growth in the local market for goods and services, and in the supply of both labor and potential entrepreneurs. Higher population growth rates may also serve to identify regions with greater tolerance of, or even appreciation for, innovative activity, including greater diversity of cultures and thoughts and generally greater dynamism, as suggested by Richard Florida (2002). Higher per capita income growth similarly suggests both better local markets for new goods and services and greater savings available for financing new firm formations.

Previous research has provided conflicting evidence on the impact of differences in unemployment rates on regional firm formation rates. We expected higher unemployment rates to reduce formation rates overall, but anticipated that in some sectors with low capital requirements, higher local unemployment might have a positive impact on formation rates. In fact, we found that regional unemployment rates do not have any significant impact on regional formation rates when all industries are aggregated together. However, when formation rates were analyzed by sector, five of our six sectors from Chapter Three showed small, but significant, positive relationships. Storey (1991) had summarized previous research as indicating that unemployment was generally positively associated with new firm formation only in time series analysis, suggesting that increases in local unemployment may lead to more firm formation, rather than locally higher rates of unemployment. Our cross-sectional analysis results, therefore, conflict with previous cross-sectional research that generally found negative relationships.

A significant and compelling contribution of the endogenous growth theory was to refocus the policy debate away from the emphasis on enhancing capital and labor, to a new priority on increasing knowledge and human capital – in particular, through a combination of taxes and subsidies. As Lucas (1993, 270) concluded, "The main engine of growth is the accumulation of human capital – of knowledge – and the main source of differences in living standards among nations is differences in human capital. Physical capital accumulation plays an essential but decidedly subsidiary role." And he further notes, "Human capital accumulation takes place in schools, in research organizations, and in the course of producing goods and engaging in trade." Thus, the debate on policies to generate growth revolved around the efficacy of such instruments as universities, secondary schools, public and private investments in research and development, training programs, and apprentice systems.

Statistical Findings on Employment Growth

The employment growth rates in Labor Market Areas, like the formation rates, also varied greatly across economic areas, but their local variations were only weakly correlated from year to year during the 1990s, generally less than 0.25 between consecutive years. Because net growth of employment in an area is affected by losses from shrinkage and closure of businesses, as well as gains from new and expanding businesses, its patterns of regional differences are much more difficult to explain. Thus, we ask a more limited question here, "What are some of the determinants of economic growth at the regional level?"

Recent theories of economic growth view local externalities, as opposed to scale economies, as the primary engine in generating growth in cities and their closely integrated surrounding counties (Labor Market Areas). Whereas scale economies operate at the plant level, externalities operate at the level of the individual or the firm, primarily through entrepreneurial activity. We investigated the impact of some of these externalities on regional economic growth from an entrepreneurial perspective by examining the relationship of local employment growth to local entrepreneurial activity. Using data on 394 local economic areas and six industrial sectors, covering the entire (nonfarm) private sector economy of the United States during the nineties, we found that higher rates of entrepreneurial activity were strongly associated with faster growth of local economies.

A model of local employment change rates was estimated in Chapter Five to analyze how differences in local socioeconomic characteristics affect growth rates. This was summarized in the second column of Table 6.1. Local differences in *firm formation rates* have the strongest impact on employment growth rates of any of our independent variables. This is probably not a direct effect of the new employment in new firms but a reflection of the impact of innovation and competition generated by the new firms, and of the same local environment that helped determined the level of entrepreneurship. Over half of the explained variation in growth rates was attributable to the local variation in new firm formation rates. Entrepreneurial activity is a key to an understanding of geographic differences in growth rates.

Average *establishment size* has a positive association with employment growth, after allowing for its negative effect through the impact of formation rates. Similarly, *sector specialization* has a negative impact on employment growth, after allowing for its positive effects through formation rates. Both of the *educational attainment* variables also have contrary effects on formation and growth. After allowing for the strong effect of formation rates on growth rates, the share of adults with high school degrees has a significantly positive estimated coefficient, while college degree share has a negative coefficient that is not significantly different from zero. The *share of proprietors* has no consistent significant impact on local employment growth rate differences.

Again, growth of manufacturing businesses proved to be an exception to the patterns exhibited by most other sectors. In this sector, coefficients estimated for entrepreneurial activity, *establishment size,* and *sector specialization* all had the opposite sign from the general case, but were not significantly different from zero. Share of adults with college degrees had a significant negative impact on growth of manufacturing employment, and *share of proprietors* was positive and significant. This evidence leads to the conclusion that the dynamics of the manufacturing sector are not indicative of those of the rest of the private sector economy, and that the extensive economic research results based on samples of manufacturing firms or establishments must be reexamined critically and not assumed to be representative of businesses in other sectors.

The physical *density* of businesses per square mile has a negative impact on growth. We had expected that denser agglomerations of businesses would increase both local demand for products and services and local supply of inputs, while also increasing network externalities among similar businesses. However, apparently the negative effects on growth of the greater competition among similar businesses within a dense area are stronger than the potential positive effects alluded to here.

When we drop firm formation rates from the model, then the picture changes radically for the contribution of the remaining factors we included. The share of adults with college degrees again becomes a significant positive influence, while the density of preexisting businesses in the area remains a significant negative influence. All other variables become small and insignificant, and the percentage of variation in growth rates explained by the model falls from 33% to only 14%.

Our research has given us a snapshot of factors that appear to influence local differences in rates of entrepreneurial activity and growth in the 1990s. Since these relationships are likely to continue in the twenty-first century, this analysis provides a basis for suggesting policies to promote formation of innovative businesses and growth of employment. However, some factors have conflicting effects on these two facets of entrepreneurship policy. First, the human capital requirement for new business formations is higher than that for employment growth, with formation levels responding positively to the local share of adults with college degrees and reacting negatively to the share with high school degrees, while growth increases with the share of high school degrees. Second, greater local sector specialization helps entrepreneurship and innovation while hurting employment growth. This sector specialization contributes to knowledge spillovers, which appear to be more important within broadly defined sectors than across the whole economy. Third, while the formation rate is by far the most important determinant of the growth rate, higher densities of local businesses depress the growth rate. Fourth, the share of proprietors already in a region does not influence future innovation or economic growth. A high proportion of the self-employed maintain stable businesses that are noninnovative, with little potential to inspire new formations or to contribute to growth. Finally, larger average size of local business establishments leads to lower formation rates, but higher growth rates.

Reconciling the Differences Between Entrepreneurship and Growth

In the introduction to this book, we suggested that several questions in urban and regional growth were important: the role of human capital in economic growth; the role of geographic structure – diversity versus specialization; and the role of culture and entrepreneurship in economic growth. Our results strongly support previous findings on the importance of human capital in economic growth. However, we find that different types of human capital might play different roles, with high-level human capital and perhaps multiple levels of skills (Lazear, 2002) being more important for entrepreneurship and innovation, while a higher level of general education might be more important for employment growth. Therefore, employment growth and technological change might be supported by different education structures.

We find a similar conclusion for the debate between specialization and diversity. If we are interested in understanding technological change (innovation, high technology, productivity), specialization seems to be an important contributing factor. This supports the Marshall-Arrow-Romer hypothesis that knowledge spillovers occur primarily within industries. However, greater specialization reduces employment growth. These results support the new models of economic geography (Fujita and Thisse, 2002, Chapter 11, 391), which argue that agglomeration and growth go hand in hand. While the positive analysis seems to give credit to the trade-off between growth and equity, the welfare analysis supports the idea that the additional growth spurred by agglomeration may lead to a Pareto-dominant outcome. When a country moves from dispersion to agglomeration, innovation follows a faster pace. As a consequence, even those who stay put in the periphery, and play no role in the innovation, are better off than under dispersion, provided that the growth effect triggered by the agglomeration is strong enough (Varga and Schalk, 2004).

Finally, our results help fill in the gap about our understanding of the relationship between entrepreneurship and economic growth. These results support not only the new growth theory but also those theories that suggest that entrepreneurship along with knowledge spillovers are important determinants of economic growth (Acs and Varga, 2005; Acs and Storey, 2004). Without adequate entrepreneurship, growth will be less than with entrepreneurship because you will have less-effective knowledge spillovers (Acs et al., 2005; Michelacci, 2003).

A weakness of the knowledge spillover formulation articulated by Romer is that it lacks microfoundations (Auerswald, 2005). The issue of how to model entrepreneurship and innovation within the context of growth and geography has not been addressed in this book. The position we have taken is one of the occupational choice model, where an individual possesses new knowledge and decides on starting a new firm after considering the relationship between current wages and future profits. This occupational choice model, while useful, has its limitations. Most importantly, it is an analysis of the labor market decision to offer one's services to a firm or to become an owner of a firm. In this sense, the occupational choice model may be considered a model of relative prices. Its shortcomings are that it is not a theory of the firm and, therefore, does not offer us any insight into why new firms are needed, only that individuals start them. If one considers the occupational choice model as an internal labor market, it comes closer to explaining why someone might want to start a new firm.

We would like to suggest a way to model entrepreneurship and innovation that would be compatible with both the new economic geography and new growth theory. What is missing in the "systems of innovation" literature is a theory of the firm. We suggest going back to Nelson and Winter (1982) and the concept of "routines" to fulfill the prerequisite required of a unit of analysis in an evolutionary framework. Over the last 20 years, routines, as the most basic unit of analysis in evolutionary economic theory, have been taken up by a growing number of authors. Routines are the firm's standard "recipies" for doing things and making decisions. For an incumbent firm, routines represent its capabilities to produce existing products or product improvements. New products and new production processes, as well as product and process innovations, are difficult for the firm to introduce since they involve new routines. If new routines cannot be incorporated into the existing "bundle of routines," *as much of the research in this book suggests*, a new organization may be needed to house a new routine. It is in this space that new firms play the most important role (Armington and Acs, 2004; Jovanovic, 1982) since new routines may best be developed in new firms. This very sketchy outline suggests a research agenda for an evolutionary theory of the firm that would be compatible with the new growth theory (Auerswald, 2005) and economic geography (Krugman, 1998). For a review of this literature, see M. C. Becker (2005).

In the next chapter, we will focus on instruments to increase both firm formation and growth and examine how these two elements fit into the bigger picture of how individuals in an entrepreneurial society play a vital role in sustaining society, as well as in propelling the economy forward.

CHAPTER SEVEN

A Formulation of Entrepreneurship Policy

Introduction

As we saw in Chapter One, the latter Schumpeter (1942) had pessimistic prognoses about the future of capitalism, while the early Schumpeter (1911) did not articulate any social feedback problems. In this volume, we propose an American solution to the social feedback mechanism, one that is consistent with the work of the early Schumpeter. American capitalism differs from all other forms of industrial capitalism in its historical focus on both the creation of wealth (entrepreneurship) and the reconstitution of wealth (philanthropy). Philanthropy is part of the implicit social contract that continually nurtures and revitalizes economic prosperity (Schramm, 2005). Much of the new wealth created historically has been given back to the community to build up the great social institutions that have a *positive* feedback on future economic growth. This entrepreneurship-philanthropy nexus has not been fully explored by either economists or sociologists. We suggest that American philanthropists – especially those who have made their own fortunes – created foundations that, in turn, contributed to greater and more widespread economic prosperity through knowledge creation (Acs and Phillips, 2002).

In traditional industrial societies, wealth creation, wealth ownership, and wealth distribution were, in great part, left up to the state or to organized religion. However, in an entrepreneurial society, individual initiative plays a vital role in propelling the economy and the society forward. We cast the United States as the first new nation – the product of a shift in human character and social roles that produced the English

Industrial Revolution and modern American civilization. This shift resulted in a new character type, the independent economic agent, who possessed unprecedented new powers of discretion and self-reliance, yet was bound to collective ends by emerging novel forms of institutional authority and internal restraint (Dewey, 1963).[1]

Entrepreneurial leadership is the mechanism by which new combinations are created, new markets are opened up, and new technologies are commercialized to form the basis for growth and prosperity. In an entrepreneurial society, entrepreneurship plays a vital role in the process of wealth creation, and philanthropy plays a crucial role in the reconstitution of wealth. In other words, the entrepreneurship-philanthropy nexus is the institutional arrangement that maintains the circular flow of wealth creation and reconstitution, by means of a positive feedback mechanism that ensures the continued economic, cultural, and social development of an entrepreneurial society.

This chapter develops a formulation for entrepreneurship policy in a modern information society (Jorgenson, 2001). We define entrepreneurship here very broadly as *the process by which agents transform knowledge into wealth through new firm formation and growth, and then reconstitute wealth into opportunity for all through philanthropy.* This formulation involves four broad levels of actors. First, individual *agents* identify business opportunities and make the personal choice to exploit them. Second, newly formed *businesses* innovate, using new knowledge and other resources to produce services and products, and play a fundamental role in the dynamics of industry evolution. Third, the *economy* includes all those institutions that play an important role in economic development and productivity growth. Finally, *society*, as the collection of all agents and the ultimate beneficiary from the increased wealth, plays a central role in social progress and equity by reconstituting a share of new wealth through philanthropy to create opportunity for others.

Each one of these facets has an appropriate policy counterpart in an entrepreneurial society. The individual agent is confronted with education and occupational choice policies that govern the boundaries by which individuals can make occupational choices. At the business level,

---

[1] One could argue that the recent antitrust case against Microsoft was as much about violating this social contract as about anticompetitive firm behavior.

Levels	Occupational Choice Policies	Enabling Policies	Supporting Policies	Social Policies
Agent	*More effective entrepreneurs*			
Business		*Continuous innovation*		
Economy			*Faster economic growth*	
Society				*Equal opportunity*

Figure 7.1. The four facets of entrepreneurship policy and their goals.

governments have enabling policies that facilitate or restrict the formation of new firms. At the level of the economy, we have a set of supporting
policies that foster the growth of businesses, and thereby the economy as
a whole. Finally, societies are sustained by social policies that are incorporated into their legal structures and regulations to ensure their continued
functioning.

As shown in Figure 7.1, this formulation gives rise to a corresponding
set of goals that are at the heart of an entrepreneurial society: *more effective
entrepreneurs, continuous innovation, faster economic growth*, and *equal
opportunity*. The first goal in an entrepreneurial society is to have more
effective entrepreneurs. By more effective entrepreneurs we mean that all
nine cells of the education levels and market dimensions discussed in the
subsectors in Chapter Four need to be covered, leading to efficient com-
pitition and production of both locally and nonlocally traded goods and
services. The second goal is continual innovation in both the product and
process areas by enabling formation of new firms. The third goal is faster
economic growth, including both employment growth and productivity growth, as discussed in Chapter Five. Only recently have academic
researchers begun to consider the importance of entrepreneurial activity
for economic growth, and the potential impact of various policies on the
quantity and quality of entrepreneurial activity (Acs and Storey, 2004).
Finally, greater equality of opportunity through wealth reconstitution is
important for an entrepreneurial society to maintain social and cultural
progress (Curti, 1957).

Although we have laid out here a broad policy framework for examining entrepreneurship policies, our research in this book has focused

primarily on the two central facets in our matrix formulation – innovation and economic growth. We have addressed them by investigating the relationships between new firm formations and human capital, and between new firm formations and employment growth. We have not examined the occupational choice issue, or what Shane (2003) calls the individual-opportunity nexus, nor have we analyzed the broader societal question of the role of philanthropy in social equity (Acs and Phillips, 2002).

In the next section, we will briefly discuss occupational choice policies. We then examine firm formation with respect to the enabling regional environment in order to help assess alternative policy instruments for increasing the rate of innovation. In the fourth section, we will examine our findings with respect to economic growth and the supporting environment for growth. In the fifth section, we will address the question "What are the societal feedback mechanisms of an entrepreneurial society that allow it to survive?" Here we will return to the early discussion about the entrepreneur in Schumpeter (1942) and examine how the conflict between wealth concentration and democracy can be defused in an entrepreneurial society. Finally, we will reexamine the matrix of policy facets and levels in order to summarize the various instruments that might be appropriate to the goals of each in an entrepreneurial society.

The Emergence of Entrepreneurial Policy

In the formulation of policy in the managed economy of the mid–twentieth century in America, issues arose at the levels of business, the economy, and society (Acs and Audretsch, 2001). Individuals were assumed to be compliant employees, limited to playing their appointed roles. The large corporation was thought to have superior productive efficiency because of economies of scale, and also believed to be the engine of technological change and innovative activity. At the economy level, this resulted in job creation, economic growth, and productivity increases. At the society level, the question of the potential conflict between efficiency and democracy went to the very heart of the matter.

The fundamental issue confronting societies at that time was how to live with this apparent trade-off between concentration and efficiency on the one hand, and decentralization and democracy on the other. This was the world so colorfully described by John Kenneth Galbraith (1956) in his theory of countervailing power, in which the power of big business was held in check by big labor and by big government. The public policy question of the day was "How can society reap the benefits of the large corporation in an oligopolistic setting while avoiding, or at least minimizing, the costs imposed by a concentration of economic power?"

In the formulation of public policy in an entrepreneurial society, we face similar questions about the role of policy with respect to individuals, business, the economy, and society. However, there are several crucial differences. In an entrepreneurial society, the role of the individual is both different and more important than in a managed economy. One of the goals of policy in the managed economy was to avoid any concentration of power in large firms, while in an entrepreneurial society, the goal is to create an enabling environment to facilitate the implementation of innovative ideas in new businesses. We now recognize in public what was formerly practiced in private to deal with the issue of unequal distribution of wealth in a pluralistic society. The societal goal is to maintain a just society where opportunity is increased and democracy is maintained through the "reconstitution of wealth" created by successful entrepreneurs for the expansion of knowledge and opportunity in society. The target at this level is the philanthropic contributions of wealthy entrepreneurs. According to *Newsweek* (September 29, 1997: 34):

> There's no escaping the brutal truth: the nation famous for capitalism, red in tooth and claw, the epicenter of the heartless marketplace, is also the land of the handout. It's not really such a paradox. Both our entrepreneurial economic system and our philanthropic tradition spring from the same root: American individualism. Other countries may be content to let the government run most of their schools and universities, pay for their hospitals, subsidize their museums and orchestras, even in some cases support religious sects. Americans tend to think most of these institutions are best kept in private hands, and they have been willing to cough up the money to pay for them.

Entrepreneurship policy has recently been examined in three books, which represent the first modern publications in English on this topic. These books focus on the individual and occupational choice; the firm, with an emphasis on new firm entry; the economy, including specific innovative sectors; and equity issues in society.

In *The Emergence of Entrepreneurship Policy: Governance, Start-Ups, and Growth in the Knowledge Economy* (2003), editor D. Hart, from the Kennedy School of Government at Harvard University, deals with the emergence of this new policy field that promotes start-ups and entrepreneurship. The authors contributing to this conference volume explicitly recognize that entrepreneurship is a societal issue, and that much of entrepreneurship is about technological innovation. Further, they recognize that entrepreneurship is a regional issue because knowledge spillovers are local (Jaffe, 1989). This is clearly a step in the right direction, and the book does a good job of discussing the relationship between entrepreneurship and technology, though it falls short of dealing with either the individual or the society issues.

In *Public Policy and the Economics of Entrepreneurship* (2004), editors Douglas Holtz-Eakin, a former member of the Council of Economic Advisors, and Harvey Rosen at Princeton University, point us in a similar direction. Most chapters in this volume employ rigorous quantitative methods that stretch marginal data as far as they can to yield limited but important insights, providing a more theoretical analysis of entrepreneurship outcomes. They examine three issues that are germane to an entrepreneurial society: the design of effective public venture capital programs; new firm formation and the deregulation of the banking industry; and the relationship among entrepreneurial activity, social mobility, and wealth inequality.

Many claim that a substantial component of the observed inequality in the distribution of wealth is a consequence of successful entrepreneurship – entrepreneurs who succeed end up with a big portion of the pie. The authors consider how the distribution of wealth over time is related to the fraction of the population engaged in entrepreneurial activity, the share of wealth held by entrepreneurs, and the inequality in wealth holdings among entrepreneurs. However, they formulate no mechanism to address the issue of the reduction of wealth inequality in an entrepreneurial society.

In their book, *Entrepreneurship Policy: Theory and Practice* (2005), Anders Lundström and Louis Stevenson also examined the importance of entrepreneurship policy. It is the first book to fully analyze the construction of entrepreneurial policy. Drawing on a study and assessment of the practices of governments in 13 countries in Europe, North America, and the Asia-Pacific regions, this book fully describes the policy area and shares new tools and methods for better understanding and explaining the how and why of an entrepreneurship policy approach. The focus is primarily on the occupational choice issue and the shift in emphasis from firms to people. However, this individual level pertains to only one facet of the broader concept of entrepreneurship policy that we are discussing.

Entrepreneurship and Occupational Choice Policy

The first facet of entrepreneurial policy focuses on the individual agent. This so-called occupational choice question has been examined by at least three disciplines. First, the sociology literature (Carroll and Hannan, 2000) offers sociological explanations for entrepreneurship, which include ethnic cultural attitudes and the lack of alternative employment opportunities due to lack of appropriate education or language skills among some groups of Americans and immigrants.

The psychology literature focuses primarily on psychological conditions in the individual agent, and Shane (2003) has extended this to include demographic conditions in his individual-opportunity nexus. The psychology literature has shown that people who engage in entrepreneurial activity are not randomly determined, but tend to share certain individual-level characteristics.

The economic explanation of occupational choice follows a long line of argument going back to Knight (1921) and Richard Kihlstrom and Jack Laffont (1979). The decision confronting each agent, to become either an employee in an incumbent enterprise or an entrepreneur starting a new firm, depends on the expected risk-adjusted profit accruing from such a new firm compared to the expected wage from employment. Certainly these expected returns would differ according to the educational attainment of the potential entrepreneur and the occupational field. The very low expected wages usually earned by high school dropouts may explain the positive relationship we found between entrepreneurship rates and share of such dropouts.

The occupational choice facet of entrepreneurship policy focuses on individual agents, rather than businesses. Lundström and Stevenson (2005, 51) suggest limiting it to this facet, Stating "the main objective of entrepreneurship policy is to stimulate higher levels of entrepreneurial activity." However, the sociological and psychological aspects of occupational choice are not subject to change, except by very long term policies. The expectations built into the economic analysis of occupational choice are difficult to change, but many of the recently developed entrepreneurial education programs are showing some success at teaching the skills and confidence necessary for successful entrepreneurship, assuming possession of some economically valuable idea on which to build an innovative new business. Some of these courses operate at the elementary or secondary school level, serving primarily to draw attention to entrepreneurship as a potential choice, and perhaps teaching the students to be attentive for knowledge spillovers that might provide the basis for an innovative new business. Other programs serve either business school students or students of the sciences, cultivating their interest, skills, and confidence for pursuing their own business opportunities.

Entrepreneurship and Enabling Policies

The second facet of entrepreneurial policy has to do with a shift from constraining to enabling policies. Such policies are targeted to enhance the spillover of knowledge and focus on enabling the commercialization of knowledge, which frequently results in new firm formation. These enabling policies are increasingly at the state, regional, or even local level, outside of the jurisdiction of the traditional federal regulatory and support agencies.

The greatest and most salient shift in small and medium-sized enterprise (SME) policy over the last 15 years has been the gradual shift of government from trying to preserve and expand SMEs that are confronted with a cost, financing, or market handicap due to size-inherent scale disadvantages, toward promoting formation and growth of small entrepreneurial firms involved in the commercialization of new knowledge, often new technology-based firms. It is important to point out that entrepreneurship and innovation go together, since almost all new firm formations are innovative to some degree. Therefore, most policies for support of research also contribute, directly or indirectly, to the new firm formation rate in the United States.

For example, both innovative new firms and existing firms benefit from the Small Business Innovation Research (SBIR) program passed by

Congress in the 1980s as a response to the loss of American competitiveness in global markets. This program mandates that major federal R&D agencies in the United States allocate around 3 percent of their research support budgets for the funding of innovative small firms, as a mechanism for restoring American international competitiveness. Four similar programs also targeted at new technology-based firms are the Small Business Technology Transfer (STTR) program, the Advanced Technology Program (ATP), the Manufacturing Extension Program (MEP), and financing programs for high-technology companies administered by the U.S. Small Business Administration (Acs, 1999).

The Advanced Research Program in Texas has provided support for basic research and the strengthening of the infrastructure of the University of Texas, which has played a central role in developing a high-technology cluster around Austin. The Thomas Edison Centers in Ohio, the Advanced Technology Centers in New Jersey, and the Centers for Advanced Technology at Case Western Reserve University, Rutgers University, and the University of Rochester, have all supported generic, precompetitive research. This support has generally provided diversified technology development involving a mix of activities encompassing a broad spectrum of industrial collaborators.

The Ben Franklin Partnership Program of Pennsylvania was established by that state as a means of transferring technology from universities and government research institutes to new firms. The Ben Franklin Partnership has served an important role as a "bridging institution" between academic research and industry, and between newly formed firms and potential sources of finance. This state-wide program promotes linkages between the leading universities and medical institutions, businesses, foundations, and civic and state agencies in order to create new business opportunities and financial support for new firm formation. This program is credited with the formation of many new high technology firms in the state.

The Research Triangle Park in North Carolina is a notable example of the research park concept. The traditional industries in North Carolina – furniture, textiles, and tobacco – had all lost international competitiveness, resulting in declines in employment and stagnating real incomes. In 1952, only Arkansas and Mississippi had lower per capita incomes than North Carolina. According to A. Link and J. Scott (2003, 2), Research

Triangle emerged from a local movement to make better use of the rich knowledge base of the region, formed by the three major universities – Duke University, the University of North Carolina-Chapel Hill, and North Carolina State. Although local businessmen looking to improve industrial growth initiated this movement, it was subsequently spearheaded by the state governor's office (Link, 1995), with great success.

Empirical evidence shows that the initiative creating Research Triangle has led to fundamental changes in the region. Link and Scott (2003) document the growth in the number of research companies in the Research Triangle Park, which began at zero in 1958 and increased to 50 by the mid-1980s and to more than 100 by 1997. At the same time, employment in these research companies grew to over 40,000 by 1997. Michael Luger (2001) credits the Research Triangle Park with directly and indirectly generating one-quarter of all jobs in the region between 1959 and 1990, and shifting the nature of those jobs toward high value-added knowledge activities.

These programs promoting entrepreneurship in a regional context are typical of the new enabling policies to promote entrepreneurial activity. While these entrepreneurial policies are evolving, they are clearly gaining in importance and impact in the overall portfolio of economic policy instruments. Whether they will ultimately prove to be successful remains the focus of coming research. The point to be emphasized in this book is that entrepreneurship policies are important instruments in the arsenal of policies to promote growth. They represent an alternative not only to the set of instruments implied in the neoclassical growth theory but also to the limitations of endogenous growth theory. As this book suggests, while generating knowledge and human capital may be a necessary condition for economic growth, it is not sufficient. Rather, a supplementary set of policies focusing on enhancing the conduits of knowledge spillovers also plays a central role in promoting economic growth.

The results in Chapter Three provide support for many of these enabling policies. By contrast, the extension of the endogenous growth model suggested in Chapter Two implies the central, although not exclusive, role played by a very different set of policy instruments. This policy focus is on instruments that will reduce the filter that generates a wedge between K and Kc, or between knowledge and economic knowledge. Such policies are targeted to enhance the spillover of knowledge and focus on enabling the commercialization of knowledge, which frequently results in new firm formation. Policies that focus on developing special industry sectors and/or clusters may be more effective than policies that have a more diverse reach for innovation. Increased spending on R&D for small-firm, science-park, and public venture capital policies to stimulate development of specialized clusters of new firms (Lerner, 2004) may also help reduce this filter.

One of the most interesting findings from Chapters Three and Four was the importance of higher education in explaining differences in formation rates. Higher shares of high school graduates in an area did not contribute to higher rates of firm formation, but higher shares of college graduates contributed strongly. This finding supports policies directed at increasing the local share of adults with college degrees, and those targeting college- and university-educated individuals for additional training in entrepreneurship and other forms of support for new firm formation. On the demographic side, both population and income growth were important predictors of firm formation rates, suggesting that policies that focus on shrinking disadvantaged areas (frequently labeled "Enterprise Zones") are swimming against the tide. The same can be said for policies that focus on the unemployed as potential entrepreneurs.

In sum, enabling policies that focus on higher education, increase access to R&D results, are sector-specific, and target highly educated agents in growing regions will have the greatest impact on entrepreneurship and innovation.

Entrepreneurship and Supporting Policies

We now shift from the enabling facet of entrepreneurship policy to the supporting facet, which applies to the whole economy. How can we help new firms to survive and grow? The policy focus of the neoclassical growth models was on deepening capital and augmenting it with labor (Solow, 1956). Thus, the policy debate revolved around the efficacy of instruments designed to induce capital investment, such as interest rates and tax credits, along with instruments to reduce the cost of labor, such as reduced income and payroll taxes and increased labor market mobility.

Since the effects of these macroeconomic instruments did not very obviously trickle down to the millions of small businesses, some special policies were designated for their assistance. In 1953, Congress created the U.S. Small Business Administration (SBA) to take affirmative action on behalf of small business by awarding loans and government contracts to a select group of small firms. The focus of this traditional SME policy was to strengthen the existing base of small enterprises by ensuring that they can compete in the marketplace and that they are not unduly prejudiced because of their small size, relative to large firms. SME policy often focuses on certain disadvantaged regions or industry sectors within a country. Storey (2003) has surveyed many countries' SME policies and identified several areas where market failure results in disadvantages for small firms and where government policies may intervene to level, or at least improve, the playing field:

- Access to equity capital – enterprise investment schemes;
- Loan finance – higher-risk small business loan schemes;
- Access to markets – organization of trade fairs and export support;
- Regulatory reform – units established within government to minimize administrative burdens on smaller firms;
- Managed workplace – property lease arrangements to assist new and very small firms;
- Training in small firms – subsidizing small business management training corporations to provide training for others;
- Targeted programs – many types of special support for businesses owned by women, indigenous peoples, the unemployed, and other groups.

While some of these programs support the growth of new and innovative firms, many are designed to facilitate survival of otherwise uneconomic firms, or to compensate for badly regulated markets or traditions that ought to be reformed. This view of SMEs as inherently disadvantaged does not lead to policies to promote growth of new businesses.

If new firm formation is a strong contributor to regional employment growth, what policies would stimulate it? According to Carl Schramm (2004), the ability to grow new businesses, and therefore the economy, depends on a set of institutional relationships that are economy-wide. They include the relationship between new firms and big businesses, government, universities, and the financial system. This facet of entrepreneurship policy we call "supporting policies." Without these supporting polices, new firms will find it very difficult, if not impossible, to grow into large successful firms. Growing firms need to be supported with money, research, people, and customers.

The first aspect of this relationship is cooperation between new firms and large firms – large firms feeding the fish instead of eating them. There are several ways that established businesses work with new firms to promote their growth. First, as mentioned in Chapter One, Williamson (1975) pointed out that large firms outsource much of their research and development to specialized small or new firms. Intel, for example, tries to build markets for its chips by investing in companies that develop new systems and products that will use the chips; it has invested in more than a thousand such new businesses. Second, once a new firm has developed a good product, a large firm will often simply buy the new firm, thereby acquiring a complete package of proven technology and expertise. Third, established firms often become major customers of new firms; for example, IBM became the largest customer of Microsoft.

The second aspect of institutional support of new firms is federal government funding and regulatory support. One form of government support is the various programs through which new firms participate in the federal research and development infrastructure. Through the Small Business Innovation Research program, for example, new technology firms can get grants for product development research. Also, through established procurement programs, new firms can qualify for limited priority in selling goods and services to the government. Many of the programs of the Small Business Administration are designed to reduce costs to small firms or to provide funds for their expansion. The SBA also works to reduce regulatory costs and tax complexities for small firms. Finally, the federal spending on R&D supports research in government labs, large firms, and both state and private universities, all of which may directly benefit new firms through knowledge spillovers from their staff and from reported results.

The third institution supporting new firms is the American university system. The universities and their staffs are a constant source of inspiration and knowledge spillovers for new businesses. The U.S. university system is also highly competitive, with an eye on technology commercialization to benefit both the staff and the university budgets. The Bayh-Dole Act of 1980 further fostered the development of new business ideas from federally funded research, and the transfer of technology from universities to the U.S. economy. The U.S. economy benefits greatly from the transfer of technology from universities, as well as from the steady flow of highly educated individuals who leave the university system each year.

Finally, the financial system plays an important role in providing the capital for high-growth companies. First, the venture capital industry invests more than $20 billion annually in growing firms. Many of the most successful firms in the United States were funded with equity capital from venture capital firms. Second, the ability to raise large amounts of money in the public equity markets also plays an important role in supporting the growth of new firms, and allows firms to buy out their venture capital investors. The deregulation of the U.S. financial system further helped promote economic growth by facilitating new firm formation. The very active competition among personal credit card issuers also contributes considerable initial debt funding from entrepreneurs for their new businesses that have not yet established their own credit.

Entrepreneurship and Social Policy

The final facet of entrepreneurship policy is the issues of equity and justice in society. It is well known that these issues are at the heart of the survival of any society. The equity issue has two sides. One is equal opportunity for all to participate in the entrepreneurial process: women, minorities, the elderly, and so on. The second is equity of outcome with respect to wealth creation, which lies at the heart of the legitimacy issue for any society. Fundamental here is the sustainability of an entrepreneurial society and the form of the feedback mechanism of wealth creation on society. We suggest that both aspects of equity – equality of access and equity of outcome – can be addressed through philanthropy, the process by which people and institutions give freely of both their wealth and their time.

Merle Curti (1957, 353) advanced the hypothesis that "philanthropy has been one of the major aspects of, and keys to, American social and cultural development." To this we would add that philanthropy has also been crucial in economic development. Solomon Fabricant states the relationship of philanthropy to economic development convincingly (in Dickinson, 1970, 8):

> [I]n this broad sense philanthropy is a necessary condition for social existence, and the extent to which it is developed influences an economy's productiveness. For decent conduct pays large returns to society

as a whole, partly in the form of a higher level of national income than would otherwise be possible. Underdeveloped countries are learning that, despite their hurry to reach desired levels of economic efficiency, time must be taken to develop the kind of business ethics, respect for the law, and treatment of strangers that keep a modern industrial society productive. Widening of the concepts of family loyalty and tribal brotherhood to include love of man "in general" is a necessary step in the process of economic development.

Therefore, when combined, entrepreneurship and philanthropy become a potent force in explaining the long-run dominance of the American economy. In an entrepreneurial society, much of the new wealth created historically has to be given back to the community to build up the social institutions *that have a positive feedback on future economic development*. This entrepreneurship-philanthropy nexus is what sustains American capitalism over time (Acs and Phillips, 2002).

The connection between philanthropy and economic prosperity is not a new idea. In *Corruption and the Decline of Rome* (1988), Ramsey MacMullen discusses how charitable foundations were partly responsible for the flourishing of Rome, and their decline coincided with the loss of the empire. The roots of American philanthropy can be found in England in the period from 1480 to 1660. By the close of the Elizabethan period, "it was generally agreed that all men must somehow be sustained at the level of subsistence" (Jordan, 1961, 401). Though the charitable organizations at the beginning of this period in England were centered on religion and the role of the church, by the close of the sixteenth century, religious charities comprised only 7% of all charities (1961: 402).

How is this philanthropic behavior explained? According to W. K. Jordan, there was an increasing awareness of the partly religious and partly secular sensitivity to human pain and suffering in sixteenth-century England (1961, 406). Doubtless, another important motivating factor was Calvinism, which taught that "the rich man is a trustee for wealth which he disposes for the benefit of mankind, as a steward who lies under direct obligation to do Christ's will" (1961, 406–407).

Andrew Carnegie exemplified the ideal Calvinist. He put philanthropy at the heart of his "gospel of wealth" (Hamer, 1998). For Carnegie, the question was not only "How to gain wealth?" but, importantly, "What to do with it?" *Wealth* suggested that millionaires, instead of bequeathing

vast fortunes to heirs or making benevolent grants by will, should admin-
ister their wealth as a public trust during life (Carnegie, 1889). Both
Carnegie (at the time) and Jordan (as a historian) suggest that *a key
motive for philanthropy is social order and harmony.*

American philanthropists – especially those who have made their own
fortunes – create foundations that, in turn, contribute to greater and
more widespread economic prosperity. This was Carnegie's hope when
he wrote about "the responsibility of wealth" over a century ago which
still inspires entrepreneurs today, though they usually express it in terms
of a duty to "give something back" to the society that helped make their
own success possible. This model of entrepreneurial capitalism with its
sharp focus on entrepreneurship and philanthropy, despite the unequal
distribution of wealth, should be encouraged.

Much of the new wealth created historically has been given back to
the community to build up the great institutions that have a *positive
feedback on future economic development.* Rather then constraining the
rich through taxes, we should allow the rich to successfully campaign
for social change through the creation of opportunity. In the past, the
fight against slavery had some very wealthy backers. If we shut off the
opportunities for wealthy individuals to give back their wealth, we will
also shut off the creation of wealth, which has far greater consequences
for an entrepreneurial society (*The Economist*, July 29, 2004).

Recently, Jeffrey Sachs has articulated a position by which to judge
our philanthropic activities based on past accomplishments. According
to Sachs, writing in *The Economist*, creating opportunity for future gen-
erations is about creating knowledge today, and the model to study is the
Rockefeller Foundation (June 24, 2000, 83):[2]

> The model to emulate is the Rockefeller Foundation, the pre-eminent
> development institution of the 20th century, which showed what grant
> aid targeted on knowledge could accomplish. Rockefeller funds sup-
> ported the eradication of hookworm in the American South; the dis-
> covery of the Yellow Fever vaccine; the development of penicillin; the
> establishment of public-health schools (today's undisputed leaders in
> their fields) all over the world; the establishment of medical facilities

---

[2] For a theory of knowledge in economic growth, see Arrow (1962) and Romer (1990).
For an application to the regional and global economy, see Acs (2002).

in all parts of the world; the creation and funding of great research centers such as the University of Chicago, the Brookings Institution, Rockefeller University, and the National Bureau of Economic Research; the control of malaria in Brazil; the founding of the research centers that accomplished the green revolution in Asia; and more.

Acs and Braunerhjelm (2004) examined the differences in how Sweden, a traditional industrial society, and the United States, an entrepreneurial society, have been impacted by philanthropic activities, commercialization of university-based knowledge, and international entrepreneurship. They conclude that the United States promotes knowledge creation with a university system based on competition and variety, with an emphasis on philanthropy. Both domestic and international entrepreneurship have been important mechanisms by which this knowledge leads to increased economic growth. Conversely, Swedish universities were characterized by less-commercialized R&D and weak links to the commercial sector, rooted traditionally in dependence on a tax-financed and homogenous university structure.

Policy Summary

This chapter has laid out a broad formulation of entrepreneurship policy. Because of the broad sweep of entrepreneurship in society, such policies affect four distinct levels of society: the individual agent, the firm, the economy, and society as a whole. The attitudes of the agent and of society as a whole toward entrepreneurship stem from historical path dependence. They are the very basic foundations of American society. It was the proliferation of this new character type, the agent, who possessed unprecedented new powers of discretion and self-reliance, yet was bound to collective ends by novel emerging forms of institutional authority and internal restraint that set the stage for an entrepreneurial society. These are summarized in Figure 7.2.

Our first goal is to have more agents consider the choice of whether to engage in entrepreneurial activity. How many entrepreneurs does an economy need and who should be an entrepreneur? These are questions for which there are no easy answers, however; an entrepreneurial society needs effective entrepreneurs. The idea of going into business is as old as America itself. It is part of the American Dream – self-reliance

	Goals	Targets	Instruments
Agent–Occupational Choice Policies	More effective entrepreneurs	Individuals	-create awareness -entrepreneurship training -facilitate networks
Business–Enabling Policies	Continuous innovation	New firm formation	-finance -regulatory relief -SBIR -science parks -tech comm
Economy–Supporting Policies	Economic growth	Institutions–universities government corporations	-R&D -education -venture capital
Society–Social Policies	Equal opportunity	Wealthy individuals	-philanthropy -taxes -social pressure -legal structure

Figure 7.2. The four facets of entrepreneurship policy: goals, targets and instruments.

and the desire to get rich. Occupational choice instruments are primarily long-run investments in higher education, more publicity for successful entrepreneurs, and building tolerance for failure. Short-run policy instruments do not easily influence them.

The second goal is to have continuing innovation in the economy – facilitating its evolution and increasing productivity, and using economic knowledge to form new firms that produce new products or services, target new markets, or increase efficiency with new processes. The target of entrepreneurship and the goal of continuing innovation can be influenced by policy instruments at both the national and local levels. Many programs to enable the translation of new knowledge into new firms have been put into place over the past two decades and have proved effective. Promoting technology transfer at universities, stimulating development of local knowledge networks, providing business incubator facilities, and funding applied research are among the many enabling programs that lead to more, and more productive, new firms in an area.

The third goal is to increase economic growth. Policies to support the growth of new firms at the level of big business, government, finance, and academia are crucial for supporting economic growth. These supporting policies are fairly short run in nature, but they also have some long-run aspects. It is clear that instruments like government venture capital resources, training courses, and research and development funding for small firms have all played an important role in supporting growth of businesses and regions.

Our fourth goal is equal opportunity for all members of society. The reconstitution of wealth and its positive feedback on society plays a central role in the sustaining of an entrepreneurial society. The societal traditions of wealth reconstitution by the wealthy in America have a long history, and they have contributed to the public image of successful entrepreneurs as paragons of society. The policy instruments that would target the reconstitution of wealth in a society do not lend themselves to short-run changes. These are instruments that are rather blunt in the short run. Here, we believe that tax policy is secondary and social institutions are far more important, and furthermore, it is the unwritten rather than the written rules that bite more in relation to issues of wealth and equity. In the United States, these instruments have been honed over several centuries.

The formulation of entrepreneurship policy needs to be carried out in the context of a broad social vision that pays attention to the longer-term positive feedback effects of entrepreneurial activity on opportunity and pluralism, in addition to the more immediate effects of such activity on local growth. Only in this context can we judge the ultimate success or failure of an entrepreneurship policy for promoting and supporting greater economic growth.

Firm Formation and Growth Data from the Longitudinal Establishment and Enterprise Microdata (LEEM)

I. Introduction

The Longitudinal Establishment and Enterprise Microdata (LEEM) comprises skeletal data on almost all U.S. private sector businesses that paid any employees during the period from 1989 through 2001. These data have been linked together over time so that there are annual observations on each business establishment, including information on the entire firm (or enterprise) to which it belongs each year. Each establishment is a business location at which goods or services are produced, and these establishments are carefully tracked over time, even as they change legal form, ownership, primary industry, or location. Potentially new businesses are identified from new entries in the Master Business List of the Internal Revenue Service, and Census Bureau programs then use additional administrative data, surveys, economic censuses, and estimates to collect more detailed information on each business and to update this annually.

These microdata facilitate research on the dynamics of American businesses – especially on their patterns of formation, employment change, mergers and acquisitions, and survival. These patterns can be analyzed for establishments in different industry sectors and regions, and for firms of various sizes and other characteristics. They constitute the only comprehensive source of longitudinal microdata covering most U.S. businesses that includes the characteristics of the firm to which each establishment belongs.

II. Brief Description of the LEEM Database

The LEEM database[1] (which the U.S. Small Business Administration refers to as the Business Information Tracking Series, or BITS) is a unique product of the complex register that Census maintains, with information on all businesses in the United States. This Standard Statistical Establishment List, or SSEL, is updated continuously with data from many other sources, but its underlying coverage is based on new business names and addresses from the Master Business File of the Internal Revenue Service. Therefore, *every business* in the United States that files any tax return is covered by the SSEL, and IRS data from quarterly payroll tax filings (including employment for the March 12 payroll period only) are used to provide comprehensive annual coverage of all U.S. employers.

The basic unit of the SSEL, and of the LEEM data, is a business establishment (location or plant). An establishment is a single physical location where business is conducted or where services or industrial operations are performed. The microdata describe each establishment in terms of its employment, annual payroll, location (state, county, and metropolitan area), primary industry, and start year, among many other characteristics. The recorded start year is the year that the establishment entered the Census register as an employer, which would normally be the year it first hired any paid employees. There are additional data for each establishment and year that identify the firm (or enterprise) to which the establishment belongs, and from these data the primary industry and the total employment and payroll of each firm can be calculated. A firm (or enterprise or company) is the largest aggregation of business establishments under common ownership or control. Most firms are composed of only a single establishment – their establishment data and firm data are identical. Only 4% of firms have more that one establishment, but more than half of all employees work for such multiunit firms.

Census's County Business Patterns (CBP) annual publication provides aggregate data on establishments with payroll expenses. These CBP tables are constructed by tabulating microdata that are selected from the SSEL

---

[1] For further documentation of the LEEM, see Acs and Armington (1998) and Robb (1999). A history of the development of the LEEM and its alternatives is found in Armington (2004), along with a discussion of issues common to all longitudinal enterprise data.

and extensively edited both at the establishment level (relative to the previous year's data) and at various aggregate levels. This CBP subset of the SSEL business population represents all active (with positive annual payroll) private sector establishments, except those in agricultural production; railroads; large pension, health, and welfare funds; and private households.

The edited microdata supporting the CBP provide the starting point for Census's Company Statistics Division to produce their annual Statistics of U.S. Business (SUSB)[2] files for each year since 1988. For this, firm-level data are constructed by aggregating data for all establishments belonging to each enterprise (industry-wide and country-wide), and the firm-level data are attached to each of the firms' component establishment records. These firm-level data are tabulated and processed for disclosure for the SUSB (public) database of the Census Bureau.

A Longitudinal Pointer File is then constructed to link each year's establishment record to the prior year's record for the same establishment, allowing for possible changes (either between years or within years) in identity or ownership of continuing establishments. Records with the same Census identification number in consecutive years are assumed to represent continuing establishments. Those that do not have a Census File Number (CFN) present in both years of data are potentially start-ups or closures of establishments, but may also be cases of change in identification number. A variety of match techniques are used to seek appropriately matched records from among these apparently discontinuing establishments, including alternative identification numbers, such as Employer Identification Numbers (EINs), Permanent Plant Numbers (PPNs), and predecessor and successor numbers, and then using combinations of other characteristics, such as industry codes, zip codes, names, and addresses. This process seeks matches not only between the newest annual data file and the prior year data but also with the next prior year, and within the latest year, looking for midyear reorganizations and for temporarily inactive establishments.[3]

---

[2] For documentation of the SUSB files, see U.S. Small Business Administration (1999).
[3] Taking the match of 1993 to 1992 as a typical example, 5.56 million records match on CFN, another 32,000 on PPN, and 3,000 on EIN. The remaining unmatched single-unit records were then grouped by zip code, and another 19,000 were matched between years and 24,000 within 1993 based on matching both industry (3-digit SIC) and street number.

The LEEM files are constructed by merging annual SUSB files using the Longitudinal Pointer Files to create a single longitudinal (multiyear) record for each establishment that appears in any of the annual files, beginning with data for 1989. Thus, each record provides comparable annual observations on the status and characteristics of an establishment, as well as summary data on the characteristics of the firm to which it belongs each year.

As with most microdata at the Census Bureau, the LEEM data are confidential, and so the microdata are available only for approved statistical analysis projects performed at Census's Center for Economic Studies (CES), and the published empirical results must be limited and approved by CES staff to avoid any disclosure potential. Most of the analysis reported in this book was carried out in the Washington CES offices, as a sequence of related research projects that were subsequently approved for disclosure. The Company Statistics Division of the Census Bureau prepares nonconfidential custom tabulations of the LEEM on a contract basis for specific research projects, and we have updated some of our analyses using firm formation counts for recent years that were prepared for the Ewing Marion Kauffman Foundation.

III. Issues for Use of LEEM Data for Measurement of Formation and Growth

The scope of the LEEM data is that of Census's County Business Patterns since 1989, and it therefore excludes agricultural production, forestry and fisheries, railroads, and domestic service workers from its coverage of private sector firms with employees. It would certainly be preferable to include railroad workers and firms for an analysis of firm formation and growth, but this sector probably has few new firm formations and little growth. The formations that do occur are primarily the result of entrepreneurs responding to right-of-way sales by larger railroads by acquiring existing track, so this is not a very serious exclusion.

The new businesses appearing in the LEEM data are identified primarily from their first filing of payroll tax withholding statements with the U.S. Internal Revenue Service. Because U.S. tax regulations consider owner/operators of corporations to be employees of the corporate entity, an incorporated self-employed person without additional employees will be considered a new firm with employees even when only the owner/operator is working there, while unincorporated firms will not be included until an additional person is hired and paid. This leads to some inconsistency in the treatment of zero-, one-, and two-employee businesses (of which there is a large number), because the numbers of workers counted vary with the legal form of these businesses. Furthermore, because partners, owners of unincorporated businesses, and unpaid family members are not considered to be employees, the number of actual workers is understated for nonincorporated firms. The microdata underlying the LEEM include a variable indicating legal form of business, but the code for "incorporated" is also the frequently used code for "unknown," and so no reliable data are available to indicate "nonincorporated."

Because these data are limited to "employee-businesses," the formation of a new business can be identified only when the new business hires an employee and begins filing taxes for that employee. Similarly, the business will appear to close in any year that it lays off all its employees for an entire calendar year, because the BITS will not have data for any year with no positive payroll, even though the proprietor may continue the business activity alone. Therefore, the closure of a business can only be tentatively identified in any year. Most businesses that remain without employees for two years, after having had employees in a prior year, are permanently closed. Nevertheless, a small fraction of the recorded new firm formations are actually reactivations of older firms that have not had any employees for over two years (nine quarters), since they may be treated as new when they reenter the SSEL.

Industry coding is often incomplete in the first year that a business appears, and a more detailed industry code may appear in subsequent years. In addition, the Census Bureau tends to place special emphasis on accuracy of industry codes in the year prior to Economic Censuses (which are in years ending with 2 or 7), because the censuses use industry-specific forms, and so a higher proportion of records have changes in industry codes in those years, and there are fewer changes in the Economic Census year and the subsequent year. The LEEM has fewer missing industry codes than CBP because the SUSB processing checks for updated codes from the subsequent year's SSEL and uses them to replace any missing or vague codes whenever possible.

All of the microdata in the LEEM have been subjected to many layers of editing before being extracted into the LEEM, and so any anomalies that appear in the data for a given establishment are probably due either to lack of information in a particular year or to actual eccentricities of the businesses' history. Just as we have found that the rates of new firm formation and closure are much higher than was realized several decades ago, more comprehensive microdata allowing the tracking of changes in establishments have shown that many businesses change their industry classification over time, often to completely different industry divisions. Many businesses also move across county lines, and even across state boundaries, often to nonadjacent states.

Because there may be differences across years during the normal life of the establishment, one must carefully choose the most appropriate year of data for classification of establishments or firms, in accord with the theory underlying the analysis and with the practicalities of the database. Thus, for example, although industry coding tends to get more detailed and more accurate as an establishment stays in the SSEL, for coding the industry of new firm formations we chose to rely on the industry that was first reported, and only use later reports if the later industry code was a more-detailed variation of a less-detailed original code. This avoids the use of codes representing new industries that some businesses may shift into as they mature.

Although all establishments with data for a given year will have positive annual payroll for that year, nearly 10% are likely to have no employment. This may be because they had not yet hired anyone by the March 12 payroll period that is reported, or had closed before then, or are seasonal and do not operate in March, or had temporarily laid off everyone in March. The establishments without employees should be excluded to get counts of establishments active at a point in time. If they are included, the count will represent all establishments that were in business at any point during the year.

Mergers, acquisitions, divestitures, and other restructuring may cause large discontinuities in the characteristics of establishments and the firms they belong to. When a small single-location firm is acquired by a larger one, that establishment changes from single-unit to multiunit, and its firm-size class is likely to change radically. Its own employment may also change, as some employees are laid off or reassigned to another location owned by the acquiring firm, and this may result in a reclassification of industry for the remaining portion of its business. When a new firm is created as a joint venture between two existing firms, it may appear as a huge new firm with a small new primary (headquarters) establishment and many large old secondary locations. A huge establishment may send most of its employees to work for an employment-leasing firm that will handle all of its former personnel management, so that its employment falls dramatically, without any reduction in output.

In spite of these difficulties, the LEEM provides far more accurate and comprehensive data on U.S. private sector businesses than any other source. With few exceptions, in comparison with the rest of the world the LEEM data offer broader coverage of the national and local economies, with more complete linkages between business firms and their owned establishments, and with more comprehensive tracking of establishments across ownership and legal changes.

IV. Definition of Firm Formations, Establishments, and Employment in the LEEM

For all of the empirical analysis and tables in this book, an establishment, and its corresponding employment, is included in a specific annual total only if the establishment has positive employment in that year (indicating that it had at least one employee in March). An establishment is included as a firm in a specific annual total only if the establishment has positive employment in that year and the establishment is either a single-unit, or a multiunit with plant number "0001" (indicating that the establishment is either a firm by itself or is the original location of a multilocation firm).[4]

Firm formations include both new single-unit firms (establishments, or locations) with fewer than 500 employees and the primary locations of new multiunit firms with fewer than 500 employees, firmwide. Those

---

[4] Many older multilocation firms no longer include their original locations, but we assume that the new firms we are identifying will still be headquartered in their original establishment.

new firms that had 500 or more employees in their first year of activity appear to be primarily offshoots of existing companies. Annually, there were somewhat fewer than 150 such large apparent births of single-unit firms, with an average of about 1,500 employees each. About a third of these larger single-unit firms were employee-leasing firms or employment agencies, while the remainder were widely distributed across industries. However, examination of the new firms with 100 to 499 employees in their first year showed that most seemed to be credible new firms, frequently in industries that are associated with large business units, such as hotels and hospitals. Since this study is not concerned with the employment impact of new firm formations, there is no danger of the bulk of the data on smaller formations being swamped by that of a few larger formations that might actually be offshoots of existing businesses. Therefore, the new firms with 100 to 499 employees were included, if they qualified otherwise.

Single-unit firm formations in year t are identified on the LEEM as nonaffiliated establishments with a start-year of t or $t-1$ that had no employment in March of year $t-1$, and had positive employment below 500 in March of year t. This avoids inclusion of either new firms that have not yet actually hired an employee or firms recovering from temporary inactivity.[5] The "start-year" is the year that the establishment entered the Census business register. About 400,000 new firms generally appear in the business register (with some positive annual payroll) the year before they have any March employment, and we postpone recording their "formation" until their first year of reported employment.

We have also included most of the relatively few multiunit firms (1,500 to 6,000 per year) that appeared to start up with fewer than 500 employees in multiple locations in their first year. We limited multiunit firm births to those whose employment in their new primary location constituted at least a third of their total employment in the first year.[6] This rule effectively eliminated the 600 to 1,000 new firms each year that were apparently set up to manage existing locations – relatively small new headquarters

---

[5] An average of 90,000 older firms each year reduce their March employment to zero and then recover the following year, but few recover after two years of zero employment.

[6] We tested a similar rule using one-half, and found that the primary difference was in quite small multiunit firms, where the smaller share was more credible for the first year.

supervising large numbers of employees in mainly older branch locations that were newly acquired or divested, or perhaps contributed to by joint venture partners.

To summarize, new firm formations were defined on the LEEM file as follows: An establishment is considered a new firm formation in a given year-to-year ("initial" to "subsequent" year, generally labeled as a formation in the subsequent year) period if it meets the following criteria: positive establishment employment in the subsequent year and zero or blank establishment employment in the initial year; the start year for the establishment is either the initial year or the subsequent year; the subsequent year enterprise employment for the establishment is fewer than 500; and the establishment is either a single-unit, or a multiunit location with plant number of 0001 where the subsequent-year establishment employment is at least 1/3 the subsequent year enterprise employment (to eliminate new headquarters of firms created by divestitures, mergers, joint ventures, and employee-leasing schemes).[7]

The Labor Market Area (LMA) for each establishment is determined using a labor market area to state/county cross-reference file for the 1990 LMA definitions specified by C. M. Tolbert and M. Sizer (1996). Specifically, the state and county codes for the first year for which the establishment has a valid state code are combined into a Federal Information Processing Standards (FIPS) code, and the corresponding LMA is retrieved from the cross-reference file. This cross-reference file was extended to deal with establishment records with missing (zero or blank) county codes, and with county codes of nines (which indicate statewide activity), by assigning them to the largest LMA in their state.

This same LMA-to-extended-FIPS cross-reference file was used to aggregate both annual county-level Labor Force data from the Bureau

[7] Firm closures, or deaths, are defined in a parallel fashion, with the additional requirement of two years of zero employment to assure that it was not a temporary layoff. An establishment is considered a firm death in a given year-to-year period if it meets the following criteria: positive establishment employment in the initial year and zero or blank establishment employment in the subsequent year; the establishment employment in the year following the subsequent year is zero or blank; the initial year enterprise employment for the establishment is fewer than 500; and the establishment is either a single-unit or a multiunit plant "0001" where the initial year establishment employment is at least 1/3 the initial year enterprise employment.

of Labor Statistics, and annual establishment counts from the LEEM for targeted industries and service subsectors, to the LMA level. These measures of the relative sizes of local area economies, and local economy-industry units, were used to calculate firm formation rates, dividing the local numbers of new firm formations by one of the measures of the size of the local economy in the year prior to the formation period.

1995 + 1996 Firm Formation Rates for U.S. Labor Market Areas with 1994 Labor Force and Establishments (average annual firm formations per 1,000 labor force in 1994, sorted by formation rate)

LMA	Biggest Place	Avg Annual Formation Rate	1994 Labor Force	1994 Establishments
287	Laramie, WY	**10.18**	87,156	6,882
72	Fort Myers, FL	**7.20**	247,519	15,400
352	Grand Junction, CO	**6.95**	88,124	5,022
71	West Palm Beach, FL	**6.84**	607,849	35,542
392	Bend, OR	**6.61**	94,522	5,225
393	Bellingham, WA	**6.60**	111,331	7,254
359	St. George, UT	**6.54**	81,879	3,737
70	Miami, FL	**6.49**	1,795,054	98,131
345	Missoula, MT	**6.47**	126,278	7,392
354	Flagstaff, AZ	**6.44**	129,736	6,927
69	Sarasota, FL	**6.23**	280,193	16,369
344	Bozeman, MT	**6.03**	112,960	6,330
353	Farmington, NM	**5.92**	70,481	3,556
88	Savannah, GA	**5.67**	173,865	9,346
15	Wilmington, NC	**5.59**	154,958	7,520
387	Longview, WA	**5.57**	92,315	5,378
298	Monett, MO	**5.55**	67,075	3,013
348	Santa Fe, NM	**5.51**	149,575	7,507
376	Reno, NV	**5.38**	251,849	12,682
78	Ocala, FL	**5.34**	123,653	6,412
364	Rock Springs, WY	**5.30**	84,384	4,414
289	Denver, CO	**5.30**	1,196,677	57,381

(*continued*)

LMA	Biggest Place	Avg Annual Formation Rate	1994 Labor Force	1994 Establishments
100	Panama City, FL	5.24	74,017	4,032
386	Spokane, WA	5.22	311,387	15,923
343	Billings, MT	5.21	160,924	9,050
346	Casper, WY	5.19	72,807	4,322
357	Twin Falls, ID	5.19	78,039	3,912
123	Traverse City, MI	5.16	114,419	6,690
368	Medford, OR	5.14	110,868	5,661
74	Orlando, FL	5.11	755,448	34,347
91	Atlanta, GA	5.08	1,714,656	76,554
284	Colorado Springs, CO	5.05	251,585	11,194
297	Springfield, MO	5.03	199,884	9,594
358	Boise City, ID	5.02	246,735	11,418
369	Roseburg, OR	5.00	89,436	4,841
276	Rapid City, SD	4.96	87,450	4,634
75	Daytona Beach, FL	4.96	215,929	10,703
73	Melbourne, FL	4.94	247,360	12,174
388	Portland, OR	4.93	934,888	43,773
394	Seattle, WA	4.91	1,765,276	85,748
303	Fayetteville, AR	4.91	158,408	6,578
194	New York, NY	4.90	5,045,508	260,283
379	Las Vegas, NV	4.88	590,750	21,745
288	Fort Collins, CO	4.84	208,228	8,985
350	Phoenix, AZ	4.84	1,288,756	54,914
251	Harrison, AR	4.81	141,508	6,463
12	Asheville, NC	4.74	237,845	11,770
67	Tampa, FL	4.74	1,078,012	50,835
312	Austin, TX	4.73	615,297	24,311
13	Myrtle Beach, SC	4.66	281,247	12,777
170	Pikeville, KY	4.66	74,740	3,807
201	Portland, ME	4.63	334,346	16,990
168	Beckley, WV	4.60	91,234	4,686
315	Laredo, TX	4.58	91,972	4,112
195	Monmouth, NJ	4.57	491,416	22,687
124	Alpena, MI	4.57	78,077	4,194
340	Hot Springs, AR	4.55	131,140	5,916
296	Columbia, MO	4.54	185,923	8,498
389	Eugene, OR	4.54	469,009	21,930
363	Pocatello, ID	4.54	149,775	6,587
360	Provo, UT	4.53	150,400	4,889

LMA	Biggest Place	Avg Annual Formation Rate	1994 Labor Force	1994 Establishments
17	Raleigh, NC	4.52	656,583	28,178
331	Dallas, TX	4.52	1,620,283	69,033
361	Salt Lake City, UT	4.51	659,266	26,192
109	Pensacola, FL	4.51	253,502	11,790
210	Houghton, MI	4.50	91,850	5,132
56	Nashville, TN	4.48	593,733	26,673
203	Claremont, NH	4.47	184,535	10,009
21	Washington, NC	4.44	57,264	3,041
86	Brunswick, GA	4.43	90,103	4,398
310	Garden City, KS	4.41	88,120	4,653
327	Brownwood, TX	4.39	50,791	2,372
377	Santa Rosa, CA	4.39	290,821	14,148
176	Charlottesville, VA	4.36	119,499	5,541
338	Oklahoma City, OK	4.36	590,487	28,416
245	FortLeonardWood, MO	4.34	42,817	1,997
31	McComb, MS	4.34	58,952	2,647
307	Roswell, NM	4.34	51,836	2,593
9	Charlotte, NC	4.34	645,310	30,061
76	Jacksonville, FL	4.33	521,936	23,846
206	Manchester, NH	4.33	590,396	27,474
314	Odessa, TX	4.32	164,802	8,482
216	Hibbing, MN	4.31	61,209	3,130
362	Logan, UT	4.30	62,922	2,115
246	Farmington, MO	4.26	56,772	2,380
19	Greenville, NC	4.26	207,186	9,637
342	Great Falls, MT	4.26	74,424	4,086
198	Wilmington, DE	4.25	283,923	13,283
77	Lake City, FL	4.25	54,701	2,322
196	Newark, NJ	4.24	2,826,381	138,408
29	Hattiesburg, MS	4.24	66,856	2,862
341	Anchorage, AK	4.24	305,089	13,986
42	Little Rock, AR	4.24	309,437	13,759
283	North Platte, NE	4.23	55,888	3,226
207	Keene, NH	4.23	62,271	3,201
257	Cape Girardeau, MO	4.21	114,595	5,820
351	Tucson, AZ	4.20	411,401	17,674
277	Cheyenne, WY	4.20	97,079	5,007

(*continued*)

LMA	Biggest Place	Avg Annual Formation Rate	1994 Labor Force	1994 Establishments
325	Abilene, TX	4.19	99,278	5,089
259	Jonesboro, AR	4.18	91,131	3,847
304	Tulsa, OK	4.16	491,696	23,246
333	Tyler, TX	4.16	180,975	7,753
82	Charleston, SC	4.16	290,290	12,768
349	Albuquerque, NM	4.15	355,847	15,433
382	Santa Barbara, CA	4.14	298,638	14,511
380	San Diego, CA	4.14	1,235,128	53,205
367	Eureka, CA	4.14	65,753	3,491
305	Enid, OK	4.13	61,187	3,417
110	Mobile, AL	4.12	304,859	13,569
299	Joplin, MO	4.11	143,870	6,808
300	Russellville, AR	4.11	63,691	2,362
378	San Francisco, CA	4.08	2,271,914	108,746
211	Rice Lake, WI	4.07	71,947	3,475
263	Minot, ND	4.06	61,955	3,423
365	Altamont, OR	4.06	71,092	3,457
39	Monroe, LA	4.06	121,861	5,428
94	Gainesville, GA	4.04	116,859	4,508
384	Lewiston, WA	4.03	79,867	3,702
200	Bangor, ME	4.01	195,348	9,897
265	Sioux Falls, SD	4.01	149,821	7,564
291	Salina, KS	4.01	54,667	3,066
103	Dothan, AL	4.01	128,330	5,645
38	Lafayette, LA	4.01	224,081	10,691
337	Ardmore, OK	4.00	51,274	2,462
385	Moses Lake, WA	4.00	91,948	4,066
356	Hilo, HI	3.99	65,665	3,323
112	Bluefield, WV	3.99	142,733	6,522
79	Gainesville, FL	3.98	132,174	5,719
202	Burlington, VT	3.98	167,645	9,028
320	Houston, TX	3.97	2,117,491	83,412
383	Los Angeles, CA	3.95	7,394,530	300,918
326	Wichita Falls, TX	3.94	92,864	4,724
107	Birmingham, AL	3.93	485,460	21,328
93	Athens, GA	3.93	126,134	5,252
85	Valdosta, GA	3.93	129,173	5,977
285	Pueblo, CO	3.92	89,040	4,417
60	Huntsville, AL	3.91	243,735	9,736

LMA	Biggest Place	Avg Annual Formation Rate	1994 Labor Force	1994 Establishments
264	Dickinson, ND	**3.91**	72,316	4,185
366	Redding, CA	**3.88**	97,494	4,801
270	Yankton, SD	**3.88**	104,458	5,824
295	Kansas City, MO	**3.88**	1,064,292	47,050
334	Longview, TX	**3.87**	133,296	6,116
58	Paris, TN	**3.86**	63,363	2,422
96	Anniston, AL	**3.86**	197,500	7,315
290	Hutchinson, KS	**3.85**	125,321	6,927
272	Sioux Center, IA	**3.85**	61,439	3,351
68	Lakeland, FL	**3.85**	237,408	10,322
306	El Paso, TX	**3.85**	404,059	15,908
101	Thomasville, GA	**3.84**	47,497	2,211
330	Fort Worth, TX	**3.84**	846,038	32,132
35	Baton Rouge, LA	**3.83**	356,585	14,563
111	Montgomery, AL	**3.83**	199,676	8,992
87	Hinesville, GA	**3.83**	84,272	3,297
51	Corinth, MS	**3.82**	61,678	2,417
199	Dover, DE	**3.81**	314,166	14,537
375	San Jose, CA	**3.81**	1,202,589	48,723
273	Fairmont, MN	**3.80**	59,329	3,249
301	Fort Smith, AR	**3.80**	145,510	6,115
308	Lubbock, TX	**3.79**	180,426	8,739
322	Lufkin, TX	**3.79**	116,804	4,880
89	Macon, GA	**3.79**	167,677	7,113
323	San Angelo, TX	**3.78**	120,410	5,143
313	San Antonio, TX	**3.78**	792,627	31,867
50	Tupelo, MS	**3.77**	96,206	4,048
336	Lawton, OK	**3.77**	89,588	4,265
104	Meridian, MS	**3.76**	69,466	2,994
45	Hazard, KY	**3.75**	56,447	2,431
309	Amarillo, TX	**3.74**	227,741	10,465
2	Morristown, TN	**3.74**	109,965	4,317
83	Greenville, SC	**3.73**	419,362	17,483
335	Texarkana, TX	**3.73**	104,242	4,382
64	Chattanooga, TN	**3.71**	273,569	11,490
108	Tuscaloosa, AL	**3.71**	143,034	5,799
81	Columbia, SC	**3.70**	336,554	14,354

(*continued*)

LMA	Biggest Place	Avg Annual Formation Rate	1994 Labor Force	1994 Establishments
317	Corpus Christi, TX	**3.70**	223,898	9,876
27	Biloxi, MS	**3.69**	200,927	7,236
142	Indianapolis, IN	**3.69**	752,557	32,767
30	Jackson, MS	**3.69**	286,885	12,056
120	Big Rapids, MI	**3.68**	75,731	3,379
254	Paducah, KY	**3.68**	82,507	3,746
286	Kearney, NE	**3.67**	94,812	5,200
266	Aberdeen, SD	**3.66**	55,116	2,966
316	Brownsville, TX	**3.66**	333,094	11,734
278	Norfolk, NE	**3.66**	60,893	3,046
261	Kirksville, MO	**3.65**	106,603	4,997
33	New Orleans, LA	**3.65**	618,733	28,417
36	Alexandria, LA	**3.65**	79,956	3,486
324	Big Spring, TX	**3.65**	44,944	2,214
99	Tallahassee, FL	**3.63**	194,722	7,712
193	Poughkeepsie, NY	**3.63**	383,296	17,384
40	Shreveport, LA	**3.62**	273,952	12,108
61	Gadsden, AL	**3.62**	141,549	5,499
130	Fort Knox, KY	**3.62**	67,577	2,697
49	Jackson, TN	**3.60**	155,382	6,331
339	Sherman, TX	**3.60**	101,501	4,274
59	Clarksville, TN	**3.58**	93,576	3,610
106	Jasper, AL	**3.57**	73,099	2,849
328	Waco, TX	**3.57**	167,446	7,072
3	Knoxville, TN	**3.56**	383,536	15,804
62	Florence, AL	**3.56**	112,388	4,459
18	Goldsboro, NC	**3.55**	90,065	3,680
167	Morgantown, WV	**3.55**	162,454	7,401
292	Topeka, KS	**3.55**	250,235	11,109
374	Sacramento, CA	**3.53**	1,125,870	46,020
98	Auburn, AL	**3.52**	58,019	1,947
24	Richmond, VA	**3.52**	516,174	22,971
118	Mount Pleasant, MI	**3.52**	57,097	2,355
173	Staunton, VA	**3.52**	88,510	3,980
43	Searcy, AR	**3.52**	60,702	2,652
268	Fargo, ND	**3.51**	136,819	6,937
293	Wichita, KS	**3.50**	334,830	15,140
255	Mount Vernon, IL	**3.49**	65,991	3,179
205	Boston, MA	**3.49**	2,492,768	111,144

LMA	Biggest Place	Avg Annual Formation Rate	1994 Labor Force	1994 Establishments
215	Minneapolis, MN	3.49	1,576,559	64,031
262	Bismarck, ND	3.48	66,994	3,420
169	Charleston, WV	3.48	169,258	7,969
243	Chicago, IL	3.47	3,927,237	168,508
302	Muskogee, OK	3.46	63,732	2,464
329	Killeen, TX	3.46	113,035	4,134
294	Bartlesville, OK	3.46	115,935	5,530
46	Somerset, KY	3.45	88,497	3,406
247	St. Louis, MO	3.45	1,170,953	53,148
90	Milledgeville, GA	3.45	114,172	4,517
84	Augusta, GA	3.45	237,430	9,591
4	Winston-Salem, NC	3.45	281,701	11,710
113	WashingtonBalti, DC	3.44	3,793,947	154,364
131	Louisville, KY	3.44	605,465	25,655
34	Houma, LA	3.44	113,183	5,293
269	Fergus Falls, MN	3.44	87,090	4,302
63	Cookeville, TN	3.44	86,532	3,056
271	Willmar, MN	3.43	69,107	3,609
47	Greenwood, MS	3.43	93,201	4,044
11	Hickory, NC	3.43	183,240	7,841
97	Columbus, GA	3.42	152,458	6,416
102	Albany, GA	3.42	79,649	3,351
41	Pine Bluff, AR	3.42	127,043	5,565
146	Bloomington, IN	3.42	137,880	5,263
14	Fayetteville, NC	3.42	249,733	9,997
20	Virginia Beach, VA	3.41	504,305	20,867
204	Providence, RI	3.41	776,295	35,794
66	Rome, GA	3.41	195,844	7,263
318	Bryan, TX	3.40	91,352	3,330
114	Marquette, MI	3.40	139,628	6,809
256	Carbondale, IL	3.39	129,219	6,053
116	Detroit, MI	3.38	2,551,266	104,694
105	Columbus, MS	3.38	84,306	3,668
5	Greensboro, NC	3.38	520,291	22,172
37	Lake Charles, LA	3.37	137,347	5,630
347	Honolulu, HI	3.37	517,209	23,918
171	Huntington, WV	3.36	146,854	6,379

(continued)

LMA	Biggest Place	Avg Annual Formation Rate	1994 Labor Force	1994 Establishments
57	Tullahoma, TN	3.35	60,355	2,257
321	Beaumont, TX	3.34	226,242	8,894
129	Lexington, KY	3.34	314,460	12,912
197	Philadelphia, PA	3.33	2,656,995	116,966
212	Hutchinson, MN	3.32	53,946	2,516
175	Cumberland, MD	3.31	124,968	5,868
218	Mason City, IA	3.31	81,943	3,966
122	Grand Rapids, MI	3.30	619,623	24,632
391	Richland, WA	3.30	155,588	6,127
166	Roanoke, VA	3.29	233,511	9,861
153	Parkersburg, WV	3.28	96,941	4,188
32	Vicksburg, MS	3.28	80,913	3,363
10	Morganton, NC	3.27	111,301	4,327
7	Spartanburg, SC	3.26	171,676	6,714
332	Paris, TX	3.26	83,693	3,153
311	Victoria, TX	3.26	106,545	4,974
248	Springfield, IL	3.26	179,374	7,902
52	Memphis, TN	3.26	543,263	22,329
231	Madison, WI	3.25	328,495	13,594
128	Greensburg, IN	3.25	67,252	2,336
23	Lynchburg, VA	3.24	110,800	4,668
147	Evansville, IN	3.24	203,012	8,878
152	Cleveland, OH	3.24	1,305,175	60,830
209	Hartford, CT	3.24	1,821,618	85,503
92	Griffin, GA	3.23	59,672	2,060
249	Alton, IL	3.22	180,695	7,435
274	Fort Dodge, IA	3.22	79,273	4,233
22	South Boston, VA	3.21	69,239	2,868
282	Omaha, NE	3.21	428,780	18,961
233	Charleston, IL	3.20	98,523	4,327
54	Bowling Green, KY	3.20	122,009	4,586
1	Johnson City, TN	3.18	276,021	10,404
232	Dubuque, IA	3.17	89,822	4,108
148	Vincennes, IN	3.17	56,629	2,606
275	Des Moines, IA	3.17	387,327	17,163
159	Columbus, OH	3.17	824,549	32,735
138	Wabash, IN	3.16	64,996	2,760
281	Lincoln, NE	3.15	184,717	8,123
260	Duluth, MN	3.15	161,990	7,531

LMA	Biggest Place	Avg Annual Formation Rate	1994 Labor Force	1994 Establishments
279	Grand Island, NE	3.14	78,704	4,150
373	Chico, CA	3.14	160,983	7,082
226	Green Bay, WI	3.13	192,664	8,404
250	Quincy, IL	3.13	75,837	3,480
214	St. Cloud, MN	3.11	127,326	4,891
280	Sioux City, IA	3.11	109,546	4,969
141	Fort Wayne, IN	3.10	287,335	12,190
119	Saginaw, MI	3.10	254,824	10,905
144	Terre Haute, IN	3.10	130,505	5,133
223	Ottumwa, IA	3.09	74,212	3,234
127	Cincinnati, OH	3.09	973,696	40,288
25	Newport News, VA	3.09	262,547	9,955
16	Rocky Mount, NC	3.08	103,284	4,370
80	Sumter, SC	3.08	86,803	3,280
65	Cleveland, TN	3.07	104,925	4,023
172	Harrisonburg, VA	3.06	86,729	3,490
188	Scranton, PA	3.06	393,777	17,711
222	Cedar Rapids, IA	3.05	136,555	5,894
28	Laurel, MS	3.04	52,529	2,005
137	Elkhart, IN	3.03	185,352	7,764
258	Blytheville, AR	3.03	48,367	1,908
44	Richmond, KY	3.02	99,551	3,688
390	Yakima, WA	3.02	124,594	4,965
156	Wheeling, WV	3.01	89,403	4,166
149	Gary, IN	3.00	320,689	12,436
355	Gallup, NM	2.99	73,589	2,509
381	Yuma, AZ	2.98	121,500	4,034
217	Rochester, MN	2.97	154,666	6,354
229	La Crosse, WI	2.97	113,082	4,710
132	Owensboro, KY	2.97	81,588	3,473
158	Athens, OH	2.97	56,992	2,212
241	Milwaukee, WI	2.96	861,594	37,563
253	Union City, KY	2.95	54,737	2,114
143	Columbus, IN	2.95	83,469	3,332
220	Waterloo, IA	2.94	132,682	5,943
230	Monroe, WI	2.94	61,586	2,566
228	Eau Claire, WI	2.94	159,394	6,570

(*continued*)

Appendix B

LMA	Biggest Place	Avg Annual Formation Rate	1994 Labor Force	1994 Establishments
150	Canton, OH	2.93	336,364	14,497
55	Columbia, TN	2.93	76,891	2,596
189	Williamsport, PA	2.92	104,668	4,545
117	Lansing, MI	2.92	233,797	8,768
115	Jackson, MI	2.91	141,539	5,495
235	Champaign, IL	2.91	196,148	7,925
6	Galax, VA	2.91	73,489	2,573
190	Allentown, PA	2.90	300,821	13,068
239	Peoria, IL	2.90	265,388	11,457
26	Roanoke Rapids, NC	2.90	58,485	2,492
186	Albany, NY	2.90	547,278	21,950
145	Lafayette, IN	2.89	172,085	6,607
95	Talladega, AL	2.88	66,858	2,208
136	South Bend, IN	2.87	334,996	13,814
252	Henderson, KY	2.86	70,510	3,103
238	Davenport, IA	2.86	230,279	10,242
48	Greenville, MS	2.86	64,767	2,600
174	Hagerstown, MD	2.85	187,881	7,489
163	Pittsburgh, PA	2.84	1,227,533	56,057
53	West Memphis, AR	2.84	59,451	2,351
164	Youngstown, OH	2.84	377,443	16,396
244	Rockford, IL	2.84	313,969	12,604
161	State College, PA	2.83	139,177	6,157
8	Gastonia, NC	2.82	198,769	7,475
267	Grand Forks, ND	2.82	147,707	6,691
319	Lake Jackson, TX	2.82	144,178	4,719
221	Iowa City, IA	2.77	113,207	4,163
184	Plattsburgh, NY	2.76	80,503	3,690
121	Kalamazoo, MI	2.76	254,016	9,971
157	Portsmouth, OH	2.75	93,485	3,524
234	Bloomington, IL	2.75	106,084	4,177
370	Modesto, CA	2.75	311,872	11,032
185	Amsterdam, NY	2.74	54,351	2,099
240	Racine, WI	2.69	291,620	11,367
162	Altoona, PA	2.67	191,102	8,769
242	Kankakee, IL	2.67	68,357	2,687
225	Appleton, WI	2.67	309,824	11,826
371	Bakersfield, CA	2.67	272,770	9,560
191	Lancaster, PA	2.64	534,161	21,816

LMA	Biggest Place	Avg Annual Formation Rate	1994 Labor Force	1994 Establishments
372	Fresno, CA	**2.63**	627,156	21,520
155	Steubenville, OH	**2.61**	58,526	2,547
160	Mansfield, OH	**2.60**	156,663	6,131
151	Lorain, OH	**2.59**	208,392	7,947
135	Toledo, OH	**2.59**	469,262	18,861
227	Wausau, WI	**2.59**	192,818	7,922
154	Zanesville, OH	**2.58**	84,720	3,376
180	Buffalo, NY	**2.56**	1,195,373	47,775
236	Burlington, IA	**2.55**	74,364	3,284
134	Lima, OH	**2.54**	130,750	5,504
182	Olean, NY	**2.54**	111,137	4,644
213	Mankato, MN	**2.53**	139,276	5,711
139	Kokomo, IN	**2.52**	93,168	3,694
125	Dayton, OH	**2.52**	640,660	25,091
237	Galesburg, IL	**2.51**	71,666	2,886
165	Erie, PA	**2.51**	314,615	13,649
192	Harrisburg, PA	**2.50**	529,389	20,937
208	Springfield, MA	**2.49**	328,979	13,579
224	Sheboygan, WI	**2.49**	103,777	3,838
140	Muncie, IN	**2.48**	212,218	7,984
133	Findlay, OH	**2.47**	126,780	5,014
177	Syracuse, NY	**2.46**	534,441	21,781
126	Richmond, IN	**2.31**	56,026	2,223
178	Oneonta, NY	**2.31**	76,191	3,143
187	Sunbury, PA	**2.28**	90,051	3,452
183	Watertown, NY	**2.28**	107,676	4,337
219	Marshalltown, IA	**2.18**	59,235	2,459
179	Binghamton, NY	**2.11**	146,255	5,457
181	Elmira, NY	**2.06**	167,896	6,439

Sources: Data calculated from tabulations of LEEM8996 and Census's *USA Counties 1998* compact disk.

Service Industry Standard Industrial Classification (4-digit SIC) Codes and Their Subsectors, with 1995 Establishment and Employment and Changes to 1998, and 1996 through 1998 Firm Formations per 100 Establishments in Subsector in 1995

Subsectors	Industry SIC	Establishments		Employment		Formations per 100 Establ.
		1995	'95–'98 Chng.	1995	'95–'98 Chng.	
Local business market, high school education						
Linen supply	7213	1,194	−4.7%	46,950	3.0%	4.33
Industrial launderers	7218	1,297	4.2%	62,821	10.6%	2.78
Photocopying & duplicating services	7334	5,163	8.0%	72,374	17.9%	7.72
Secretarial & court reporting	7338	6,548	7.5%	36,260	25.6%	15.50
Disinfecting & pest control services	7342	10,165	2.7%	78,782	9.8%	7.85
Building cleaning & maintenance services, n.e.c.	7349	45,098	6.3%	794,517	10.3%	16.41
Equipment rental & leasing, n.e.c.	7359	17,891	1.4%	167,861	10.5%	5.90
Detective & armored car services	7381	11,090	6.1%	514,011	13.5%	11.69
Security systems services	7382	2,980	30.8%	57,924	35.6%	14.22
Business services, n.e.c.	7389	60,765	15.6%	747,252	28.6%	16.22
Truck rental & leasing, no drivers	7513	4,140	12.5%	36,950	34.1%	3.40

Subsectors	Industry SIC	Establishments		Employment		Formations per 100 Establ.
		1995	'95–'98 Chng.	1995	'95–'98 Chng.	
Refrigeration & air-conditioning services	7623	3,557	1.2%	26,978	9.7%	7.77
Electrical & electronic repair shops, n.e.c.	7629	9,412	−4.0%	64,051	3.9%	7.50
Welding repair	7692	5,857	0.4%	35,066	12.6%	8.56
Armature rewinding shops	7694	2,335	−6.5%	24,459	−3.4%	2.56
Local consumer market, high school education						
Rooming & boarding houses	7021	1,523	2.0%	10,915	0.0%	10.11
Organization hotels & lodging houses	7041	2,090	−8.1%	14,048	2.9%	2.87
Power laundries, family & commercial	7211	1,680	3.5%	24,998	−4.7%	9.62
Garment pressing & agents for cleaners	7212	3,061	−0.5%	14,198	6.9%	8.34
Coin-operated laundries & cleaning	7215	12,473	−0.6%	53,307	5.0%	9.92
Dry cleaning plants, except rug cleaning	7216	20,734	−3.6%	165,597	−1.8%	6.44
Carpet & upholstery cleaning	7217	7,499	6.0%	41,019	10.3%	15.16
Laundry & garment services, n.e.c	7219	3,069	−3.7%	19,159	−5.0%	10.01
Photographic studios, portrait	7221	11,628	8.1%	71,151	−7.3%	7.33
Beauty shops	7231	73,386	−1.3%	390,050	4.0%	9.21
Barber shops	7241	4,444	−6.6%	15,744	−2.9%	6.71
Shoe repair shops & shoeshine parlors	7251	2,194	−16.6%	6,654	−13.4%	7.06

(*continued*)

Subsectors	Industry SIC	Establishments		Employment		Formations per 100 Establ.
		1995	'95–'98 Chng.	1995	'95–'98 Chng.	
Miscellaneous personal services, n.e.c.	7299	16,214	9.9%	110,545	11.2%	16.83
Medical equipment rental & leasing	7352	2,570	6.4%	28,256	2.2%	7.43
Photofinishing laboratories	7384	6,675	−13.4%	71,974	−0.7%	4.77
Utility trailer & recreational vehicle rental	7519	661	−2.4%	4,087	5.1%	7.06
Automobile parking	7521	8,370	6.2%	56,590	13.4%	2.22
Auto top & body repair & paint shops	7532	32,403	1.4%	186,647	10.7%	7.98
Auto exhaust system repair shops	7533	5,203	0.2%	26,152	−1.6%	4.95
Tire retreading & repair shops	7534	2,071	0.5%	17,633	−5.4%	8.59
Automotive glass replacement shops	7536	4,092	20.7%	22,346	28.8%	8.17
Automotive transmission repair shops	7537	5,912	2.0%	27,227	9.0%	8.56
General automotive repair shops	7538	67,205	5.0%	288,119	8.9%	10.22
Automotive repair shops, n.e.c.	7539	9,615	−4.4%	45,270	4.0%	5.49
Car washes	7542	11,290	5.5%	113,585	6.8%	14.45
Automotive services, n.e.c.	7549	10,818	20.0%	83,063	22.9%	13.54
Radio & television repair shops	7622	5,446	5.5%	31,319	4.9%	7.63
Watch, clock, & jewelry repair	7631	1,706	1.3%	6,555	4.1%	9.30
Reupholstery & furniture repair	7641	6,282	−4.6%	24,452	4.1%	9.65
Repair services, n.e.c.	7699	34,028	0.6%	233,730	6.4%	8.70

Subsectors	Industry SIC	Establishments		Employment		Formations per 100 Establ.
		1995	'95–'98 Chng.	1995	'95–'98 Chng.	
Motion picture theaters, except drive-in	7832	5,610	−4.2%	107,422	17.7%	2.83
Drive-in motion picture theaters	7833	361	−24.7%	3,263	−2.1%	3.05
Videotape rental	7841	18,707	3.0%	154,980	−1.0%	6.65
Bowling centers	7933	5,608	−7.6%	93,357	−7.2%	4.10
Sports clubs, managers & promoters	7941	1,279	17.6%	38,423	19.9%	18.11
Racing, including track operators	7948	2,437	−1.1%	53,692	2.3%	12.67
Coin-operated amusement devices	7993	4,324	0.3%	41,271	29.2%	8.33
Amusement parks	7996	771	1.9%	72,033	26.1%	8.95
Membership sports & recreation clubs	7997	11,751	1.9%	261,628	4.5%	4.50
Amusement & recreation services, n.e.c.	7999	20,840	5.2%	357,092	18.3%	11.97
Child day care services	8351	49,193	9.2%	519,021	13.3%	9.66
Residential care	8361	27,495	11.8%	537,332	14.3%	6.94
Civic, social, & fraternal associations	8641	42,371	−4.1%	393,030	2.1%	3.00
National market, high school education						
Hotels & motels	7011	40,179	7.2%	1,450,076	4.8%	8.22
Sporting & recreational camps	7032	2,277	1.7%	16,068	12.0%	4.98
Recreational vehicle parks & campsites	7033	2,778	3.2%	16,753	1.0%	8.70
Heavy construction equipment rental	7353	3,743	17.3%	44,202	27.4%	7.51
Passenger car rental	7514	3,950	−3.9%	84,792	21.5%	5.64

(*continued*)

Subsectors	Industry SIC	Establishments		Employment		Formations per 100 Establ.
		1995	'95–'98 Chng.	1995	'95–'98 Chng.	
Local business market, advanced education						
Computer-related services, n.e.c.	7379	14,951	76.2%	113,906	94.1%	39.08
Legal services	8111	151,358	1.9%	949,165	3.5%	7.68
Account'g, audit'g & bookkeep'g services	8721	76,299	0.7%	553,725	19.2%	7.86
Management services	8741	23,077	24.5%	429,774	23.8%	17.01
Local consumer market, advanced education						
Offices & clinics of medical doctors	8011	183,532	−2.6%	1,559,081	9.3%	5.10
Offices & clinics of dentists	8021	106,936	2.0%	613,709	8.2%	4.16
Offices & clinics of doctors of osteopathy	8031	7,038	−3.7%	44,361	2.2%	7.88
Offices & clinics of chiropractors	8041	27,009	1.3%	88,417	3.6%	8.27
Offices & clinics of optometrists	8042	16,151	1.6%	74,213	10.1%	5.77
Offices & clinics of podiatrists	8043	7,574	−1.9%	30,081	1.4%	5.20
Offices & clinics of health practitioners, n.e.c.	8049	22,644	12.7%	146,088	28.2%	13.54
General medical & surgical hospitals	8062	4,382	−0.5%	2,919,713	1.9%	1.16
Psychiatric hospitals	8063	603	−6.1%	90,289	−14.0%	2.71
Medical laboratories	8071	7,501	8.0%	137,977	−1.7%	7.43
Specialty outpatient facilities, n.e.c	8093	10,171	32.6%	224,583	18.5%	8.28
Elementary & secondary schools	8211	15,158	6.0%	550,225	10.6%	4.09
Junior colleges & technical institutes	8222	555	−3.8%	56,071	0.4%	2.88
Religious organizations	8661	148,451	4.3%	1,308,329	10.6%	4.48

Subsectors	Industry SIC	Establishments		Employment		Formations per 100 Establ.
		1995	'95–'98 Chng.	1995	'95–'98 Chng.	
National market, advanced education						
Advertising agencies	7311	13,170	3.1%	144,935	15.4%	10.93
Computer programming services	7371	20,190	47.3%	301,811	49.4%	25.60
Prepackaged software	7372	5,298	41.6%	121,341	43.7%	19.53
Computer integrated systems design	7373	5,310	29.9%	101,882	45.5%	17.06
News syndicates	7383	485	2.1%	8,738	15.3%	5.02
Botanical & zoological gardens	8031	416	10.6%	13,885	19.0%	8.65
Specialty hospitals, except psychiatric	8069	621	12.4%	203,385	2.6%	3.81
Colleges, universities, & profess'l schools	8221	2,312	7.4%	909,798	7.6%	3.55
Museums & art galleries	8412	3,450	9.6%	60,720	11.6%	6.44
Professional membership organizations	8621	5,778	7.3%	58,331	9.7%	5.98
Engineering services	8711	38,924	12.8%	651,725	17.9%	10.60
Architectural services	8712	17,304	7.6%	139,428	20.6%	9.67
Commercial physical research	8731	5,152	17.0%	159,564	11.9%	14.03
Commercial econ., soc., & ed. research	8732	5,114	3.3%	117,740	18.5%	7.80
Noncommercial research organizations	8733	3,216	5.0%	82,687	11.4%	7.51
Management consulting services	8742	36,378	24.8%	356,324	41.4%	20.01
Business consulting, n.e.c.	8748	15,458	20.1%	123,091	15.4%	19.11

(*continued*)

Subsectors	Industry SIC	Establishments		Employment		Formations per 100 Establ.
		1995	'95–'98 Chng.	1995	'95–'98 Chng.	
Local business market, college education						
Advertising, n.e.c.	7319	2,083	17.3%	39,270	25.8%	16.07
Commercial photography	7335	3,615	−1.5%	21,028	−11.6%	8.47
Commercial art & graphic design	7336	11,689	11.0%	65,727	26.4%	14.90
Employment agencies	7361	12,314	16.2%	382,453	36.0%	14.32
Help supply services	7363	17,842	33.9%	1,974,710	41.3%	10.38
Computer process'g & data prep. & process'g	7374	7,364	14.4%	228,356	18.2%	6.81
Computer facilities management	7376	646	31.4%	25,674	15.0%	12.02
Computer rental & leasing	7377	843	3.4%	12,005	16.3%	7.55
Computer maintenance & repair	7378	4,440	1.1%	50,987	14.3%	12.45
Passenger car leasing	7515	999	−11.6%	11,145	3.5%	6.37
Business associations	8611	13,922	0.3%	103,424	−3.2%	3.75
Labor unions & similar labor organizations	8631	18,159	−6.3%	159,167	−1.0%	2.08
Surveying services	8713	8,503	3.4%	53,121	17.0%	7.69
Facilities support management services	8744	881	77.2%	58,032	10.9%	10.18
Local consumer market, college education						
Funeral services & crematories	7261	15,291	1.8%	98,423	6.9%	2.74
Tax return preparation services	7291	7,990	16.8%	144,908	−0.6%	13.71
Dance studios, schools, & halls	7911	4,998	2.9%	26,792	11.6%	10.21
Theatrical producers & services	7922	5,769	10.8%	82,003	17.0%	13.30

Subsectors	Industry SIC	Establishments		Employment		Formations per 100 Establ.
		1995	'95–'98 Chng.	1995	'95–'98 Chng.	
Entertainers & entertainment groups	7929	6,143	10.4%	69,524	6.6%	14.52
Physical fitness facilities	7991	8,644	11.2%	152,430	19.7%	15.93
Public golf courses	7992	3,544	16.3%	55,261	18.6%	8.97
Skilled nursing care facilities	8051	10,546	−12.5%	1,115,205	−7.2%	0.37
Intermediate care facilities	8052	4,452	−12.8%	229,765	−9.1%	0.26
Nursing & personal care facilities, n.e.c.	8059	2,507	−18.9%	124,619	−13.6%	0.93
Home health care services	8082	11,615	33.3%	607,283	16.3%	14.74
Kidney dialysis centers	8092	1,450	46.0%	34,021	25.8%	3.66
Health & allied services, n.e.c.	8099	4,977	−8.3%	99,201	5.5%	5.11
Libraries	8231	2,078	5.6%	20,294	16.2%	4.51
Data processing schools	8243	1,423	46.2%	15,959	58.0%	26.68
Business & secretarial schools	8244	651	−12.7%	16,251	−8.5%	6.45
Vocational schools, n.e.c.	8249	3,156	16.5%	48,200	20.0%	12.53
Schools & educational services, n.e.c.	8299	13,982	15.7%	136,885	20.6%	14.21
Individual and family services	8322	35,606	19.3%	516,329	19.3%	8.89
Job training & vocational rehabilitation	8331	7,570	3.1%	292,757	3.9%	3.85
Social services, n.e.c.	8399	16,283	6.9%	231,952	1.6%	6.16
Political organizations	8651	1,539	16.8%	7,638	24.6%	23.93
Membership organizations, n.e.c.	8699	9,338	−0.4%	77,261	12.5%	3.32

(*continued*)

Subsectors	Industry SIC	Establishments		Employment		Formations per 100 Establ.
		1995	'95–'98 Chng.	1995	'95–'98 Chng.	
National market, college education						
Outdoor advertising services	7312	1,172	10.3%	12,023	7.5%	11.77
Radio, TV, publisher representatives	7313	1,874	21.0%	20,938	40.9%	13.73
Adjustment & collection services	7322	5,037	−5.5%	75,075	14.7%	7.41
Credit reporting services	7323	1,718	−10.5%	29,132	28.8%	5.67
Direct mail advertising services	7331	4,024	−4.3%	83,890	8.0%	8.37
Information retrieval services	7375	1,082	257.7%	25,183	188.9%	101.97
Motion picture & video production	7812	7,622	7.8%	70,992	9.6%	14.82
Services allied to motion pictures	7819	2,807	25.0%	37,321	53.3%	15.88
Motion picture & tape distribution	7822	1,041	−4.6%	18,480	81.4%	8.07
Motion picture distribution services	7829	159	−8.8%	1,095	4.7%	6.08
Dental laboratories	8072	7,080	−1.7%	41,473	2.1%	6.13
Testing laboratories	8734	4,603	5.0%	71,049	11.5%	6.75
Public relations services	8743	5,037	10.2%	38,148	25.6%	12.92
Services, n.e.c.	8999	22,167	−2.5%	168,746	3.7%	7.95

Note: Change rates are calculated as the three-year difference from 1995 to 1998, divided by the 1995 base in the subsector. Formation rates are the sum of new firms first appearing in 1996, 1997, and 1998, divided by the number of establishments (in hundreds) in the subsector in 1995.

n.e.c. = indicates not elsewhere classified.

APPENDIX D

1991–1996 Employment Growth Rates and Share of High-Growth Establishments in Labor Market Areas, with 1991 Employment, Establishments, and Population, and 1991–1996 Population Growth and Relative Employment Growth Rates

LMA	Biggest Place	Empl't Growth	1991 Empl't	High-growth Establ. Share	1991 Establ.	1991 Population	Population Growth	Emp.gr'th–Pop.gr'th
USA	Total US	**10.7%**	92,265,576	4.7%	5,544,033	252,046,485	5.2%	5.5%
1	Johnson City, TN	**12.6%**	180,455	3.7%	9,839	529,052	3.6%	9.0%
2	Morristown, TN	**15.2%**	61,344	5.0%	3,853	184,204	11.4%	3.8%
3	Knoxville, TN	**16.9%**	247,965	5.0%	15,166	709,720	6.7%	10.2%
4	Winston-Salem, NC	**13.5%**	231,693	4.3%	11,221	518,243	5.2%	8.3%
5	Greensboro, NC	**11.8%**	405,091 .	4.4%	21,345	917,113	5.7%	6.1%
6	Galax, VA	**9.3%**	41,831	3.6%	2,456	141,287	3.4%	5.9%
7	Spartanburg, SC	**14.6%**	124,794	4.3%	6,441	320,678	5.3%	9.3%
8	Gastonia, NC	**6.4%**	139,179	4.4%	7,457	372,034	4.5%	1.9%
9	Charlotte, NC	**17.7%**	550,375	5.4%	28,383	1,126,690	10.9%	6.8%
10	Morganton, NC	**9.7%**	68,055	3.9%	4,158	209,777	6.2%	3.6%
11	Hickory, NC	**16.7%**	146,979	4.6%	7,462	314,585	7.9%	8.8%
12	Asheville, NC	**18.9%**	148,026	4.8%	11,000	467,570	8.4%	10.4%
13	Myrtle Beach, SC	**19.3%**	179,033	4.7%	12,091	545,500	5.5%	13.8%

(continued)

203

LMA	Biggest Place	Empl't Growth	1991 Empl't	High-growth Establ. Share	1991 Establ.	1991 Population	Population Growth	Emp.gr'th–Pop.gr'th
14	Fayetteville, NC	18.5%	153,928	4.5%	9,448	569,156	5.3%	13.2%
15	Wilmington, NC	24.2%	89,758	5.9%	6,805	285,590	13.9%	10.3%
16	Rocky Mount, NC	5.2%	82,523	4.6%	4,303	201,526	4.8%	0.5%
17	Raleigh, NC	22.6%	474,572	5.8%	25,768	1,122,386	14.1%	8.5%
18	Goldsboro, NC	16.0%	52,393	4.1%	3,495	194,193	5.6%	10.4%
19	Greenville, NC	21.2%	118,417	4.7%	8,956	491,785	3.3%	18.0%
20	Virginia Beach, VA	15.2%	308,863	4.9%	20,291	1,056,323	4.7%	10.5%
21	Washington, NC	7.0%	34,643	4.3%	2,918	114,270	5.2%	1.8%
22	South Boston, VA	3.5%	39,845	3.0%	2,799	145,423	3.6%	−0.1%
23	Lynchburg, VA	10.3%	79,774	4.0%	4,455	208,275	4.9%	5.5%
24	Richmond, VA	13.1%	386,333	4.7%	21,831	917,618	6.2%	6.9%
25	Newport News, VA	4.9%	172,144	4.1%	9,548	517,634	5.9%	−1.0%
26	Roanoke Rapids, NC	4.3%	34,153	2.4%	2,550	135,167	2.0%	2.3%
27	Biloxi, MS	25.0%	100,170	4.8%	6,656	391,507	9.5%	15.5%
28	Laurel, MS	32.9%	24,645	4.7%	1,938	113,317	2.0%	30.9%
29	Hattiesburg, MS	28.7%	35,476	5.0%	2,666	141,168	6.9%	21.8%
30	Jackson, MS	13.8%	200,420	4.8%	11,677	570,895	4.4%	9.4%
31	McComb, MS	19.8%	30,105	4.1%	2,532	142,173	2.2%	17.5%
32	Vicksburg, MS	25.3%	37,865	3.9%	3,241	175,888	0.9%	24.4%
33	New Orleans, LA	7.8%	500,912	4.8%	27,031	1,332,716	1.4%	6.4%
34	Houma, LA	15.1%	71,965	5.4%	5,083	265,179	1.5%	13.7%
35	Baton Rouge, LA	22.8%	228,955	5.7%	13,449	718,774	5.4%	17.3%

36	Alexandria, LA	**18.7%**	45,006	**4.3%**	3,238	188,187	−1.5%	20.2%
37	Lake Charles, LA	**21.9%**	74,655	**4.7%**	5,324	326,206	0.7%	21.3%
38	Lafayette, LA	**16.5%**	142,120	**5.4%**	10,065	501,613	4.6%	11.9%
39	Monroe, LA	**18.2%**	69,286	**4.8%**	5,084	269,537	1.8%	16.4%
40	Shreveport, LA	**17.0%**	171,360	**4.6%**	11,617	609,838	1.3%	15.8%
41	Pine Bluff, AR	**13.4%**	77,126	**4.6%**	5,430	284,081	−1.9%	15.2%
42	Little Rock, AR	**18.7%**	230,324	**5.8%**	13,036	559,655	5.8%	12.9%
43	Searcy, AR	**19.0%**	31,101	**4.0%**	2,553	126,259	3.2%	15.9%
44	Richmond, KY	**15.3%**	52,025	**3.8%**	3,559	230,259	7.1%	8.2%
45	Hazard, KY	**2.7%**	28,934	**4.1%**	2,413	173,122	0.7%	1.9%
46	Somerset, KY	**16.0%**	47,581	**4.6%**	3,265	147,964	6.1%	9.9%
47	Greenwood, MS	**20.0%**	48,738	**3.7%**	3,914	212,693	2.0%	18.0%
48	Greenville, MS	**12.0%**	36,772	**2.8%**	2,626	153,643	−2.1%	14.0%
49	Jackson, TN	**14.8%**	100,732	**4.9%**	6,004	299,442	4.7%	10.1%
50	Tupelo, MS	**17.6%**	69,948	**5.0%**	3,792	179,315	5.6%	12.0%
51	Corinth, MS	**12.4%**	35,407	**4.3%**	2,216	119,492	3.1%	9.3%
52	Memphis, TN	**20.2%**	420,504	**5.2%**	21,553	1,080,737	5.5%	14.7%
53	West Memphis, AR	**13.1%**	28,723	**3.7%**	2,287	138,250	−0.5%	13.6%
54	Bowling Green, KY	**18.6%**	70,920	**4.4%**	4,273	227,454	6.3%	12.3%
55	Columbia, TN	**17.5%**	45,530	**4.2%**	2,429	133,756	12.3%	5.3%
56	Nashville, TN	**23.5%**	468,787	**6.0%**	24,458	1,013,921	11.1%	12.3%
57	Tullahoma, TN	**10.6%**	37,163	**3.8%**	2,101	112,007	7.7%	2.9%
58	Paris, TN	**27.0%**	31,157	**5.3%**	2,275	122,238	7.1%	19.9%

(continued)

LMA	Biggest Place	Empl't Growth	1991 Empl't	High-growth Establ. Share	1991 Establ.	1991 Population	Population Growth	Emp.gr'th–Pop.gr'th
59	Clarksville, TN	27.3%	44,113	5.5%	3,301	207,316	13.8%	13.5%
60	Huntsville, AL	16.4%	163,959	4.5%	9,020	464,818	7.5%	8.9%
61	Gadsden, AL	19.9%	84,557	4.4%	5,048	275,698	5.2%	14.7%
62	Florence, AL	21.7%	64,507	4.0%	4,133	211,058	4.7%	17.0%
63	Cookeville, TN	15.3%	48,887	5.2%	2,869	156,547	7.1%	8.1%
64	Chattanooga, TN	11.3%	193,327	4.6%	11,066	535,222	5.3%	6.0%
65	Cleveland, TN	20.1%	63,516	5.3%	3,689	200,463	8.2%	11.9%
66	Rome, GA	16.3%	136,927	5.0%	6,874	351,927	7.9%	8.4%
67	Tampa, FL	14.8%	777,522	4.5%	48,882	2,098,345	4.6%	10.2%
68	Lakeland, FL	21.4%	150,305	4.2%	10,129	502,622	6.6%	14.8%
69	Sarasota, FL	9.7%	203,626	3.5%	15,683	642,751	6.4%	3.3%
70	Miami, FL	16.0%	1,213,815	4.5%	90,179	3,344,744	8.4%	7.5%
71	West Palm Beach, FL	12.8%	420,601	4.4%	32,743	1,216,268	10.6%	2.2%
72	Fort Myers, FL	17.8%	169,616	4.2%	14,543	507,718	11.4%	6.4%
73	Melbourne, FL	3.7%	165,555	4.0%	11,461	507,371	8.4%	–4.6%
74	Orlando, FL	21.5%	552,754	5.3%	31,405	1,306,676	11.7%	9.8%
75	Daytona Beach, FL	17.4%	122,047	3.9%	10,071	481,404	9.0%	8.4%
76	Jacksonville, FL	17.4%	374,439	5.2%	22,442	993,843	8.8%	8.5%
77	Lake City, FL	15.1%	27,522	4.1%	2,226	122,126	11.7%	3.4%
78	Ocala, FL	18.9%	70,391	4.3%	6,079	300,146	13.1%	5.8%
79	Gainesville, FL	21.9%	72,433	4.7%	5,413	268,046	7.6%	14.3%
80	Sumter, SC	20.5%	47,008	3.7%	3,185	194,332	5.2%	15.3%

206

81	Columbia, SC	**13.8%**	230,480	**4.5%**	13,577	636,073	5.6%	8.2%
82	Charleston, SC	**12.6%**	179,723	**4.1%**	12,350	627,842	0.1%	12.5%
83	Greenville, SC	**13.7%**	338,800	**4.7%**	16,330	776,804	6.2%	7.5%
84	Augusta, GA	**7.6%**	174,730	**4.3%**	9,106	508,287	5.0%	2.6%
85	Valdosta, GA	**25.3%**	75,195	**4.1%**	5,619	271,615	5.8%	19.5%
86	Brunswick, GA	**18.0%**	56,563	**4.8%**	4,161	184,326	6.3%	11.7%
87	Hinesville, GA	**23.7%**	40,640	**5.1%**	3,043	204,384	8.4%	15.3%
88	Savannah, GA	**18.8%**	126,111	**5.2%**	8,734	367,003	9.5%	9.2%
89	Macon, GA	**19.0%**	105,078	**4.7%**	6,863	347,897	6.0%	13.0%
90	Milledgeville, GA	**14.0%**	69,810	**3.5%**	4,311	241,283	4.2%	9.8%
91	Atlanta, GA	**27.8%**	1,315,328	**6.5%**	69,279	2,809,317	15.8%	12.0%
92	Griffin, GA	**11.7%**	31,942	**3.2%**	1,955	121,002	4.5%	7.2%
93	Athens, GA	**9.9%**	77,755	**4.3%**	4,952	248,538	8.0%	1.9%
94	Gainesville, GA	**27.6%**	65,474	**5.7%**	4,103	196,180	13.8%	13.8%
95	Talladega, AL	**21.4%**	39,005	**4.5%**	2,070	138,066	2.8%	18.6%
96	Anniston, AL	**13.6%**	121,694	**4.7%**	6,823	402,345	8.1%	5.5%
97	Columbus, GA	**15.7%**	104,797	**4.3%**	6,225	351,996	3.3%	12.4%
98	Auburn, AL	**27.2%**	30,361	**4.2%**	1,775	123,863	5.2%	22.0%
99	Tallahassee, FL	**18.4%**	95,979	**5.0%**	7,420	359,913	8.6%	9.8%
100	Panama City, FL	**24.3%**	44,903	**5.2%**	3,719	150,759	11.5%	12.8%
101	Thomasville, GA	**13.9%**	29,231	**4.1%**	2,122	100,653	4.6%	9.3%
102	Albany, GA	**17.9%**	45,832	**4.4%**	3,239	167,874	4.1%	13.8%
103	Dothan, AL	**11.9%**	82,427	**4.3%**	5,316	268,709	2.1%	9.8%

(continued)

LMA	Biggest Place	Empl't Growth	1991 Empl't	High-growth Establ. Share	1991 Establ.	1991 Population	Population Growth	Emp.gr'th– Pop.gr'th
104	Meridian, MS	16.5%	43,586	3.6%	2,886	148,895	3.1%	13.3%
105	Columbus, MS	14.8%	50,058	4.1%	3,544	191,600	1.4%	13.4%
106	Jasper, AL	18.8%	41,040	4.6%	2,690	153,417	3.4%	15.4%
107	Birmingham, AL	13.4%	388,112	5.3%	20,177	951,928	5.5%	7.9%
108	Tuscaloosa, AL	15.5%	87,464	4.0%	5,528	311,616	2.4%	13.2%
109	Pensacola, FL	25.1%	147,285	5.9%	10,863	529,718	10.5%	14.6%
110	Mobile, AL	15.3%	199,367	5.0%	12,520	616,938	6.1%	9.2%
111	Montgomery, AL	16.6%	131,151	5.0%	8,400	409,839	5.0%	11.6%
112	Bluefield, WV	2.1%	82,359	3.8%	6,311	353,149	-1.5%	3.6%
113	WashingtonBalti, DC	7.4%	2,639,292	4.9%	147,063	6,642,841	3.8%	3.6%
114	Marquette, MI	14.4%	77,956	3.8%	6,424	289,703	-0.9%	15.4%
115	Jackson, MI	15.1%	81,766	4.2%	5,330	288,455	3.1%	12.0%
116	Detroit, MI	13.0%	1,921,754	5.1%	101,475	5,116,443	3.6%	9.4%
117	Lansing, MI	9.1%	145,501	5.0%	8,500	437,006	2.7%	6.4%
118	Mount Pleasant, MI	15.7%	29,119	4.9%	2,232	120,962	3.9%	11.8%
119	Saginaw, MI	9.0%	165,724	4.4%	10,324	529,299	1.4%	7.6%
120	Big Rapids, MI	22.9%	36,946	4.4%	3,200	153,540	6.4%	16.5%
121	Kalamazoo, MI	15.1%	170,344	4.8%	9,478	482,873	2.9%	12.2%
122	Grand Rapids, MI	18.9%	436,811	5.8%	22,999	1,129,403	6.6%	12.3%
123	Traverse City, MI	21.4%	65,758	5.1%	6,119	196,089	9.6%	11.7%
124	Alpena, MI	18.3%	38,340	4.5%	4,002	173,533	2.4%	15.9%
125	Dayton, OH	12.6%	469,155	4.6%	24,505	1,276,093	1.1%	11.5%

126	Richmond, IN	**6.4%**	38,023	**3.2%**	2,127	105,001	0.4%	5.9%
127	Cincinnati, OH	**9.2%**	786,797	**4.7%**	38,716	1,873,235	4.0%	5.2%
128	Greensburg, IN	**20.5%**	29,532	**4.6%**	2,147	121,889	8.6%	11.9%
129	Lexington, KY	**18.4%**	206,554	**4.6%**	12,460	570,907	6.2%	12.2%
130	Fort Knox, KY	**17.6%**	35,341	**4.6%**	2,525	161,156	5.6%	12.0%
131	Louisville, KY	**14.8%**	456,782	**5.1%**	24,267	1,118,711	4.1%	10.7%
132	Owensboro, KY	**9.2%**	50,184	**4.3%**	3,380	169,052	3.1%	6.0%
133	Findlay, OH	**13.7%**	83,517	**4.4%**	4,938	241,681	1.6%	12.1%
134	Lima, OH	**9.9%**	91,394	**4.5%**	5,312	259,233	0.9%	9.0%
135	Toledo, OH	**10.5%**	330,839	**4.8%**	18,372	914,129	0.6%	9.9%
136	South Bend, IN	**12.3%**	219,822	**5.1%**	13,128	632,837	2.1%	10.2%
137	Elkhart, IN	**28.4%**	133,163	**6.5%**	7,336	326,147	6.1%	22.2%
138	Wabash, IN	**9.6%**	44,711	**4.2%**	2,668	119,261	4.4%	5.2%
139	Kokomo, IN	**22.3%**	61,490	**4.2%**	3,585	186,123	-0.9%	23.2%
140	Muncie, IN	**7.8%**	136,679	**4.7%**	7,760	414,471	0.0%	7.8%
141	Fort Wayne, IN	**15.1%**	228,875	**5.1%**	11,622	509,247	3.4%	11.7%
142	Indianapolis, IN	**12.9%**	597,888	**5.2%**	30,310	1,306,385	6.4%	6.4%
143	Columbus, IN	**19.3%**	56,921	**5.5%**	3,014	148,308	6.6%	12.7%
144	Terre Haute, IN	**11.2%**	80,977	**3.7%**	4,805	247,908	2.8%	8.4%
145	Lafayette, IN	**15.9%**	103,919	**3.8%**	6,419	329,167	2.2%	13.6%
146	Bloomington, IN	**17.6%**	70,238	**4.6%**	4,927	257,524	5.8%	11.8%
147	Evansville, IN	**11.7%**	154,255	**4.6%**	8,672	370,605	2.4%	9.3%
148	Vincennes, IN	**24.8%**	28,860	**3.1%**	2,588	113,103	-0.9%	25.7%

(continued)

LMA	Biggest Place	Empl't Growth	1991 Empl't	High-growth Establ. Share	1991 Establ.	1991 Population	Population Growth	Emp.gr'th– Pop.gr'th
149	Gary, IN	7.1%	217,894	4.5%	11,637	649,379	2.2%	4.9%
150	Canton, OH	11.8%	233,852	4.5%	13,910	668,597	2.9%	8.9%
151	Lorain, OH	11.7%	130,028	4.6%	7,632	407,675	2.9%	8.8%
152	Cleveland, OH	9.4%	1,094,482	4.8%	58,794	2,603,202	1.2%	8.2%
153	Parkersburg, WV	13.5%	60,423	4.5%	4,017	198,186	1.9%	11.6%
154	Zanesville, OH	7.4%	48,811	4.0%	3,302	178,795	3.6%	3.7%
155	Steubenville, OH	−0.7%	44,629	3.4%	2,464	141,810	−2.6%	1.9%
156	Wheeling, WV	3.0%	60,021	3.7%	4,058	202,625	−1.7%	4.7%
157	Portsmouth, OH	16.7%	50,123	3.9%	3,431	217,305	4.3%	12.4%
158	Athens, OH	10.7%	26,508	4.1%	2,110	139,297	3.2%	7.6%
159	Columbus, OH	16.8%	617,393	5.4%	30,915	1,475,641	5.7%	11.1%
160	Mansfield, OH	15.0%	102,911	3.9%	5,990	314,930	2.4%	12.6%
161	State College, PA	8.9%	85,444	4.2%	6,121	294,773	3.4%	5.5%
162	Altoona, PA	5.5%	122,567	3.5%	8,562	420,563	−0.2%	5.7%
163	Pittsburgh, PA	4.4%	979,189	3.9%	55,858	2,601,959	−0.9%	5.3%
164	Youngstown, OH	2.9%	270,619	4.0%	16,109	820,001	−0.6%	3.4%
165	Erie, PA	3.0%	221,386	4.0%	13,602	657,082	0.2%	2.8%
166	Roanoke, VA	5.8%	169,865	4.3%	9,415	437,136	1.6%	4.2%
167	Morgantown, WV	9.4%	93,896	4.2%	7,051	355,478	1.7%	7.7%
168	Beckley, WV	12.5%	49,984	4.5%	4,441	231,756	1.7%	10.7%
169	Charleston, WV	6.2%	118,059	4.2%	7,696	374,492	1.0%	5.2%

170	Pikeville, KY	**2.8%**	44,711	**4.0%**	3,686	213,945	0.6%	2.3%
171	Huntington, WV	**7.1%**	93,239	**3.6%**	6,248	340,734	1.0%	6.2%
172	Harrisonburg, VA	**14.2%**	53,655	**4.7%**	3,361	151,981	5.8%	8.4%
173	Staunton, VA	**9.1%**	54,191	**3.7%**	3,825	175,814	2.5%	6.6%
174	Hagerstown, MD	**11.9%**	108,679	**3.7%**	7,182	371,235	4.9%	7.0%
175	Cumberland, MD	**10.7%**	77,935	**3.3%**	5,616	250,594	3.5%	7.2%
176	Charlottesville, VA	**11.3%**	72,845	**3.9%**	5,277	230,396	9.0%	2.3%
177	Syracuse, NY	**−1.5%**	401,336	**3.4%**	22,325	1,116,147	−2.0%	0.5%
178	Oneonta, NY	**2.8%**	41,107	**3.0%**	3,281	160,160	0.2%	2.6%
179	Binghamton, NY	**−3.6%**	103,907	**3.3%**	5,557	305,908	−3.4%	−0.1%
180	Buffalo, NY	**2.9%**	912,651	**3.8%**	47,738	2,362,199	−0.1%	3.0%
181	Elmira, NY	**0.6%**	115,364	**3.1%**	6,501	349,945	−0.4%	1.0%
182	Olean, NY	**9.1%**	67,512	**3.8%**	4,677	240,959	0.4%	8.7%
183	Watertown, NY	**−3.5%**	60,656	**3.2%**	4,342	252,745	1.3%	−4.8%
184	Plattsburgh, NY	**2.6%**	41,363	**2.9%**	3,603	171,240	−2.4%	5.0%
185	Amsterdam, NY	**4.8%**	28,539	**2.4%**	2,174	111,784	−1.0%	5.7%
186	Albany, NY	**7.3%**	345,040	**3.4%**	22,286	1,046,584	1.2%	6.1%
187	Sunbury, PA	**−2.5%**	60,697	**2.8%**	3,509	187,905	3.0%	−5.6%
188	Scranton, PA	**2.3%**	282,633	**3.2%**	17,781	812,275	2.1%	0.2%
189	Williamsport, PA	**7.4%**	70,356	**3.6%**	4,486	224,117	0.1%	7.3%
190	Allentown, PA	**4.7%**	230,272	**3.7%**	13,106	601,098	1.9%	2.8%
191	Lancaster, PA	**3.5%**	397,306	**4.0%**	21,503	1,038,699	3.0%	0.5%
192	Harrisburg, PA	**6.7%**	402,556	**4.3%**	20,484	974,193	4.5%	2.2%

(*continued*)

LMA	Biggest Place	Empl't Growth	1991 Empl't	High-growth Establ. Share	1991 Establ.	1991 Population	Population Growth	Emp.gr'th–Pop.gr'th
193	Poughkeepsie, NY	−5.8%	238,525	3.2%	17,426	809,565	1.6%	−7.4%
194	New York, NY	0.6%	4,290,264	3.9%	260,341	10,878,328	1.1%	−0.5%
195	Monmouth, NJ	9.8%	257,518	4.5%	21,510	996,736	6.9%	2.9%
196	Newark, NJ	3.1%	2,359,911	4.1%	136,485	5,387,046	2.4%	0.7%
197	Philadelphia, PA	2.5%	2,154,296	4.3%	117,115	5,398,276	0.4%	2.0%
198	Wilmington, DE	6.0%	249,464	3.8%	12,471	522,896	5.9%	0.1%
199	Dover, DE	8.4%	179,371	3.5%	14,042	552,546	6.9%	1.5%
200	Bangor, ME	9.4%	111,968	4.1%	9,698	406,623	−2.0%	11.5%
201	Portland, ME	8.9%	248,976	4.3%	16,567	662,568	0.9%	8.0%
202	Burlington, VT	9.5%	113,380	4.5%	8,711	295,119	4.4%	5.0%
203	Claremont, NH	9.8%	115,932	4.0%	9,804	343,267	2.0%	7.9%
204	Providence, RI	4.3%	549,978	4.3%	35,133	1,528,745	−0.4%	4.8%
205	Boston, MA	7.1%	2,143,471	5.0%	109,369	4,663,184	1.9%	5.1%
206	Manchester, NH	15.0%	378,075	5.3%	26,459	1,053,485	5.2%	9.8%
207	Keene, NH	10.6%	44,302	3.5%	3,204	111,867	2.1%	8.5%
208	Springfield, MA	−2.0%	241,400	3.7%	13,904	670,664	−1.4%	−0.6%
209	Hartford, CT	0.3%	1,497,514	4.1%	86,247	3,461,062	−0.8%	1.1%
210	Houghton, MI	17.9%	48,153	4.5%	4,868	183,716	4.5%	13.4%
211	Rice Lake, WI	19.7%	35,019	4.1%	3,247	132,924	6.7%	13.0%
212	Hutchinson, MN	25.7%	28,630	3.7%	2,377	102,251	1.3%	24.4%
213	Mankato, MN	12.3%	91,530	4.3%	5,430	243,591	2.4%	9.9%
214	St. Cloud, MN	22.2%	76,456	5.4%	4,491	214,565	9.6%	12.6%

212

215	Minneapolis, MN	**15.6%**	1,249,031	**5.8%**	59,091	2,571,425	6.7%	9.0%
216	Hibbing, MN	**20.5%**	30,113	**4.7%**	2,807	121,278	9.4%	11.1%
217	Rochester, MN	**9.4%**	107,420	**3.3%**	5,954	276,779	2.1%	7.3%
218	Mason City, IA	**13.8%**	49,931	**3.5%**	3,883	151,317	-0.8%	14.6%
219	Marshalltown, IA	**10.1%**	35,318	**3.3%**	2,360	109,171	1.5%	8.6%
220	Waterloo, IA	**15.8%**	77,780	**3.8%**	5,787	248,424	-0.8%	16.6%
221	Iowa City, IA	**13.0%**	65,555	**4.1%**	3,958	186,132	3.5%	9.5%
222	Cedar Rapids, IA	**19.4%**	99,455	**4.8%**	5,462	227,597	5.5%	13.8%
223	Ottumwa, IA	**19.1%**	40,936	**4.2%**	3,125	139,550	1.2%	17.9%
224	Sheboygan, WI	**10.4%**	74,420	**4.4%**	3,717	185,273	3.4%	7.0%
225	Appleton, WI	**14.0%**	211,466	**4.6%**	11,083	495,665	5.7%	8.3%
226	Green Bay, WI	**17.7%**	131,419	**5.1%**	7,871	334,560	6.2%	11.5%
227	Wausau, WI	**12.0%**	129,046	**4.3%**	7,506	347,856	3.8%	8.2%
228	Eau Claire, WI	**20.9%**	91,139	**4.3%**	6,208	285,771	3.0%	17.9%
229	La Crosse, WI	**9.7%**	74,759	**4.2%**	4,513	202,185	4.4%	5.3%
230	Monroe, WI	**11.0%**	31,083	**3.9%**	2,497	111,802	3.0%	8.1%
231	Madison, WI	**19.3%**	214,701	**5.3%**	12,505	521,827	9.5%	9.7%
232	Dubuque, IA	**16.5%**	58,975	**3.7%**	3,906	159,669	1.1%	15.5%
233	Charleston, IL	**18.6%**	57,099	**4.0%**	4,133	195,379	2.0%	16.6%
234	Bloomington, IL	**9.1%**	80,273	**4.0%**	3,974	187,161	5.1%	4.0%
235	Champaign, IL	**7.0%**	129,181	**4.3%**	7,728	376,578	-1.6%	8.6%
236	Burlington, IA	**10.3%**	49,039	**3.9%**	3,208	138,217	0.0%	10.3%
237	Galesburg, IL	**9.2%**	38,951	**3.1%**	2,861	148,611	-0.9%	10.1%

(continued)

LMA	Biggest Place	Empl't Growth	1991 Empl't	High-growth Establ. Share	1991 Establ.	1991 Population	Population Growth	Emp.gr'th–Pop.gr'th
238	Davenport, IA	7.1%	163,670	3.9%	9,893	448,189	0.7%	6.4%
239	Peoria, IL	8.9%	184,060	3.9%	11,092	519,934	1.0%	7.9%
240	Racine, WI	12.1%	185,836	4.6%	10,942	526,763	6.1%	6.1%
241	Milwaukee, WI	9.5%	730,001	5.0%	36,121	1,590,472	1.6%	7.9%
242	Kankakee, IL	38.8%	41,609	3.5%	2,518	128,373	3.6%	35.2%
243	Chicago, IL	7.0%	3,302,354	4.8%	161,118	7,413,944	4.5%	2.5%
244	Rockford, IL	7.7%	219,554	4.2%	12,058	574,218	4.1%	3.6%
245	FortLeonardWood, MO	11.9%	19,895	3.5%	1,919	105,942	−1.0%	12.9%
246	Farmington, MO	9.0%	31,406	3.8%	2,320	125,058	6.3%	2.7%
247	St. Louis, MO	7.1%	998,832	4.6%	51,457	2,268,736	1.7%	5.4%
248	Springfield, IL	6.4%	115,102	4.0%	7,533	342,445	3.5%	2.9%
249	Alton, IL	7.1%	100,966	3.9%	7,105	371,571	2.1%	5.0%
250	Quincy, IL	8.4%	46,107	3.7%	3,328	146,233	1.0%	7.4%
251	Harrison, AR	18.2%	74,242	4.3%	5,868	298,270	9.6%	8.7%
252	Henderson, KY	2.0%	45,808	3.8%	3,016	148,807	1.7%	0.3%
253	Union City, KY	11.7%	33,280	4.1%	2,031	111,118	1.8%	9.9%
254	Paducah, KY	23.7%	50,899	5.4%	3,463	163,326	4.0%	19.7%
255	Mount Vernon, IL	11.6%	38,392	3.7%	3,079	135,995	1.8%	9.7%
256	Carbondale, IL	6.9%	72,853	3.7%	5,828	300,058	1.3%	5.6%
257	Cape Girardeau, MO	11.9%	73,830	4.4%	5,673	245,679	3.4%	8.5%
258	Blytheville, AR	19.9%	25,229	2.8%	1,905	111,682	−5.8%	25.7%

259	Jonesboro, AR	14.5%	52,507	4.5%	3,542	178,169	5.4%	9.0%
260	Duluth, MN	12.9%	99,990	4.2%	7,200	320,583	−0.2%	13.1%
261	Kirksville, MO	12.0%	52,822	3.5%	4,859	219,270	−0.2%	12.2%
262	Bismarck, ND	15.3%	39,958	4.2%	3,281	124,722	2.8%	12.4%
263	Minot, ND	18.5%	31,713	4.2%	3,320	134,063	0.7%	17.8%
264	Dickinson, ND	5.8%	33,612	3.2%	4,112	144,193	−2.7%	8.6%
265	Sioux Falls, SD	19.3%	106,001	4.6%	7,028	262,369	7.0%	12.3%
266	Aberdeen, SD	12.3%	27,685	2.8%	2,939	109,700	−0.8%	13.2%
267	Grand Forks, ND	19.8%	69,954	4.6%	6,372	268,546	1.7%	18.1%
268	Fargo, ND	21.3%	90,137	5.2%	6,430	247,603	3.1%	18.1%
269	Fergus Falls, MN	24.6%	43,773	4.5%	3,981	173,767	3.1%	21.5%
270	Yankton, SD	16.6%	49,768	3.2%	5,568	200,595	0.6%	16.1%
271	Willmar, MN	28.9%	39,568	3.9%	3,441	134,994	0.9%	28.0%
272	Sioux Center, IA	15.3%	35,861	3.7%	3,157	118,529	0.1%	15.1%
273	Fairmont, MN	15.1%	33,767	3.6%	3,134	112,820	−1.6%	16.6%
274	Fort Dodge, IA	12.3%	47,815	3.2%	4,166	156,417	−1.9%	14.2%
275	Des Moines, IA	12.8%	279,076	4.6%	16,291	649,250	4.5%	8.3%
276	Rapid City, SD	16.8%	49,435	4.4%	4,189	173,651	4.0%	12.8%
277	Cheyenne, WY	12.2%	51,477	3.7%	4,822	193,573	4.1%	8.1%
278	Norfolk, NE	19.1%	36,956	3.5%	2,986	113,444	2.7%	16.5%
279	Grand Island, NE	15.6%	48,343	3.2%	3,927	140,477	1.9%	13.7%
280	Sioux City, IA	21.4%	72,701	3.9%	4,801	200,426	3.9%	17.5%
281	Lincoln, NE	15.0%	123,238	4.2%	7,616	316,239	4.8%	10.2%

(continued)

LMA	Biggest Place	Empl't Growth	1991 Empl't	High-growth Establ. Share	1991 Establ.	1991 Population	Population Growth	Emp.gr'th–Pop.gr'th
282	Omaha, NE	15.1%	329,633	4.7%	18,123	777,960	4.4%	10.7%
283	North Platte, NE	15.9%	24,722	3.1%	3,107	110,398	1.5%	14.4%
284	Colorado Springs, CO	35.8%	138,892	6.1%	9,790	455,513	18.9%	16.9%
285	Pueblo, CO	16.6%	49,399	4.3%	4,290	200,544	5.5%	11.1%
286	Kearney, NE	16.8%	47,762	2.9%	5,032	174,563	1.4%	15.4%
287	Laramie, WY	27.9%	69,812	6.4%	5,898	140,363	14.4%	13.5%
288	Fort Collins, CO	27.6%	108,647	6.8%	7,870	347,813	14.2%	13.4%
289	Denver, CO	20.1%	842,615	6.2%	51,542	1,923,771	12.3%	7.9%
290	Hutchinson, KS	11.0%	72,696	3.2%	6,702	240,478	-0.6%	11.6%
291	Salina, KS	13.6%	35,851	2.9%	2,992	104,809	0.1%	13.5%
292	Topeka, KS	18.3%	140,676	4.4%	10,525	479,998	2.4%	15.9%
293	Wichita, KS	7.6%	254,920	4.3%	14,402	627,745	5.3%	2.3%
294	Bartlesville, OK	4.1%	76,634	3.5%	5,383	242,443	-0.4%	4.5%
295	Kansas City, MO	13.2%	775,865	5.1%	44,852	1,949,759	5.1%	8.1%
296	Columbia, MO	18.3%	110,183	4.3%	7,782	326,097	8.6%	9.8%
297	Springfield, MO	22.7%	131,580	5.0%	8,682	369,013	10.2%	12.5%
298	Monett, MO	39.9%	27,362	5.7%	2,442	104,658	18.6%	21.4%
299	Joplin, MO	19.2%	92,175	4.2%	6,397	288,461	4.9%	14.3%
300	Russellville, AR	27.4%	33,115	4.0%	2,133	119,149	7.9%	19.5%
301	Fort Smith, AR	22.1%	89,624	5.2%	5,737	294,865	5.9%	16.2%

302	Muskogee, OK	**10.4%**	31,142	**5.0%**	2,329	139,008	5.0%	5.4%
303	Fayetteville, AR	**27.6%**	98,213	**6.9%**	5,517	276,065	18.4%	9.3%
304	Tulsa, OK	**9.1%**	352,748	**4.8%**	22,025	954,553	6.6%	2.4%
305	Enid, OK	**12.0%**	32,518	**3.0%**	3,336	129,191	−1.7%	13.7%
306	El Paso, TX	**16.9%**	212,765	**4.8%**	14,891	886,832	11.5%	5.4%
307	Roswell, NM	**6.5%**	30,313	**3.6%**	2,469	115,112	5.8%	0.7%
308	Lubbock, TX	**12.2%**	105,719	**4.9%**	8,396	362,925	1.9%	10.3%
309	Amarillo, TX	**14.0%**	121,150	**3.7%**	10,183	445,744	5.0%	9.1%
310	Garden City, KS	**24.7%**	43,550	**4.1%**	4,423	167,579	4.5%	20.2%
311	Victoria, TX	**16.8%**	53,237	**3.4%**	4,855	206,494	5.5%	11.3%
312	Austin, TX	**38.8%**	321,222	**7.2%**	20,915	951,312	18.5%	20.3%
313	San Antonio, TX	**22.6%**	473,471	**5.3%**	29,491	1,539,945	10.5%	12.1%
314	Odessa, TX	**7.3%**	93,676	**4.1%**	8,253	330,273	3.0%	4.3%
315	Laredo, TX	**15.4%**	41,362	**3.9%**	3,506	197,799	19.0%	−3.6%
316	Brownsville, TX	**21.3%**	143,495	**4.7%**	10,677	731,245	19.5%	1.7%
317	Corpus Christi, TX	**14.0%**	123,886	**5.0%**	9,499	471,310	6.9%	7.1%
318	Bryan, TX	**21.9%**	38,832	**5.5%**	2,996	171,129	7.4%	14.5%
319	Lake Jackson, TX	**5.8%**	70,935	**4.0%**	4,578	276,362	7.7%	−2.0%
320	Houston, TX	**8.2%**	1,567,212	**5.2%**	78,217	3,717,382	9.8%	−1.5%
321	Beaumont, TX	**6.1%**	136,354	**4.2%**	8,501	458,808	5.9%	0.2%
322	Lufkin, TX	**19.2%**	59,864	**5.1%**	4,643	261,153	4.5%	14.8%
323	San Angelo, TX	**15.7%**	53,928	**4.0%**	4,950	251,156	7.4%	8.3%
324	Big Spring, TX	**10.7%**	21,698	**3.2%**	2,223	101,174	1.9%	8.8%

(continued)

LMA	Biggest Place	Empl't Growth	1991 Empl't	High-growth Establ. Share	1991 Establ.	1991 Population	Population Growth	Emp.gr'th–Pop.gr'th
325	Abilene, TX	12.2%	55,737	4.1%	4,967	201,602	3.2%	9.0%
326	Wichita Falls, TX	17.9%	53,099	3.6%	4,654	190,876	4.4%	13.5%
327	Brownwood, TX	19.6%	23,711	4.4%	2,276	102,891	5.4%	14.2%
328	Waco, TX	11.8%	101,123	4.1%	6,662	341,084	5.2%	6.6%
329	Killeen, TX	29.6%	57,063	6.1%	3,747	264,563	18.9%	10.7%
330	Fort Worth, TX	18.9%	508,149	5.8%	29,981	1,480,095	8.7%	10.1%
331	Dallas, TX	18.5%	1,313,495	5.8%	64,298	2,652,685	10.6%	7.9%
332	Paris, TX	13.0%	44,459	4.8%	3,038	162,684	4.7%	8.3%
333	Tyler, TX	22.7%	90,022	5.1%	7,404	369,343	8.4%	14.3%
334	Longview, TX	13.3%	77,427	4.6%	5,820	271,938	4.6%	8.7%
335	Texarkana, TX	11.5%	62,617	4.6%	4,231	219,926	2.5%	9.0%
336	Lawton, OK	13.4%	46,065	3.9%	4,114	227,266	2.1%	11.2%
337	Ardmore, OK	16.4%	26,068	3.9%	2,385	110,138	3.5%	12.9%
338	Oklahoma City, OK	14.6%	392,017	4.7%	26,722	1,167,444	5.1%	9.4%
339	Sherman, TX	12.9%	56,508	4.2%	4,110	217,665	5.3%	7.7%
340	Hot Springs, AR	21.2%	68,946	4.4%	5,400	276,160	5.9%	15.3%
341	Anchorage, AK	11.9%	163,984	5.8%	12,861	569,054	6.4%	5.5%
342	Great Falls, MT	11.2%	37,515	3.7%	4,034	154,989	2.5%	8.8%
343	Billings, MT	16.2%	86,110	4.7%	8,271	288,943	7.4%	8.8%
344	Bozeman, MT	24.2%	55,678	5.2%	5,696	197,681	9.7%	14.6%
345	Missoula, MT	21.5%	64,207	5.0%	6,520	226,774	14.8%	6.7%
346	Casper, WY	12.7%	41,625	3.7%	4,109	133,411	3.9%	8.8%

347	Honolulu, HI	-3.8%	400,509	3.3%	23,851	1,004,690	4.3%	-8.1%
348	Santa Fe, NM	18.7%	69,559	4.9%	6,801	277,398	10.5%	8.1%
349	Albuquerque, NM	25.9%	221,866	6.3%	14,240	653,411	11.1%	14.7%
350	Phoenix, AZ	30.8%	886,681	7.1%	50,608	2,378,478	19.4%	11.3%
351	Tucson, AZ	19.0%	237,967	5.9%	16,663	806,411	13.3%	5.7%
352	Grand Junction, CO	34.5%	45,682	6.0%	4,319	160,311	15.0%	19.5%
353	Farmington, NM	27.3%	38,409	7.3%	3,157	133,109	12.7%	14.6%
354	Flagstaff, AZ	34.4%	60,529	6.6%	6,037	249,243	18.5%	15.9%
355	Gallup, NM	19.9%	29,285	5.5%	2,331	204,201	11.7%	8.2%
356	Hilo, HI	-5.9%	41,089	2.3%	3,226	127,350	9.7%	-15.7%
357	Twin Falls, ID	20.9%	41,154	5.2%	3,631	140,299	10.1%	10.8%
358	Boise City, ID	30.5%	144,503	6.2%	9,885	416,783	18.7%	11.8%
359	St. George, UT	47.1%	34,400	7.3%	3,187	156,204	24.0%	23.0%
360	Provo, UT	37.2%	87,500	8.0%	4,170	288,248	18.1%	19.1%
361	Salt Lake City, UT	30.9%	427,866	6.9%	23,391	1,161,330	12.2%	18.8%
362	Logan, UT	19.4%	34,436	5.9%	1,857	122,411	13.5%	6.0%
363	Pocatello, ID	14.7%	81,273	4.7%	5,949	269,781	7.8%	6.9%
364	Rock Springs, WY	16.1%	46,583	4.1%	3,956	160,350	6.5%	9.6%
365	Altamont, OR	8.4%	31,772	4.2%	3,426	154,057	4.8%	3.7%
366	Redding, CA	2.8%	52,020	4.1%	4,934	205,074	5.0%	-2.2%
367	Eureka, CA	6.1%	35,628	4.2%	3,433	133,699	1.6%	4.5%
368	Medford, OR	16.3%	61,805	5.3%	5,253	215,033	11.8%	4.5%
369	Roseburg, OR	8.1%	50,224	4.4%	4,755	202,205	4.5%	3.7%

(*continued*)

LMA	Biggest Place	Empl't Growth	1991 Empl't	High-growth Establ. Share	1991 Establ.	1991 Population	Population Growth	Emp.gr'th– Pop.gr'th
370	Modesto, CA	0.5%	151,049	3.7%	11,315	636,182	5.7%	−5.2%
371	Bakersfield, CA	−3.1%	138,692	3.6%	9,887	569,841	8.5%	−11.6%
372	Fresno, CA	5.1%	289,751	4.2%	21,510	1,210,845	8.5%	−3.3%
373	Chico, CA	4.5%	77,139	3.3%	7,280	355,180	4.9%	−0.4%
374	Sacramento, CA	8.1%	646,472	4.2%	46,983	2,208,210	6.8%	1.3%
375	San Jose, CA	7.3%	951,459	5.4%	48,592	2,136,221	4.0%	3.3%
376	Reno, NV	19.3%	179,147	5.2%	11,736	441,569	14.6%	4.7%
377	Santa Rosa, CA	9.1%	156,925	4.4%	14,360	530,955	5.0%	4.1%
378	San Francisco, CA	3.1%	1,772,575	4.7%	108,795	4,221,067	3.6%	−0.5%
379	Las Vegas, NV	35.9%	391,494	6.5%	19,322	965,892	28.1%	7.8%
380	San Diego, CA	4.6%	835,145	4.6%	53,871	2,554,242	4.7%	−0.1%
381	Yuma, AZ	12.7%	46,555	4.3%	3,919	227,565	16.8%	−4.1%
382	Santa Barbara, CA	0.2%	183,857	4.4%	14,887	593,126	3.0%	−2.8%

383	Los Angeles, CA	-1.6%	5,639,265	4.5%	309,194	14,805,135	3.9%	-5.5%
384	Lewiston, WA	17.6%	34,058	4.3%	3,468	150,790	6.4%	11.2%
385	Moses Lake, WA	19.6%	39,306	4.7%	3,636	151,858	14.2%	5.3%
386	Spokane, WA	21.4%	181,145	5.5%	13,837	585,800	12.8%	8.6%
387	Longview, WA	6.4%	60,881	4.5%	5,025	205,054	6.0%	0.4%
388	Portland, OR	20.7%	644,102	5.9%	39,656	1,568,527	11.4%	9.3%
389	Eugene, OR	22.1%	254,169	5.3%	20,237	868,045	9.5%	12.6%
390	Yakima, WA	11.6%	56,949	4.5%	4,625	221,314	10.8%	0.8%
391	Richland, WA	17.1%	83,358	5.6%	5,611	277,373	11.8%	5.3%
392	Bend, OR	24.5%	48,028	5.6%	4,608	166,956	14.9%	9.7%
393	Bellingham, WA	14.6%	68,390	3.9%	6,509	223,412	13.2%	1.4%
394	Seattle, WA	9.5%	1,282,396	4.8%	79,123	3,239,609	8.8%	0.7%

Note: High-growth establishments have increased their employment by an average of at least 15% per year for the five years from 1991 to 1996, and a minimum of 5 additional employees.

Sources: Aggregated from LEEM8996 and Census's *USA Counties 1998*, compact disc using Tolbert and Sizer 1990 LMA definitions.

References

Acs, Z. J. 1984. *The Changing Structure of the U.S. Economy*. New York: Praeger.
　1999. Public policies to support new technology-based firms (NTBFs). *Science and Public Policy* 26 (4): 247–257.
　2002. *Innovation and the Growth of Cities*. Cheltenham, UK: Edward Elgar.
Acs, Z. J., L. Anselin, and A. Varga. 2002. Patents and innovation counts as measures of regional production of new knowledge. *Research Policy* 31 1069–1085.
Acs, Z. J., and C. Armington. 1998. Longitudinal Establishment and Enterprise Microdata (LEEM) Documentation. Washington DC: Center for Economic Studies, U.S. Bureau of the Census, CES 98–99.
　2004a. The Impact of Geographic Differences in Human Capital on Service Firm Formation Rates. *Journal of Urban Economics* 56: 244–278.
　2004b. Employment Growth and Entrepreneurial Activity in Cities. *Regional Studies* 38: 911–928.
　2005. *Using Census BITS To Explore Entrepreneurship, Geography, and Economic Growth*. Washington, DC: Office of Advocacy, U.S. Small Business Administration.
Acs, Z. J., and D. Audretsch. 1990. *Innovation and Small Firms*. Cambridge, MA: MIT Press.
　2001. *The Emergence of the Entrepreneurial Society*. Handout by Swedish Foundation for Small Business, Stockholm, Sweden, May.
　eds. 2003. *Handbook of Entrepreneurship Research*. The Netherlands: Kluwer Academic Publishers.
Acs, Z. J., D. Audretsch, P. Braunerhjelm, and B. Carlsson. 2004. The missing link: The knowledge filter and endogenous growth. Working paper No. 4783, Center for Economic Research, London.
　2005. A knowledge spillover theory of entrepreneurship. Max Planck Institute of Economics, Jena, Germany. Mimeographed.
Acs, Z. J., D. Audretsch, and M. P. Feldman. 1992. Real effects of academic research: Comment. *American Economic Review* 82: 363–367.

1994. R&D spillovers and recipient firm size. *Review of Economic Statistics* 99: 336–340.

Acs, Z. J., and P. Braunerhjelm. 2005. The entrepreneurship-philanthropy nexus: Implications for internationalization. *Management International Review* 45 (3): 111–144.

Acs, Z. J., B. Carlsson, and C. Karlsson. 1999. *Entrepreneurship, Small & Medium-Sized Enterprises and the Macroeconomy.* Cambridge: Cambridge University Press.

Acs, Z. J., F. FitzRoy, and I. Smith. 2002. High technology employment and R&D in cities: Heterogeneity vs. specialization. *Annals of Regional Science* 36: 269–371.

Acs, Z. J., and R. J. Phillips. 2002. Entrepreneurship and philanthropy in American capitalism. *Small Business Economics* 19 (3): 189–204.

Acs, Z. J., and D. J. Storey. 2004. Introduction: Entrepreneurship and economic development. *Regional Studies* 38 (8): 871–877.

Acs, Z. J., and A. Varga. 2002. Geography, endogenous growth and innovation. *International Regional Science Review* 25: 132–148.

2005. Entrepreneurship, agglomeration and technological change. *Small Business Economics* 24 (3): 323–334.

Aghion, P., and P. Howitt. 1992. A model of growth through creative destruction. *Econometrica* 60: 323–351.

1998. *Endogenous Growth Theory.* Cambridge, MA: MIT Press.

Alvarez, S. A., and J. B. Barney. 2005. How do enterpreneurs organize under conditions of uncertainty? *Journal of Management* 31 (5): 776–793.

Anselin, L., A. Varga and Z. J. Acs. 1997. Local geographic spillovers between university research and high technology innovation. *Journal of Urban Economics* 42: 422–448.

2000. Geographic spillovers and university research: A spatial econometric approach. *Growth and Change* 31: 501–515.

Armington, C. 1995. Deriving establishment births from unemployment insurance data. *Proceedings of the 1995 Annual Research Conference.* Washington, DC: Bureau of the Census, U.S. Dept. of Commerce.

1997. Statistics of U.S. business – microdata and tables of SBA/Census data on establishment size. Washington, DC: Office of Advocacy, U.S. Small Business Administration.

2004. Development of business data: Tracking firm count, growth, and turnover by size of firms. Washington, DC: Office of Advocacy, U.S. Small Business Administration.

Armington, C., and Z. J. Acs. 2002. The determinants of regional variation in new firm formation. *Regional Studies* 36: 33–45.

2004. Job creation and persistence in services and manufacturing. *Journal of Evolutionary Economics* 14: 305–329.

Arrow, K. 1962. The economic implication of learning by doing. *Review of Economics and Statistics* 80: 155–173.

Audretsch, D. 1995a. Innovation, growth and survival. *International Journal of Industrial Organizations* 13: 441–458.

1995b. *Innovation and Industry Evolution.* Cambridge, MA: MIT Press.

1999. *Small Firms and Efficiency. Are Small Firms Important? Their Role and Impact.* Massachusetts: Kluwer Academic Publishers.

Audretsch, D., and M. P. Feldman. 1996. R&D spillovers and the geography of innovation and production. *American Economic Review* 86: 630–640.

Audretsch D., and M. Fritsch. 1994. The geography of firm births in Germany. *Regional Studies* 28: 359–365.

2002. Growth regimes over time and space. *Regional Studies* 36: 113–124.

Audretsch, D., and M. Keilbach. 2004. Entrepreneurship capital and economic performance. *Regional Studies* 38: 949–960.

Auerswald, P. 2005. Entrepreneurship in the theory of the firm: The microeconomics of long term growth. George Mason University. Manuscript.

Autant-Bernard C. 2001. Science and knowledge flows: Evidence from the French case. *Research Policy* 30: 1069–1078.

Baldwin, R., R. Forslid, Ph. Martin, G. Ottaviano, and F. Rober-Nicoud. 2003. *Economic Geography and Public Policy.* Princeton, NJ: Princeton University Press.

Barro, R. J., and X. Sala-i-Martin. 1995. *Economic Growth.* New York: McGraw Hill.

1996. Convergence across state and region. *Brookings Papers in Economic Activity* 2: 107–158.

Bartik, T. J. 1989. Small business start-ups in the U.S.: Estimates of the effects of characteristics of states. *Southern Economic Journal* 55: 1004–1018.

Bates, T. 1991. Commercial bank financing of white and black owned small business start-ups. *Quarterly Review of Economics and Business* 13: 64–80.

Baumol, W. J. 1993. *Entrepreneurship, Management, and the Structure of Payoffs.* Cambridge, MA: MIT Press.

2003. *The Free Market Innovation Machine: Analyzing the Growth Miracle of Capitalism.* Princeton, NJ: Princeton University Press.

2004. Entrepreneurship, enterprises, large established firms and other components of the free-market growth machine. *Small Business Economics* 23: 9–21.

Becker, M. C. 2005. The concept of routines twenty years after Nelson and Winter (1982): A review of the literature. Working Paper 03–06, Druid, Copenhagen Business School.

Bhide, A. 2000. *The Origin and Evolution of New Businesses.* New York: Oxford University Press.

Birch, D. 1987. *Job Creation in America: How Our Smallest Companies Put the Most People to Work.* New York: The Free Press.

Blanchflower, D., and A. Oswald. 1998. What makes an entrepreneur? *Journal of Labor Economics* 16: 26–60.

Braunerhjelm, P., and B. Borgman. 2004. Geographical concentration, entrepreneurship and regional growth: Evidence from regional data in Sweden, 1975–99. *Regional Studies* 38: 929–948.

Braunerhjelm, P., and B. Carlsson. 1999. Industry clusters in Ohio and Sweden, 1975–1995. *Small Business Economics* 12: 279–293.

Bresnahan, T., A. Gambardella, and A. Saxenian. 2001. Old economy inputs for 'New Economy' outcomes: Cluster formation in the new Silicon Valleys. *Industrial and Corporate Change* 10: 835–860.

Carnegie, A. 1889. Wealth. *North American Review,* June.

Carree, M., and L. Klomp. 1996. Small business and job creation: A comment. *Small Business Economics* 8: 317–322.

Carree, M., A. van Stel, R. Thurik, and S. Wennekers. 2002. Economic development and business ownership: An analysis using data of 23 OECD countries in the period 1976–1996. *Small Business Economics* 19 (3): 271–290.

Carroll, G. R., and M. T. Hannan. 2000. *The Demography of Corporation and Industries.* Princeton, NJ: Princeton University Press.

Casson, Mark. 1995. *Entrepreneurship and Business Culture.* Aldershot, UK, and Brookfield, VT: Edward Elgar.

  2003. Entrepreneurship, business culture and the theory of the firm. In Z. Acs and D. Audretsch, eds. *Handbook of Entrepreneurial Research.* Boston: Kluwer Academic Publishers, 223–246.

  2005. The individual-opportunity nexus: A review of Scott Shane: A General Theory of Entrepreneurship. Small Business Economics 24 (5): 423–430.

Chandler, Alfred. 2000. *A Nation Transformed by Information: How Information Has Shaped the United States from Colonial Times to the Present.* Oxford: Oxford University Press.

Ciccone, Antonio. 2002. Agglomeration effects in Europe. *European Economic Review* 46: 213–327.

Ciccone, C., and R. E. Hall. 1996. Productivity and the density of economic activity. *American Economic Review* 86: 54–70.

Cohen W., and D. Levin. 1989. Innovation and learning: The two faces of R&D. *Economic Journal* 99: 569–696.

Curti, M. 1957. The history of American philanthropy as a field of research. *American Historical Review* 62 (2): 352–363.

Daily, C. M., P. P. McDougall, J. G. Covin, and D. R. Dalton. 2002. Governance and strategic leadership in entrepreneurial firms. *Journal of Management* 28 (3): 387–412.

Davidson, P., L. Lindmark, and C. Olofsson. 1994. New firm formation and regional development in Sweden. *Regional Studies* 38: 395–410.

Davis, S., J. Haltiwanger, and S. Schuh. 1996. *Job Creation and Job Destruction.* Cambridge, MA: MIT Press.

Denison, E. 1967. *Why Growth Rates Differ.* Washington DC: Brookings Institute.

Dewey, J. 1963. *Philosophy and Civilization.* New York: Capricorn Books.

Dickinson, F. G. 1970. The changing position of philanthropy in the American economy. New York: National Bureau of Economic Research. Distributed by Columbia University Press, New York.

Dixit, A., and J. E. Stiglitz. 1977. Monopolistic competition and optimum product diversity. *American Economic Review* 67: 297–308.

Domar, E. 1946. Capital Expansion, rate of growth, and employment. *Econometrica* 14: 137–147.

Dunford, M., D. Perrons, B. Really, and R. Bull. 2002. Citations, authors and referees, regional studies, 1981–2002. *Regional Studies* 36: 1053–1065.

Duranton, Gilles, and Diego Puga. 2000. Diversity and specialization in cities: Why, where and when does it matter. *Urban Studies* 37: 533–555.

Economist, The. 2000. Sachs on globalization. June 24: 81–83.

    2004. Doing well and doing good. July 29: 83–84.

Edquist, C. 1997. *Systems of Innovation: Technologies, Institutions and Organizations.* London: Pinter.

Evans, D., and B. Jovanovic. 1989. Estimates of a model of entrepreneurial choice under liquidity constraints. *Journal of Political Economy* 95: 657–674.

Evans, D., and L. S. Leighton. 1990. Small business formation by unemployed and employed workers. *Small Business Economics* 2: 319–330.

Executive Office of the President, Office of Management and Budget. 1987. *Standard Industrial Classification Manual.* Washington, DC: NTIS Order No 87-100012.

Feldman, M. P. 1994. The university and economic development: The case of Johns Hopkins University and Baltimore. *Economic Development Quarterly* 8: 66–67.

Feldman, M. P., and D. B. Audretsch. 1999. Innovation in cities: Science-based diversity, specialization and localized competition. *European Economic Review* 43: 409–429.

Fischer, I. 1930. *The Theory of Interest.* New York: Macmillan.

Fisher, M., and A. Varga. 2003. Spatial knowledge spillovers and university research: Evidence from Austria. *Annals of Regional Science* 37: 303–322.

Florida, R. 2002. *The Rise of the Creative Class.* New York: Basic Books.

Fölster, S. 2002. Do lower taxes stimulate self-employment. *Small Business Economics* 19: 135–145.

Fritsch, M. 1997. New firms and regional employment change. *Small Business Economics* 9: 437–447.

Fujita, M., P. Krugman, and A. Venables. 1999. *The Spatial Economy.* Cambridge, MA.: MIT Press.

Fujita, M., and J.-F. Thisse. 2002. *Economics of Agglomeration.* New York: Cambridge University Press.

Galbraith, J. K. 1956. *American Capitalism.* Boston: Houghton Mifflin.

Garten, J. E. 1992. A Cold Peace: America, Japan, Germany, and the Struggle for Supremacy. New York: Times Books.

Gartner, W. T. 1989. "Who is an entrepreneur?" is the wrong question. *Entrepreneurship Theory and Practice* 13: 47–68.

Geroski, P. 1995. What do we know about entry? *International Journal of Industrial Organization* 13: 421–441.

Glaeser, E. L. 2000. The new economics of urban and regional growth. In *The Oxford Handbook of Economic Geography,* edited by G. L. Clark, M. P. Feldman, and M. S. Gertler. New York: Oxford University Press.

Glaeser, E. L., H. D. Kallal, J. A. Scheinkman, and A. Shleifer. 1992. Growth in cities. *Journal of Political Economy* 100: 1126–1152.

Glaeser, E. L., J. A. Scheinkman, and A. Shleifer. 1995. Economic growth in a cross-section of cities. *Journal of Monetary Economics* 36: 117–143.

Glendon, S. 1998. Urban life cycles. Harvard University. Mimeographed.

Global Entrepreneurship Monitor. 2001. London Business School.
  2002. London Business School.

Greenwood, J., and B. Jovanovic. 1998. Accounting for growth. Working Paper 6647, NBER, Cambridge, MA.

Griliches, Z. 1979. Issues in assessing the contributions of research and development to productivity growth. *Bell Journal of Economics* 10: 92–116.

Grossman, G., and E. Helpman. 1991. *Innovation and Growth in a Global Economy.* Cambridge, MA: MIT Press.

Guesnier, B. 1994. Regional variations in new firm formation in France. *Regional Studies* 28: 347–358.

Gylfasson, T. 1999. *Principles of Economic Growth.* Oxford: Oxford University Press.

Haltiwanger, J., and C. J. Krizan. 1999. Small business and job creation in the United States: The role of new and young business. In *Are Small Firms Important?* edited by Z. J. Acs. Boston: Kluwer Academic Publishers.

Hamer, J. H. 1998. Money and the moral order in late nineteenth and early twentieth-century American capitalism. *Anthropological Quarterly* 71: 138–150.

Hannan, M. T., and J. Freeman. 1989. *Organizational Ecology.* Cambridge, MA: Harvard University Press.

Harrison, B., and S. Kanter. 1978. The political economy of states: Job-creation business incentives. *American Institute of Planning Journal* 44 (4): 425–435.

Harrod, R. 1939. An essay in dynamic theory. *Economic Journal* 49: 14–33.

Hart, D., ed. 2003. *The Emergence of Entrepreneurship Policy: Governance, Start-Ups, and Growth in the Knowledge Economy.* New York: Cambridge University Press.

Hart, M., and E. Hanvey. 1995. Job generation and new small firms: Some evidence from the late 1980s. *Small Business Economics* 7: 97–110.

Hayek, F. 1945. The use of knowledge in society. *American Economic Review* 35: 519–530.

Hebert, R. F., and A. N. Link. 1982. *The Entrepreneur.* New York: Praeger.

Heilbroner, R. L. 1984. Economics and political economy: Marx, Keynes and Schumpeter. *Journal of Economics Issues* 18 (September): 681–695.

Henderson, V., A. Kuncore, and M. Turner. 1995. Industrial development in cities. *Journal of Political Economy* 103: 1067–1090.

Holtz-Eakin, D., and C. Kao. 2003. Entrepreneurship and economic growth: The proof is in the productivity. Center for Policy Research, Syracuse University. Mimeographed.

Holtz-Eakin, D. and H. Rosen, eds. 2004. *Public Policy and the Economy of Entrepreneurship.* Princeton, NJ: Princeton University Press.

Hoover, E., and R. Vernon. 1959. *Anatomy of a Metropolis.* Cambridge, MA: Harvard University Press.

Howitt P. 1996. *The Implications of Knowledge-Based Growth for Micro-Based Policies.* Calgary: University of Calgary Press.

Illeris, S. 1986. New firm creation in Denmark: The importance of the cultural background. In *New Firms and Regional Development in Europe,* edited by B. Keeble and E. Wever. Croom Helm, UK: Beckerham.

Jacobs, J. 1969. *The Economy of Cities.* New York: Vintage.

Jaffe, A. 1989. The real effects of academic research. *American Economic Review* 79: 957–970.

Jaffe, A., M. Trajtenberg, and R. Henderson. 1993. Geography, location of knowledge spillovers as evidence of patent citations. *Quarterly Journal of Economics* 108: 483–499.

Johannisson, B. 1984. A cultural perspective on small business – local climate. *International Small Business Journal* 2 (2): 31–41.

Jones, C. I. 1995a. R&D-based models of economic growth. *Journal of Political Economy* 103: 759–784.

———. 1995b. Time series test of endogenous growth models. *Quarterly Journal of Economics* 110: 495–525.

———. 2002. Sources of U.S. economic growth in a world of ideas. *American Economic Review* 92: 220–239.

Jordan, W. K. 1961. The English background of modern philanthropy. *American Historical Review* 66 (2): 401–408.

Jorgenson, D. W. 2001. Information technology and the U.S. economy. *American Economic Review* 91: 1–32.

Jovanovic, B. 1982. Selection and evolution of industry. *Econometrica* 50: 649–670.

2001. New technology and the small firm. *Small Business Economics* 16: 53–55.

Jovanovic, B., and R. Rob. 1989. The growth and diffusion of knowledge. *Review of Economic Studies* 56: 569–582.

Judd, Kenneth L. 1985. On the performance of patents. *Econometrica* 53 (3): 567–585.

Kaldor, N. 1961. Capital accumulation and economic growth. In *The Theory of Capital*, edited by F. Lutz and D. Hague. New York: St. Martin's Press.

Karlsson, C., and Z. J. Acs. 2002. Institutions, entrepreneurship and firm growth: The case of Sweden. Special issue of *Small Business Economics* 19 (2): 1–4.

Keeble, D., and S. Walker. 1994. New firms, small firms and dead firms: Spatial patterns and determinants in the United Kingdom. *Regional Studies* 28: 411–427.

Keller, W. 2002. Geographic localization of international technology diffusion. *American Economic Review* 92: 120–142.

Keynes, J. M. 1963. *Essays in Persuasion.* New York: W. W. Norton.

Kieschnick, M. D. 1981. *Taxes and Growth: Business Incentives and Economic Development.* Washington, DC: Council of State Planning Agencies.

Kihlstrom, R., and J. Laffont. 1979. A general equilibrium entrepreneurial theory of firm formation based on risk aversion. *Journal of Political Economy* 59: 719–748.

Kirchoff, B. 1994. *Entrepreneurship and Dynamic Capitalism.* Westport, CT: Praeger.

Kirchhoff, B. A., C. Armington, I. Hasan, and S. Newbert. 2002. The influence of R&D expenditures on new firm formation and economic growth. Washington, DC: Office of Advocacy, U.S. Small Business Administration.

Kirchhoff, B. A., and P. G. Greene. 1998. Understanding the theoretical and empirical content of critiques of U.S. job creation research. *Small Business Economics* 10: 153–159.

Kirzner, I. M. 1997. Entrepreneurial discovery and the competitive market process: An Austrian approach. *Journal of Economic Literature* 35: 60–85.

Knight, F. 1921. *Risk, Uncertainty and Profit.* Boston: Houghton Mifflin.

1944. Diminishing returns from investment. *Journal of Political Economy* 52: 26–47.

Krugman, P. 1991a. Increasing returns and economic geography. *Journal of Political Economy* 99: 483–499.

1991b. History and industry location: The case of the manufacturing belt. *American Economic Review* 81: 80–83.

1998. Space: The final frontier. *Journal of Economic Perspectives* 12: 161–174.

Lazear, E. P. 2002. Entrepreneurship. Working Paper 9106, National Bureau of Economic Research, Cambridge, MA.

Lee, A. Y., R. Florida, and Z. J. Acs. 2004. Creativity and entrepreneurship: A regional analysis of new firm formation, *Regional Studies* 38 (8): 879–892.

Lerner, J. 2004. When bureaucrats meet entrepreneurs: The design of effective public venture capital programs. In *Public Policy and the Economics of Entrepreneurship*, edited by D. Holtz-Eakin and H. Rosen. Princeton: Princeton University Press, 1–22.

Levy, J. D. 1999. *Tocqueville's Revenge: State, Society and Economics in Contemporary France*. Boston: Harvard University Press.

Link, A. 1995. *A Generosity of Spirit: The Early History of the Research Triangle Park*. Research Triangle Park: The Research Triangle Foundation of North Carolina.

Link, A., and J. Scott. 2003. The growth of Research Triangle Park. *Small Business Economics* 20: 167–175.

Littunen, Hannu. 2000. "Networks and Locan environmental characteristics in the survival of new firms." *Small Business Economics* 15 (1): 59–71.

Lucas, R. E. 1979. On the size distribution of business firms. *Bell Journal of Economics* 9: 508–523.

1988. On the mechanics of economic development. *Journal of Monetary Economics* 22: 3–42.

1993. Making a miracle. *Econometrica* 61: 251–272.

Luger, Michael. 2001. "Technology-led development." Invited speech at National Economic Development Forum, Washington, DC, May 31.

Lundström, A., and L. Stevenson. 2005. *Entrepreneurship Policy: Theory and Practice*. Berlin: Springer.

MacMullen, R. 1988. *Corruption and the Decline of Rome*. New Haven, CT: Yale University Press.

Marshall, A. 1890. *Principles of Economics*. 8th ed., London: Macmillan.

Mason, C. 1994. Spatial variations in enterprise: The geography of new firm formation. In *Deciphering the Enterprise Culture*, edited by R. Burows. New York: Routledge.

McKenzie, L. 1959. On the existence of a general equilibrium for a competitive market. *Econometrica* 27: 54–71.

Michelacci, C. 2003. Low returns in R&D due to the lack of entrepreneurial skills. *Economic Journal* 113: 207–225.

Nelson, R. 1992. *National Innovation Systems: A Comparative Analysis*. New York: Oxford University Press.

Nelson, R., M. J. Peck, and E. D. Kalachek. 1967. *Technology, Economic Growth and Public Policy*. Washington, D.C.: The Brookings Institution.

Nelson, R., and S. Winter. 1982. *An Evolutionary Theory of Economics Change*. Cambridge, MA: Harvard University Press.

Newsweek. 1997. The land of the handout. September 29: 34–36.

Nijkamp, P., and J. Poot. 1998. Spatial perspectives on new theories of economic growth. *Annals of Regional Science* 32: 7–38.

Parker, S. 2004. *The Economics of Self-Employment and Entrepreneurship*, Cambridge: Cambridge University Press.

Polanyi, M. 1967. *The Tacit Dimension*. New York: Doubleday Anchor.

Porter, M. E. 1990. *The Competitive Advantage of Nations*. New York: The Free Press.

———. 2000. *Can Japan Compete?* London: Macmillan.

Ramsey, F. 1928. A mathematical theory of saving. *Economic Journal* 38: 543–559.

Rauch, J. E. 1993. Productivity gains from geographic concentration of human capital: Evidence from the cities. *Journal of Urban Economics* 34: 380–400.

Reynolds, P. D. 1994. Autonomous firm dynamics and economic growth in the United States, 1986–1990. *Regional Studies* 28: 429–442.

———. 1999. Creative destruction. In *Entrepreneurship, Small & Medium-Sized Enterprises and the Macroeconomy*, edited by N. J. Acs, B. Carlsson and C. Karlsson. Cambridge: Cambridge University Press, 97–136.

Reynolds, P. D., B. Miller, and W. R. Maki. 1994. Explaining regional variation in business births and deaths: U.S. 1976–88. *Small Business Economics* 7: 387–407.

Reynolds P. D., D. Storey, and P. Westhead. 1994. Cross national comparisons of the variation in new firm formation rates. *Regional Studies* 28: 443–456.

Robb, A. 1999. New data for dynamic analysis: The Longitudinal Establishment and Enterprise Microdata (LEEM) File. Washington, DC: Center for Economic Studies, U.S. Bureau of the Census, CES 99–18.

Rocha, H. O. 2004. Entrepreneurship and development: The role of clusters. *Small Business Economics* 23: 363–400.

Romer, P. 1986. Increasing returns and economic growth. *American Economic Review* 94: 1002–1037.

———. 1990. Endogenous technological change. *Journal of Political Economy* 98: S71–S102.

———. 1994. New goods, old theory and the cost of welfare restrictions. *Journal of Development Economics* 39 (1): 5–38.

Rosenberg, N. 1963. Technological change in the machine tool industry, 1840–1910. *Journal of Economic History* 23: 414–443.

Rostow, W. 1990. *Theories of Economic Growth from David Hume to the Present*. Oxford: Oxford University Press.

Samuelson, P. 1983. Thunen at two hundred. *Journal of Economic Literature* 21: 1468–1488.

Savage, M., P. Dickens, and T. Fielding. 1988. Some social and political implications of the contemporary fragmentation of the service class in Britain. *International Journal of Urban and Regional Studies* 12 (3): 238–247.

Saxenian, A. 1994. *Regional Advantage: Culture and Competition in Silicon Valley and Route 128*. Cambridge: Cambridge University Press.

Schmitz, J. 1989. Imitation, entrepreneurship, and long-run growth. *Journal of Political Economy* 97: 721–739.

Schmookler, Jacob. 1966. *Invention and Economic Growth*. Cambridge, MA: Harvard University Press.

Schramm, C. F. 2004. Building entrepreneurial economies. *Foreign Affairs* July/August: 104–115.

Schramm, Carl. J. 2005. Law outside the market: The social utility of the private foundation. The Kauffman Foundation, Kansas City, MO.

Schumpeter, J. 1911. *Theorie der Wirtschaftlichen Entwicklung*. [English translation: *The Theory of Economic Development*.] Cambridge, MA: Harvard University Press.

——— 1934. *The Theory of Economic Development*. Cambridge, MA: Harvard University Press.

——— [1942] 1950. *Capitalism, Socialism, and Democracy*. 3d. ed. New York: Harper and Row.

——— 1947. The creative response in economic history. *Journal of Economic History* 7: 149–159.

——— 2005. Development. *Journal of Economic Literature* 43 (March): 108–120.

Shane, S. 2003. *A General Theory of Entrepreneurship: The Individual-Opportunity Nexus*. Cheltenham, UK: Edward Elgar Publishing.

Shane, S., and S. Venkataraman. 2000. The promise of entrepreneurship as a field of research. *Academy of Management Review* 25: 217–221.

Sharma, P., and J. J. Chrisman. 1999. Towards a reconciliation of the definitional issues in the field of corporate entrepreneurship. *Entrepreneurship Theory & Practice* 23 (3): 11–27.

Sheshinski, E. 1967. Optimal accumulation with learning by doing. In *Essays on the Theory of Optimal Economic Growth*, edited by K. Shell. Cambridge, MA: MIT Press, 31–52.

Simon, C., and C. Nardinelli. 1996. The talk of the town: Human capital, information and the growth of English cities, 1861–1961. *Explorations in Economic History* 33: 384–413.

——— 2002. Human capital and the rise of American cities, 1900–1990. *Regional Science and Urban Economics* 32: 59–96.

Solow, R. M. 1956. A contribution to the theory of economic growth. *Quarterly Journal of Economics* 94: 614–623.

——— 1957. Technical change and the aggregate production function. *Review of Economics and Statistics* 39: 312–320.

Sternberg, Rolf, and Sander Wennekers. 2005. Determinants and effects of new business creation using global entrepreneurship monitor data. Special issue on Causes and Effects of New Business Creation, guest eds. Sternberg and Wennekers. *Small Business Economics* 24 (3): 193–203.

Stiglitz, J. E. 1997. *Wither Socialism?* Cambridge, MA: MIT Press.

2002. *The Roaring Nineties.* New York: W. W. Norton.

Storey, D. J. 1984. Editorial. *Regional Studies* 18: 187–188.

1991. The birth of new firms – does unemployment matter? A review of the evidence. *Small Business Economics* 3: 167–178.

2003. Entrepreneurship, small and medium sized enterprises and public policies. In *Handbook of Entrepreneurship Research,* edited by Z. J. Acs and D. Audretsch. Boston: Kluwer, 473–514.

Storey, D. J., and A. M. Johnson. 1987. *Job Generation and Labour Market Change.* London: Macmillan.

Streech, W., and K. Yamamura. 2002. *The Origins of Non-liberal Capitalism: Germany and Japan in Comparison.* New York: Cornell University Press.

Sutton, J. 1997. Gibrat's legacy. *Journal of Economic Literature* 35: 40–59.

Swan, T. 1956. Economic growth and capital accumulation. *Economic Record* 32: 334–361.

Sweeney, G. P. 1987. *Innovation, Entrepreneurship and Regional Development.* London: Macmillan.

1991. Technical culture and the local dimension of entrepreneurial vitality. *Entrepreneurship and Regional Development* 3: 363–378.

Sweeney, G. P. 1996. Learning efficiency, technological change and economic progress. *International Journal of Technology Management* 11: 5–27.

Thornton, P., and K. Flynn. 2003. Entrepreneurship, networks and geographies. In *Handbook of Entrepreneurship Research,* edited by Z. J. Acs and D. Audretsch. Boston: Kluwer.

Tolbert, C. M., and M. Sizer. 1996. U.S. commuting zones and Labor Market Areas: A 1990 update. Staff Paper No. AGES-9614, Rural Economy Division, Economic Research Service, U.S. Department of Agriculture, Washington, DC.

U.S. Office of Management and Budget. 1987. *Standard Industrial Classification Manual,* Washington, DC: Executive Office of the President.

U.S. Small Business Administration. 1999. *Statistics of U.S. Business – Microdata and Tables of SBA/Census Data.* Washington DC: Office of Advocacy.

Utterback, J. M. 1994. *Mastering the Dynamics of Innovation.* Cambridge, MA: Harvard Business School Press.

Varga, A. 1998. *University Research and Regional Innovation: A Spatial Econometric Analysis of Academic Technology Transfers.* Boston: Kluwer Academic Publishers.

Varga, A., and H. J. Schalk. 2004. Knowledge spillovers, agglomeration and macroeconomic growth: An empirical approach. *Regional Studies* 38: 977–989.

Washington Post, The. 1996. US sails on tranquil economic seas. December 2.

Weizman, M. 1998. Recombinant growth. *Quarterly Journal of Economics* 113: 331–360.

Wennekers, S., and R. Thurik. 1999. Linking entrepreneurship and economic growth. *Small Business Economics* 13: 27–55.

Williamson, O. E. 1975. *Markets and Hierarchies: Analysis and Antitrust Implications.* New York: The Free Press.

——— 1985. *The Economic Institutions of Capitalism.* New York: The Free Press.

Winter, S. 1984. Schumpeterian competition in alternative technological regimes. *Journal of Economic Behavior and Organization* 5: 297–320.

Index